POSTMODERN SEXUALITIES

The sexual occasions an opportunity to consider some of the most fundamental issues of the confused and uncertain human response to a world in
continuing transformation.

In this collection of essays derived from ten year's work on the subject of
sexuality and its meanings, William Simon argues that we can only make
sense of our sexuality within the larger project of making sense of our
humanity. *Postmodern Sexualities* explores the meanings and uses of sexuality as a social construct and offers the most intensive elaboration of
"scripted theory" to sexual behaviour currently available. The essays
range widely, from changes in the social construction of deviance and
perversion to the experience of adolescence and the myth of the Wild West.
Through them all, Bill Simon rethinks the Freudian model, showing how
sexuality has become for us not, as we might once have thought, a unifying
thread in our experience, but rather the ultimate postmodern discourse.

Intellectually profound, politically engaged, and consistently challenging, this book will be essential reading for all those with an interest in
sexuality in a world of continuing transformation.

William Simon is Professor of Sociology at the University of Houston,
Texas.

POSTMODERN SEXUALITIES

William Simon

London and New York

First published 1996
by Routledge
11 New Fetter Lane, London EC4P 4EE

Simultaneously published in the USA and Canada
by Routledge
29 West 35th Street, New York, NY 10001

Routledge is an International Thomson Publishing company

© 1996 William Simon

Typeset in Palatino by Routledge
Printed and bound in Great Britain by Clays Ltd, St. Ives PLC

British Library Cataloguing in Publication Data
A catalogue record for this book is available from the British Library

Library of Congress Cataloguing in Publication Data
Simon, William, 1930 –
Postmodern Sexualities / William Simon.
p. cm.
Includes bibliographical references and index.
1. Sex – Social aspects. 2. Sexuality in popular culture
3. Social change 4. Postmodernism I. Title.
HQ23.S53 1996
306.7 – dc20   95 – 25972

ISBN 0–415–10626–5 (hbk)
ISBN 0–415–10627–3 (pbk)

For Lynn

CONTENTS

FOREWORD
Symbols of change

William Simon argues, among many other things, that sexuality – that "inconstant universal" – is conducted at an angle: it is never just sex. Indeed, as he says in his preface, "all discourses of sexuality are inherently discourses about something else; sexuality rather than serving as a constant thread that unifies the totality of human experience, is the ultimate dependent variable, requiring explanation more often than it provides explanation". Sexuality for humans never just is: it has no reality *sui generis*, and a concern with it always brings wider social and psychic issues in their wake. Human sexualities have to be socially produced (no human can ever just do it), socially organized, socially maintained and socially transformed. And, as cultures change, so do sexualities. The most recent changes have been brought about alongside feminism, postmodernism, multiculturalism and globalization and mean that new sexual meanings are everywhere in the making. This underpins much of what Simon argues in this important book. Understanding sexualities may indeed help us make sense of many wider things.

The radical import of Simon's view – developed over the last thirty years with his colleague John Gagnon – has only just begun to be recognised (and often as if it constituted a new and original view). William Simon and John Gagnon were the founders of what has now become commonly known as the "social constructionist" approach to sexuality. Both worked at the Kinsey Institute for Sexual Behaviour in the 1960s, collecting and unearthing mounds of empirical data. And yet in the midst of this, both felt the need to theorize – to take the data out of the simple realm of the biological, the 'natural' and the merely factual – that most obvious and commonsensical view of sex and sex research available – and to place it squarely in the realms of the social, the symbolic and the theoretical. Starting in 1966, a highly fruitful partnership emerged which produced over 30 articles and linked books which culminated in their pathbreaking study *Sexual Conduct* in 1973.[1] Partially drawing on the work of the literary critic Kenneth Burke for whom symbolism was so central; partially drawing upon their Chicago-based training in symbolic interactionism and especially the dramaturgical metaphors of Erving Goffman; partially just being sociologists who recognized the social when they saw it; they argued that sex, far from being natural, was located well within the realms of the social and the symbolic. Parting intellectual company in the mid-1970s, it would be fair to say that Gagnon's work took a more Durkheimian and research-oriented direction while Simon's became more influenced by neo-Freudianism – a turn that infuses many chapters of this book.

Theoretically, there is an undeniable coincidence of drift between those theories of sexuality developed in the past 30 years by Simon and Gagnon and now called constructionist, the general theoretical stance of symbolic interactionism, the philosophical position of pragmatism and the tottering towards a kind of social thought and social world which has been called postmodernism. They are not synonymous, but there is an affinity. All deny the essentialist world of foundational truth – of nature, of psychology, of history; all deny any 'strong truth' (some deny all truth) and seek pluralities and multiplicities; all highlight the role of language and symbols, signs and signifiers. For the pragmatist, there has been a hundred-year war on Foundational truth and Grand theory alongside a concern with "plural universes", an avoidance of essentialists and "totalizers", dualists and "splitters". In the interactionist version, there has long been a concern with the plurality of truths, the ambiguity of meaning, the struggle of a social self in the dialectics of "I and Me", the ceaseless flux, the localized context and the deconstructed, decentered life in story telling. And in the more general constructionist account of sexuality, an "extremely outrageous idea" has been proposed: that "one of the last remaining outposts of the 'natural' in our thinking was fluid and changeable, the product of human action and history rather than the invariant result of the body, biology or an innate sex drive".[2] Pragmatism, interactionism, constructionism and postmodernism, then, all throw into doubt Grand Narratives of Sexuality.

Simon challenges us to think theoretically about sexualities in a way that few contemporary writers do. It is a supreme irony that most writing about sexuality is not about sexuality at all but about many other things – gender, power, discourse, identity; and yet, while Simon claims that "sexual desire is always inherently something else" (Chapter 6), he is one of the few writers to enter the world of the theoretical with sex on his mind. This is first and foremost a contribution to social theory that takes the sexual more seriously than most.

Two themes of Simon's constructionist account shine through this book. The first is the power of symbolism in sexualities – every page drips with the significance of language, symbol and metaphor as constitutive of human sexualities. The second theme is the apocalyptic social change that has slowly been descending upon us. As Simon says, we now increasingly live our lives in ways that are "different from any that humanity has previously known". This is the postmodern (or postparadigmatic) age. It is characterized by an intense pluralization, individuation and a multiplicity of choices that were simply unknown in any other era. Rapid social change has become our normal condition.

At the heart of Simon's theory is the recognition that sexuality for humans is profoundly not like that of other animals. It is social and symbolic through and through: nothing can be grasped without recognizing this symbolic nature. There is here a de-essentializing and de-naturalizing thrust, and Simon recognizes everywhere that sexuality is massively prone to contingent context and metaphorical muddle. Human beings have devised a myriad of metaphors to talk about, think about, write about and perform human sexualities. Sexual life thus gets framed as the machine that pumps or the disease that plagues us, as the beast within or the spiritual force without; as a biological drive, as an evolutionary force, as a tool of repression, as a liberatory act, as joyful lust, as romantic longing, as violence and hate, as natural or unnatural. Sex is, among many other things, an achievement, an act, an aggression, a boredom, a body, a chase, a commodity, a form of filth, an expression of love, a feeling, a game, a gender, a hormone, an identity, a hunt, a hobby, a medical problem, a microdot, a pathology, a play, a performance, a perversion, a possession, a script, a scarred experience, a therapy, a mode of transgression, a form of violence, a form of work, a kind of war.

In the western world, the list of metaphors for sexuality is enormous and they may each have their contextual moment. Sometimes only one of these metaphors is at work, and at other times they are blended into a massive contradictory web. The narratives of our sexuality feed directly from and into these wider frames of metaphorical miasma. Yet, though our sexual lives are locked in an extensive metaphorical world, most of it has become so tired, so repeated, so "dead" that we can no longer see them as in any way metaphorical: they have "become" our sex. For instance, what does it mean to say that "sex is natural!" or "sex is dirty" or even "the male sex"? Is there an essence hanging around the word "sex" that intrinsically implies this? Is sex really natural, really dirty or really male? Or have these terms – natural, dirty, male – captured the term so pervasively that we can no longer grasp their symbolic and invented character? The postmodern serves as a challenge to the tired habitualization of old metaphors.

The biological metaphor is perhaps the tiredest yet most pervasive and powerful, and it is certainly Simon's major target of critique in this book. It will not endear him to common sense or mainstream sexology. However, much writing on human sexuality is couched in metaphors derived from biology and medicine. Thus, the languages of both biology and essence converge on a unitary view of the goals of sexuality: sex is driven for the reproduction of the species. From this flows a key idea: an ideal form of sexuality as heterosexual coitus in which the male must be sufficiently aroused to penetrate and the female sufficiently receptive to the man and capable of at least bearing the child – and usually raising it too. Key images follow: images of *heterosexuality, coital sex, male arousal, female nurturance, motherhood, procreation, children* – images which certainly seem to have informed much of western thinking, no less in the past than in the present. Some writers have referred to this as compulsory heterosexuality.[3] And the relevance of these metaphors is not surprising, as they get enormous support from "science" and "sexology" – another of Simon's objects of critique. Most of our contemporary understanding of sex comes from the work of biologists, medics and sexologists who, by virtue of their scientific training, have no difficulty in finding everything of significance about sex to be located within the "natural" worlds of hormones, brain structures, drives and instincts. From the writings of the earliest social Darwinians to the contemporary sociobiologists; from research on hormones to research on sex differences in the brain; from theories of aggression to theories of male bonding – most writers who have claimed the authority of science have been concerned with laying out the biological foundations.

Now what is distinctive about Simon's work is his wish to supplant these biologically grounded metaphors with socially grounded ones. The metaphor of *script* is his favorite and it emerges many times in this book. Appropriately for someone so influenced by the work of Burke and Goffman, scripting theory suggests that human sexualities are best seen as drama. An elaborate set of stagecraft rules and performance guides engulf our sexualities and bring them into passion. There is no simple rubbing of ticks here, no simple unmediated orgasmic release: sexuality for humans must have life breathed into it through drama. Often this leads to "slow changing, rule bound genre" (Chapter 2). Fixed formulae for drama make life and sexuality easier. But there is always room too for improvised performance. While human sexuality may have a goal of reproduction, it is not the only goal and tells us really very little about the role of sexuality in human affairs. How often does sex result in procreation? The very question poses a challenge – the widening of metaphors of the sexual. There is nothing simple about its definition. As this book makes abundantly clear, it is multiple, fragmented, diffuse, split and contested. And it is becoming more and more so.

For Simon, psychoanalytic writing is an important aid in deciphering the symbolism of sex. (Kohut seems a major influence.) And it is everywhere to be found in this book. But Simon is no simple follower or canonical believer. Rather, his task is more "to engage with it deconstructively" (Chapter 3). He merges his interactionist concerns with recognition that psychoanalysis handles desire and symbolism better than any extant theory to date; it has a profound importance in grasping the intrapsychic script and the representational world. Yet it is often hopelessly time-bound and muddled. Intrapsychic life has to be seen as socially contingent. And there is a clear reversal of Freud at many points: the sexual does not shape the social, rather the sexual is put to social and psychic use. More for Simon is the critical period of sexual development childhood: rather the moments of most salience occur in adolescence. And yet "latency" often occurs in childhood. The linearity of chronological age in Freud breaks down, just as it has in the wider social world. There is a "blurring of the boundaries" (cf. Chapter 2).

There is an interesting emphasis in this book on adolescence and the emergence of the symbolic at this time. The suggestion is that landscapes of desire or cultural scenarios of sexual scribing have a prime focus in adolescence; most of our images of sex are derived from the young not the old, and this itself creates tensions – for the old of course, but for the young as they grow. Simon's concern with adolescence stems from a concern with how desires become eroticized, a task which is centrally performed during the long and troublesome periods of youth. Hence three chapters of this book, no less, turn to this period of life. They can be read as a deconstruction of Freud, but they can also be read as providing signs of an opening internal dialogue which helps slowly to construct an eroticized self of the adolescence – one that is currently forged out of the contingent circumstances of choice, pluralism and complexity. Cultural scenarios provide the contexts for the building of psychic scripts that ultimately link to sexual habits and the creation of a sexual self. The youth market may also be breaking down the traditional distinctions between youth and child-hood so that children enter these erotic scenarios increasingly earlier. There can, in these changing times, no longer be any simple model of psycho-sexual development that holds for all or most. Complexity, difference and contingency are the hallmarks of the modern development. (Families, for instance, now exist in many more different forms and create earlier settings that provide many more different pathways into sexualities, and so too do communities and the wider culture which are undergoing radical trans-formations.) The construction of the self is highlighted, then, through contexts of complexity, pluralism and choice and the question of how sexuality acquires its significance in youth is posed. For Simon, the motivations for sex are "rarely, if ever, in the exclusive control of 'sexual desire' " (Chapter 4). "Social puberty" becomes important rather than biological maturation.

If symbolism and metaphor is one theme underpinning this book, change is the other. For Simon, the modern world has seen change speeding up and increasingly impacting more and more lives: it has entered a postparadigmatic phase where consensual meanings have dis-solved into pluralism, authority has been weakened, "choices" have proliferated, time and space have become reordered and the natural has been deconstructed and denaturalized. Modernity brought in its wake the seeds of its own destruction – "To Make It New". Processes were put into play which recognized differences, relativities, changes: potential chaos yet enormous possibility. With this came the radical options for new sexualities divorced from traditional religions, traditional family structures, traditional communities, traditional politics, traditional limited and restricted communication channels. Here, a space emerges for new kinds of sexualities. The new "postmodernist culture", so widely discussed, is the latest stage of modernity: accelerated, expanded, extended.

The postmodern has been endlessly described. The most famous definition comes from Baudrillard, for whom it is:

> the characteristic of a universe where there are no more definitions possible. It is a game of definitions which matters.... It has all been done. The extreme limit of... possibilities has been reached. It has destroyed itself. It has deconstructed its entire universe. So all that are left are pieces. All that remains to be done is play with the pieces. Playing with the pieces – that is postmodern.[4]

For Giddens, late modernity (a term I prefer) is a time when we have become increasingly cut off from local social relations and become "disembedded"; a period of increasing "risk" for all society's members, largely because all the old verities have ceased to be; and a time of growing self reflexivity, when the very knowledge produced in the world helps shape the emergence of that world.[5] For others it is "the time of the sign". A time when media images, modes of information, "regimes of signification" and the "aestheticization of everyday life" have become the engulfing feature of modern experience; we live in through the media which become experiences in themselves. For others, it is the time of consumer cultures,[6] and for others still, it is the time of a new hypertechnology.[7]

It is a time when the Grand Narratives have come to an end; a period of fragmentation, differentiation, indeterminacies, immances, de-structurings, de-unification, de-centering. The quest for the grand truth, the scientific solution, the correct political position, the linear progression and the theoretical purity are now all seen as flawed. Indeed, such pursuits have been used in the past as a means of coercion and tyranny; the need now is to recognize the fragments, the bits, the pastiches, the movements to and fro, the immanent divisions, ubiquitous and fluctual. I use the term "late modern" to describe all this.

And all of this must impact out sexualities. It is no longer the source of a truth as it was for the moderns with their strong belief in science. Instead, human sexualities become destabilized, decentered and de-essentialized; the sexual life is no longer seen as harboring an essential unitary core locatable within a clear framework (like the nuclear family) with an essential truth waiting to be discovered: there are only fragments. It is, as Simon says, "accompanied by the problematic at every stage" (Chapter 1). Sexualities are likely to become more and more

- self-conscious and reflective: the very terms we use to discuss sexuality will become more discussed, elaborated upon, contexted;
- different in form from telephone sex to music video erotica, from virtual sex to internet sex cafés;
- differentiated and variable: a plurality of meanings, acts, identities will emerge;
- more recursive, or dependent upon borrowings from the mass media and, indeed, from social science;[8]
- indeterminate: a supermarket of sexual possibilities pervades;
- pastiched: thus, sexual identities blur and change.[9] In the most extreme versions of this story, we move beyond human beings ("The Death of the Subject") and identities (the word "postidentitarian" has already been invented).[10] The "Human Being" vanishes altogether from the story;
- excessive: hyperbolic madness starts to invade sexuality. The Krokers, for instance, talk about "panic sex" and "excremental sex".[11]

Simon's study is about the postmodern, and he raises many important insights as to where our sexualities may be heading in the twenty-first century. His postmodernism is evidenced not just in what he says but in the way that he says it. Boldly he "abandons any pretence at linear coherence" in his writing, and suggests that his readers (i.e. you) "read selectively" anyway. So not only can the various chapters be read in any order, not only is there significant repetition, not only are there chapters which seem strangely out of place – the one on *Who Killed Liberty Vallance?* is a fascinating oddity – but by the final chapter, what we are treated to is a new mode of writing: epigrammatic non-linear, pastiched. The reader may be advised to dip into this chapter selectively – there is a thought here for each day!

There is, then, no closure of any kind to this book. Simon's project is to open theoretical spaces to examine the sexual as it is socially constituted, and along the way he discusses many important topics. Homosexuality assumes an important role. It signposts the problematizing of desire and "has become a presence in the everyday order of things' (Chapter 1). Masturbation is accorded a more significant role than usual in nearly every chapter. Paedophila emerges as an issue which has made "adult child" sex more plausible than before, hence raising greater fears. Sado-masochism becomes a key script of late twentieth-century desire. The nature of the self and identity changing is everywhere. And so on. This is an important book which deserves to be savored in its reading and influential in its impact.

NOTES

1 See John Gagnon and William Simon, *Sexual Conduct: The Social Sources of Human Sexuality* (1973), Aldine.

2 See Carole S. Vance, "Social Constructionism" in D. Altman *et al.* (eds) *Homosexuality, Which Homosexuality* (1989), Gay Men's Press: 13.

3 See Adrienne Rich, "Compulsory Heterosexuality and Lesbian Existence" in Ann Snitow, Christine Stansell and Sharon Thompson (eds) *Desire, The Politics of Sexuality* (1983), Virago: 212–40.

4 Douglas Kellner, *Jean Baudrillard: From Marxism to Postmodernism and Beyond* (1989), Polity Press: 116.

5 Anthony Giddens, *The Consequences of Modernity* (1990), Polity Press.

6 Mike Featherstone, *Consumer Culture and Postmodernity* (1991), Sage.

7 See Allucquere Rosanne Stone, *The War of Desire and Technology at the Close of the Mechanical Age* (1995), MIT Press.

8 See Ken Plummer, *Telling Sexual Stories: Power, Change and Social Worlds* (1995), Routledge.

9 This is part of a wider story now well documented in social sciences; of *The Protean Self, The Mutable Self, The Homeless Mind, The Narcissistic Personality; the Saturated Self*. Here, identities in the late modern world are no longer stable or fixed. This literature is now enormous, and hugely recursive; it often features among the best-selling non-fiction. See, for example, Ken Gergen, *The Saturated Self* (1991), Basic Books.

10 See Douglas Kellner, "Popular Culture and the Construction of Postmodern Identities" in Scott Lash and Jonathan Friedman (eds) *Modernity and Identity* (1992), Blackwell: 173.

11 See "Panic Penis", in Arthur and Marilouise Kroker, *Panic Encyclopaedia* (1989), MacMillan: 181.

Ken Plummer
Professor of Sociology, University of Essex

PREFACE

The work that follows is drawn from papers and essays, published and unpublished, written over the past decade (1984–94). It is not, however, merely a collection of such papers and essays. Each has been revised, frequently incorporating concepts and insights developed in others. By the same token, it is not intended to represent a single, continuous text offering a comprehensive theory of human sexuality. Indeed, it is a major contention of this work that such a comprehensive theory of human sexuality necessarily implies otherwise questionable essentialisms; such an effort must adopt a view of sexualities that are significantly independent of specific sociocultural contingencies. I will argue that all discourses of sexuality are inherently discourses about something else; sexuality, rather than serving as a constant thread that unifies the totality of human experience, is the ultimate dependent variable, requiring explanation more often than it provides explanation. At best, this book aims at developing a conceptual apparatus for dealing with this complex and profoundly variable topic.

One consequence of my abandonment of any pretense at a linear coherence is an inevitable redundancy. This is particularly true when the concepts most central to the effort, such as "scripting" and the distinction between "paradigmatic" and "postparadigmatic" social orders, are applied. Such redundancies might be defended on two grounds. First, as one considers for whom one is writing, it is necessary to recognize that many readers will not read this book from beginning to end. One of the most prominent aspects of the current, postmodern condition can only be described as a crisis of intellectual overproduction. As a result, increasing numbers of us, particularly those involved in multidisciplinary topics, learn to read selectively. At the same time, an attending pluralization of perspectives leaves little by way of common conceptual meanings. Few of even the most generic of sociological concepts can currently be used without specification of specific meanings. Second, appearing in different contexts, each presentation of central concepts provides what are often critically different shades of meaning.

xvii

A second concern, one repeated throughout this book, is the inevitable biases found in the unexamined assumption of the author. As one who has tried to call attention to the ways in which Freud's vision of human sexuality was colored by his experiences within a specific historical setting, I cannot exempt myself from the same accusation: the risk of having one's perceptions and preferred images of representation be tainted by a multi-dimensional ethnocentrism. I am a white, late middle-aged male who has lived his entire life in North America, and whose sexual experience has been predominantly heterosexual. And while I have attempted to limit the effects of such inevitable biases by being as cognizant as possible of available research and commentary, such efforts may actually serve as much as a mask for biases as serving as protection from such biases.

The best defense against the biases of time, place, and experience is an effort to avoid allowing the sometimes powerful imagery of sexuality to create a seemingly isolated culture of its own, and to place such considerations in as broad an intellectual frame of reference as possible. This, to the best of my ability, I have tried to do: to try to make sense out of sexuality by applying the larger text of making sense out of being human. As Darnton (1994) observed:

> As carnal knowledge works its way into cultural patterns, it supplies endless material for thought, especially when it appears in narratives – dirty jokes, male braggadocio, female gossip, bawdy songs, and erotic novels. In all these forms, sex is not simply a subject but also a tool, used to pry the top off things and explore their inner things. *It does for ordinary people what logic does for philosophers; it helps make sense of things.*
>
> (Italics added)

To which I can only add: I hope so.

William Simon
Houston, Texas

ACKNOWLEDGMENTS

During the decade in which the following essays were composed, I was fortunate in having as initial readers some remarkable persons. First among these was my wife, Lynn Randolph, who suffered through successive drafts and my persistent irritation at her persistent insight.

A very special reader was the late Robert J. Stoller. Bob read early versions of everything except the last essay and his responses were generous in criticism and enthusiasm. Beyond our too few conversations and exchanges of letter, he came to constitute a significant other whose understanding I could assume and whose approval I wanted; writing, in part, often became a one-sided conversation with him. This, of course, is in addition to all I learned from conversing with his substantial writings.

A similar role was played by Martin Levine, whose premature death also represents a great loss. He, too, was a person whose understanding and approval were important considerations for more than two decades.

Virginia Carmichael was one of the first persons to read this as a single manuscript. She returned a document thoroughly scarred by the application of her intelligence, her substantive knowledge, and her severe editorial pencil. In responding to her numerous comments and suggestions, I found myself approaching a clarity that I had previously been successful in avoiding. In subsequent tampering with these essays I can only hope that I have not undone too much of what she helped me realize.

John Gagnon, friend since graduate school days, colleague at the Institute for Sex Research, and collaborator for two decades (1965–85) is obviously a continuing presence in this work. Many of the ideas that constitute this work were initially articulated in the course of this very fruitful collaboration. John co-authored the essays on "sexual scripts" that provided the basis for what, after considerable revision, became Chapter 2. While I am sure that much of what is contained in Chapter 2 is still consistent with his thinking, I am also sure that in the decade since the end of our collaborative efforts our thinking has moved in different directions. His most recent views on sexual scripting and its uses can be found in Lauman and Gagnon (1995) and Lauman et al. (1994).

The earliest versions of what came to be Chapters 3 and 4 were written while on a faculty development leave from the University of Houston, for which I am very appreciative. I must also acknowledge the succession of students in my course on Sexuality and Society. Being as much a talker as a writer, I talked through with them much that is contained in what follows, in ways that sometimes may have served me more than them.

During this period, my life and work have been enriched by the interaction with many persons – colleagues, students, friends and many who were these in combination. Among these are: C. Alan Haney, Russell Curtis, Ed Willems, Ed Hill, Suzanne Bloom, Artis Bernard, John Bernard, Simon Moss, George Reiter, Patricia Y. Miller, Howard Kaplan, Simon Gotshalk, Diane Kraft, Denise Bullock, Jill Ross, Nancy Stevens, Tony Fuller, and, most recently, Zack Schiller, Greg Carlton, Yvonne Carlton, and Jim Townsend. And almost from the very beginning, James and Veronica Elias and Richard Green.

Writing, like sex itself, can be served as much by argument as by affection. My children, David Simon, Jonathan Simon, Adam Simon, Cean Randolph and Grayson Randolph, by their persistent arguments, shared discoveries, and numerous provocations continuously challenged and often humbled me. From each I continue to learn. Lastly, my brother, Myron Simon, generously shared the reading of page proofs. More importantly, he was the one who led the way into the once alien landscape of North American Academia.

An early version of Chapter 1 appeared in *Psychology and Sexual Behavior*. Earlier versions of Chapter 2 appeared in *Archives of Sexual Behavior* and *Theories of Human Sexuality* (edited by J. Geer and W. O'Donoghue, New York: Plenum). A version of Chapter 5 initially appeared in *The Southwest Media Review* under the title, "They Lied: Liberty Valance Lives".

INTRODUCTION

There is no emotion,
Only a collage of emotions;
There is no desire,
Only an ecology of desires;
There is no pleasure,
Only an economy of pleasures.

All attempts at theorizing social life are, at the same time, works of autobiography. This is the most basic insight of the sociology of knowledge and, as such, it stands as an additional reminder of the tendency for discourse to create the conditions of its own subversion. The problematics posed by the conditions of postmodernity for the individual also exist for the individual theorist as well as for communities of theorists. Individuation at the individual level and differentiation at the collective level make it increasingly difficult to continue to maintain the illusion that science can achieve some privileged position of neutral observation reported in unbiased language.[1]

At this point, it should be clear that, as a sociologist, I conceive of postmodernism as not being merely a new intellectual perspective, but rather as an expression of or a response to the dramatic changes in the character of social life and the human experiences these changes have occasioned. This development is clearly what is suggested by Daniel Bell when he observed "[T]here are disjunctures everywhere, and more and more in contemporary society there are radical disjunctures. What I've argued is that beliefs are independent of changes in the social structure" (*New York Times*, 7 February 1989). Another, more personal view is expressed by Richard Ford in his novel, *The Ultimate Good Luck* (1981), as he described his hero in the following terms:

He had a sense when he joined the marines that the country he was skying out of was a known locale, with a character that was exact and coordinate and that maintained a patterned feel. A thing you could get back with if you had a reason. But that patterned feel had gotten

1

disrupted somehow, as though everything whole had separated a little inch, and he had dropped back in between things, to being on the periphery without a peripheral perspective.

The postmodern perspective begins with the decentering perception that a peripheral perspective is the best we can hope for when the surrounding social order, once perceived as an encompassing continent, is experienced as a dense and confusing archipelago.

ADMITTING TO CHANGE

Approximately at mid-century, two seminal works appeared that defined the most influential approaches to the interactions that simultaneously create individuals and societies. These two works were by writers fully aware of each other. One was Erik Erikson's *Childhood and Society* (1950); the other was David Riesman's amazingly prescient work *The Lonely Crowd* (1969). *Childhood and Society*, while mindful of the precarious nature of the culture–personality relationship, like much of the modernist tradition, was assertively ahistorical, focusing upon what were seen as the timeless requirements of the individual. It served as one of the most influential statements within the behavioral sciences and psychotherapeutic communities. The latter, while sharing to an extraordinary degree a common tradition, outlined a dialectic that sought to chart the reciprocal transformations of individual personality and the institutionalized practices of social life. The cumulative experiences of the past several decades, decades that have borne witness to dramatic changes along many of the most crucial dimensions of social and personal life, necessarily have returned our attention to the broad historical perspective. As a result, there is increased recognition that humanity can no longer be comfortably viewed as a species that merely experiences history, but must itself be viewed as the continuing and changing product of history (Castoriades 1987).

Where Erikson, among others, pointed to the continuities in the shaping of human behavior, to what can be viewed as the sources of its inevitable "over-determination", Riesman clearly sensitized us to its "under-determined" qualities, allowing us to view both social orders and individuals as part of a permanent revolution. This latter point, which I shall emphasize, is of critical significance for consideration of gender and sexuality, two aspects of the human experience that more than others have been shrouded in illusions of biophysical species constancy. All but the most committed of social constructionists tend to display a reluctance to diminish the significance of the apparent universality of these two categories, their manifest relevance in all social orders, or their seeming rootedness in the constant (or slowly changing) nature of the body. It becomes increasingly important, perhaps for this very reason, to assert

2

boldly the contextually specific nature of the behaviors we associate with these concepts. *Many of the uses of gender and sexuality, observable within the context of the rapidly changing present, may in fact be different than any that humanity has previously known.*

As a result, we must risk interpretations that are keyed to specific contextual implications without attempting to make such interpretations congruent with overarching generalizations abstracted from cross-cultural or transhistorical comparisons. Such comparative efforts are important, but their importance may rest as much in recognition of the similarities of differences as in recognition of the implicit differences of similarities. While this approach may be seen as encouraging an excessively reckless and uninformed relativism, the dangers of this are limited, at least for the moment, by the heavy, if not burdensome, weight of more traditional conceptions of social science scholarship.

POSTMODERNISM AND POSTMODERNITY

The contemporary situation may represent a more revolutionary time than any the Western world – and now the entire globe – has ever known. The idioms and images we associate with postmodernism are not merely matters of styles, fashionable clichés, or intellectual fashions; rather they are an expression of a shift as profound as any we have known since the Renaissance and, in many respects, this shift may represent an even more profound change, since it directly touches many more lives and many more facets of our lives than did the one we associate with the Renaissance, and it does so much more immediately. The "decentering" that followed the Copernican Revolution initially touched relatively few lives compared to the pervasive impact of satellite transmission of information and images along with near global access to technologies of reception. I speak of changes and the experience of changes that not only directly altered our concepts of time and space but also altered the very experience of time and space for masses of people.

The proliferation of choices currently available, a proliferation typified by the expanding universes of cable television and the shopping mall, has been devalued by many critics as involving relatively trivial choices. Choices, they assert, that are superficial and that, in their superficiality, prevent the individual from perceiving alternatives that are more con-sequential in their lives. In considerable measure, such criticisms are not without validity. However, as trivial as such choices may be, they are greater in number than what was previously available to most people. More importantly, it can be the very practice of choosing, albeit between superficial differences, that has a characterological consequence of greater significance than found in most specific choices.

Moreover, we must speak of changes in behavior and its meanings and,

3

moving beyond the superficialities and elasticities of identity, we must speak directly to altered and altering dimensions of subjectivity, of altered and altering dimensions of being human. Not the least of which, as we shall see, is a markedly heightened need for intrapsychic processing of experience in contexts where others and ourselves can less and less be taken for granted (Van de Berg 1974).

The technologies of a postmodern world compel it to mirror itself in the broadest terms and in ways that penetrate all but the most isolated, all but the most self-consciously isolated. By that very quality, postmodernity becomes a contextualizing aspect of almost all social settings. However, the ability of the qualities of postmodernity to pervade all sectors of social life does *not* mean that all individuals then become models of the postmodern or are immediately converted into uniform postmodern personalities. To the contrary, the speed with which these changes have occurred affects many persons in many different ways. We might learn from Riesman (1969), who reminded us that there is rarely any one-to-one relationship between the qualities of social life and individual psychology; rather, it is a matter of the relative distribution of various types of persons and the varied problematics of the fit between the ways social life is organized and the experienced requirements of specific types of persons.

Most individuals, at any one time, will adapt to prevailing social conditions, some easily and some with only the most self-conscious efforts and distress. It is this very sense of pluralization, one carried to unprecedented lengths by the conditions of postmodernity, that becomes the central issue when one considers specific forms of behavior. One of the most difficult aspects of discussing the very social conditions and qualities of subjective experience that are essential to an understanding of an emergent postmodernity is a pluralism of meaning: a pluralism of meaning derived from a heightened pluralism of voices, perspectives, and – of greatest importance – a pluralization and heightened individuation of human experience.

THE NORMALIZATION OF CHANGE

Among the more critical aspects of postmodernity is the *normalization of change*, the unprecedented degree to which change permeates virtually every aspect of our lives and the immediate landscape of our lives and the unprecedented degree to which we have come to live with it, expect it, and even come to desire it as the normal condition of our lives. Change occurs in things (the furnishing of our lives with objects, relationships, and experiences), change occurs in the order of things (the value and meaning of these furnishings), and, as a result, change occurs pervasively across the trajectory of individual lives. Mobilities become a near constant. Individuals in increasing numbers and frequencies move between varied social and physical locations. Even those individuals who stay in place find many of the most significant, even the most commonplace, aspects of their everyday life undergoing constant revision, if not transformation. There is the mobility of others who constitute the interpersonal involvements of such individuals, as well as the continuing renovations of their own social worlds.

Very few individuals currently living in North America expect successive generations of family members to live in the same house, the same neighborhood, or even in the same community. Vast numbers no longer expect to live in the same dwelling even during the larger part of their own adult lives, though many have learned to live in the same kind of house, neighborhood, or community despite frequent mobilities. Similarly, most expect that the objects that furnish their lives at home, work, and leisure will frequently change in appearance, concept, and social significance. *Communities of memory*, to use Bellah's term (Bellah *et al.* 1986), give way to more abstract *audiences of memory* as "the community of limited liability" – communities that command our attention only to the degree that we require its services and only for as long as we plan to reside there – gives way to a more abstract self of limited liabilities where careers and relationships are no longer necessarily viewed as life-long commitments.

At the individual level, change occurs in ever-shortening spans of time and, as a result, proximate cohorts tend to share fewer and fewer "natural paradigms".[2] In other words, interaction across cohorts is persistently threatened by an undercutting of the ability to share a "taken for granted" sense of what otherwise appear to be shared worlds. This loss, in turn, often engenders mistrust of others, of one's self, and often of both; in consequence of which empathy frequently emerges not from assumed shared experience, but as a cultivated ability to detect, decipher, and transpose the mysteries of others, including the self as other. Decentering comes to describe the realms of both the intrapsychic and the interpersonal.

Within this context of pervasive change, what the future – which was, and still is, for many persons the justification of their lives – might look like upon its realization is rarely guaranteed. The familiar cliché that there are two sources of human misery, "not having what you want and having what you want", takes on a new significance. It is only in the past several decades that we have learned on a massive basis the hard truth of the latter, as we learned that success under certain circumstances can occasion painful dissatisfactions as much as they are occasioned by failure (Simon and Gagnon 1975). Moments of achievement, which once promised consummatory gratification, often become a shallow, if not mocking, experience because either the achiever or the meaning of the achievement has changed during the interval.

We meet the future in the present with what we are, which includes what we have been. Few prior generations have had to live their own futures with the speed, comprehensiveness, and intensity with which we have lived ours *as a normal condition*. Even our self-conscious attempt to preserve the past evokes a kind of nervousness as if we expect to encounter signs that announce that some part of the past is currently "closed for repairs".

Continuing change creates unevenly intense levels of stress. Perhaps it is experienced as less stressful for those for whom the constancy of change is becoming normal, but in any case it is stressful for all to some degree. All too often, strategic responses to the stress of change are either an adaptation to the requirements of the present, which must risk the pains of alienation from what we once were, or a tiring, self-conscious regulation of patterns of behavior that once were mindless affirmations of our being in the world. For example, many trained in one set of rules of gender conduct must now learn to conform to radically modified rules, often at the expense of feelings of alienation from earlier identity claims, or to resist newer expectations at the expense of risking alienation from the world, as well as from other aspects of themselves. This dilemma would be typified by many women's feelings that loyalty to the desires currently experienced by the self are often experienced as a kind of disloyalty to prior constructions of the self as well as a betrayal of a legacy of significant others. Such inner conflict often includes issues of getting married, staying married, having children, and commitments to work and other employments.

INDIVIDUATION

A second critical aspect of postmodernity is an extraordinary heightening of *individuation* which can be described as the consequence of the *multiplication* and *segregation* of roles available to, in some measure forced upon, the individual. One result is that persons can share a nearly identical portfolio of roles without sharing similar commitments or coming to them from similar origins. More importantly, such persons will have little reason to experience themselves as sharing a common collective identity, except in the increasingly specific categories with which "actuarial" social bookkeeping describes a public (J. Simon 1988). Far more typical of the ways common interest finds expression in postmodern settings is the *class action* lawsuit, whose participants tend to be and remain strangers to each other.

This is not to say that strong group identities do not exist, but rather to note that most of us experience these identities commonly as *partial*, where the experiences of collective membership almost instantaneously become occasions for consciousness of difference with other group members, and *provisional*, where both social life and attachment to such groups lose a sense of permanence. A social landscape emerges where the self and its self-affirming, self-sustaining and self-inventing narratives are recited by an increasingly decentered self that is more than the sum of its current portfolio of social roles.[3] *As a result, the continuing standardization or apparent uniformities of social life tend to obscure a growing and possibly critical pluralism at the level of individual experience.*

More than anything else, the individual experiences postmodernity as a proliferation of *choices*, choices that are often uncertain in their outcomes and irregular in their availability. As Charles Horton Cooley observed regarding choice some ninety years ago:

> Choice is like a river; it broadens as it comes down through history – though there are always banks – and the wider it becomes the more persons drown in it. Stronger and stronger swimming is required and types of character that lack vigor and self-reliance are more and more likely to go under.
>
> (Cooley 1902: 39)

What Cooley was suggesting is that the self is not a given within social life, but a continuing production of social life, a production given to change, even at the most fundamental levels, as significant change occurs within social life. *The proliferation of choice must occasion a qualitative increment in the internal dialogues of the self and, in doing so, must also occasion a shift in the politics of the self* (Simon *et al.* 1993).

Choice, once the rarest and most calamitous of human experiences, becomes an everyday experience in all aspects of social life and mandates equally unprecedented occasions for self-reflexivity, the self scrutinizing itself. Let me pose this in its most pedestrian instance. Enormous numbers of us almost daily ask ourselves a question, a question that most of humanity asked, if ever, on only the rarest of occasions, "What shall I wear today?" This question joins conceptions of the self with the individual's perceptions of the expectations of others; the individual self-consciously anticipating her or his subsequent role as a text that will be read by others. The transparency of coded (costumed and postured) social roles may increasingly render opaque the inner self, often isolating the self, sheltering it and, at times, transforming it (Davis 1992).

The social roles we occupy are increasingly experienced, as Ortega y Gasset (1963) would have it, not as natural and fixed representations of the self, not as we experience the constraints of our skins, but as optional appliances, as costumes that celebrate, and at times disguise, *assertions* about who and what we have been, as well as what we are and what we desire to be. This enlarged domain of reflexive management of the self is the major source of the development of a more managerial and more abstract self. Though we might speak of an empowering of the self, this does not necessarily mean a more powerful self, except in the sense of the more conscious role it plays in the production of itself.

> So then I am the one who looks at himself (myself), a sort of impotent God. I am not only a watchful eye. I am also the one who experiences

7

the passions, desires, and so forth, which are both myself and not myself. I am within, I am without: the one who makes, who is made, who sees what is done and how it is done, without really under-standing .... I have a sort of impression that events are taking place within me, that things and passions are conflicting within me; that I am watching myself and seeing the struggle of these opposing forces, and that now one, now the other follows; a melee, a mental battlefield. And that the real self is the "I" who watches "myself" who am the scene of these happenings, these conflicts. I am not these passions, it seems, I am the one who beholds them, watches, comments, considers. I am also the one who yearns for a different self .... I am not my passions, I am in my passions.

(Ionesco 1987: 30–1)

Where complexity and change at the broad social level and individuation and uncertainty at the individual level create ever-expanding alternatives and uncertainties, other latent sources of individual diversity begin to find increased expression and heightened significance. One such source is the remarkable diversity rooted in genetic variability, which currently may become more significant as individuals become less singularly encapsu-lated within institutional settings more enduring than themselves. An-other derives from the weight of innumerable idiosyncratic, marginally significant events and traumas of life. A relevant insight can be found in Freud's *Three Essays on a Theory of Sexuality* (1905), where he notes that the experiences of childhood are of as little significance in "primitive" societies as they are of great significance in modern societies. I take this to mean that in social contexts where there is little choice and little uncertainty regard-ing the destinies of individuals, where most of the features of everyday existence come in only one model, variations that derive from either inborn characteristics, such as tolerance for discomfort, or the common or un-common traumas of childhood are of little consequence, having only a limited capacity to influence behaviors already ordered by tradition. In such settings, where there is relative uniformity in expectations about behavior, where others mirror back the nearly identical image of the individual, and where individual and group identities are virtually synonymous, it takes a remarkable person to resist calls for conformity in social worlds where alternative ways of doing things are literally unthinkable.

As Trilling (1972) and Elias (1978) both noted, it is only when there is sufficient heterogeneity in social experience, and a pluralism of mirrored images of the self, that a significant expansion of the domain and powers of psychic reality occurs. This development can be seen as the beginnings of the modern self; an occasion marked by an increase in uncertainty about our ultimate destinies and a diversity of alternatives open to the individual mandates an enlarged internal dialogue as well as a strategic appraisal of the environment.[4] A social world that requires that we negotiate for our desires must simultaneously train us to negotiate with ourselves; a complexity of social experience creates a comparable complexity of psychological life. Increasingly, how rare is the characteristic that Riesman (1969) found so essential to worlds bound in tradition, the characteristic of not being able to think of oneself as being anything but what one is? How much more scarce are those who cannot think of the surrounding world as being anything other than what it presents itself as being?

THE PARADIGMATIC AND POSTPARADIGMATIC

These developments can be described as an evolutionary drift from being what I have called a *paradigmatic* social order to its current and possibly permanent *postparadigmatic* social condition. Paradigmatic contexts are those that realize a high degree of consensual meanings, shared meanings that tend to fit together almost seamlessly, since they are often experienced as being derived from a smaller number of master paradigms that, in turn, are all authorized by some universally shared, ultimate source of truth. Thus *patriarchy* as a cultural practice described (and proscribed) patterns of behavior, not only within the family but also between the monarch and the subject, the employer and the employee, the healer and the patient, the priest and the parishioner, and the teacher and the student. As individuals moved from role to role, the dominant cultural styles remained constant. Ultimately, the principle of hierarchy was viewed as being as natural and as universal as the relationship between the individual and God the father.

Postparadigmatic contexts are those where this seamless integration of consensual meanings begins to dissolve. Appearing in pluralized forms, with their underlying assumptions stripped of their unquestionable authority, even the most familiar aspects of social life become sites for conflicting or alternative options. This can be observed where the legacy of modernism meets the legacy of traditional society, since there are currently as many alternative forms of psychotherapy as there are forms of religious practice. Even more expressive of the impact of postmodernity are the wide divergences of practice and theory within most current religions and schools of psychotherapy.

In effect, postparadigmatic conditions are precisely what occasion this dense introduction. One can less and less assume that there is any depth of shared meanings or common knowledge, particularly when discussing that in which we are all participants – the human experience. The mid-century's dream of realizing a systematically integrated human science remains just that – a dream, possibly a deceptive and deceiving dream and, like all dreams, regulated more by a wish than by reality.

Much of the foregoing might best be paraphrased in the concluding remarks of Ernest Gellner in his recent work, *Reason and Culture*:

> In a stable traditional world, [persons] had identities, linked to their social roles, and confirmed by their overall vision of nature and society. Instability and rapid change both in knowledge and in society has deprived such self-images of the erstwhile feel of reliability. Identities are perhaps more ironic and conditional than once they were, or at any rate, when confident unjustifiably so.
>
> (Gellner 1992: 182)

PROBLEMS OF THEORY

The postmodern condition, then, calls into question what is perhaps the most fundamental assumption of traditional sociological theory: that society, more than having conceptual utility, constitutes an organic reality, an objective reality that coercively frames our considerations of social life. Society, so described, was viewed as constituting a continuing truth of our lives, against which competing claims for being a more true understanding of our lives can be judged (Denzin 1991). So much of our common training makes it difficult to accept that there is no one truth of society around which differently located perspectives may contest, but rather only a shared moment containing a plurality of articulated perspectives, each attempting to realize the full power of its version of reality.

The invoking of the concept of society and its interests, then, is almost always viewed as fraudulent from some points of view. This implicit intracultural relativism appears negative and, in a literal sense, endlessly committed to the "unmasking" or "debunking" of prior understandings. Such "negativity" in cultural criticism is not unique to our day. The unmasking of an existing understanding about the nature or meaning of given social phenomena has been a near constant thread in cultural criticism from the very beginnings of the modern era in the West. It was the particular hallmark of the creation of the social sciences in the nineteenth century. The negative or deconstructive aspects of much earlier work – Marx and Freud come to mind – also provoked accusations of cultural nihilism, accusations of facilitating the erosion of basic beliefs that were viewed in their day as necessary for the sustaining of everyday life.[5]

Science, which traditionally requires the practice of persistent skepticism, always promised a kind of nihilism, which is why its history of triumphs is also a chronicle of what were originally viewed as dangerous and demoralizing heresies. However, in recent times, the organized institutions of science have moved to a more central and authoritative social role. This ascendancy, after much early resistance, followed because it emerged in ways that were inseparable from modernity's promise of continuous progress; science provided the direct imagery of continuous progress towards the collapsing of all truths into a single formula or password. During the interim, science offered an implicit promise that all previously outmoded or embarrassed "truths" or "understandings" would ultimately be replaced by other understandings that were certifiably more true, closer to ultimate truth. At the level of social science, this assurance generated a kind of conceptual incest where the "negative dialectic", its deconstructive mode, appears to germinate a positive vision of the "new". Such visions of the new often preceded the critique, serving as the inspiration for the critique of previous understandings and practices.[6]

What is so problematic for the contemporary cultural critic is that it has become far more difficult to move from the deconstructive mode to the constructive (or reconstructive) mode. The illuminations of contemporary social science are born tainted by the almost immediate recognition that, at their best, they may represent little more than "enlightened false consciousness" (Sloterdijk 1987). This "false consciousness" remains haunted by the awareness of the inevitability of having its own products subsequently proven "false", not only when viewed from the elevations or descents of an unknowable future, but when viewed as the fractional interests that derive from distinct social locations. For possibly the first time, critique of the canon, once offered as a self-generated and universal heritage, calls into question the very concept of canon, which is increasingly seen as the strategic and contingent manipulations of factional interests. Both truth and beauty become objects of suspicion as we learn to ask, "Whose truth?" "Whose beauty?" "Serving what purpose?"

One of the major reasons for what currently appears as an unusual hyperdeconstructivity is that conventional social science – indeed, in the Popperian sense, science generally – is foremost among the targets of postmodern cultural criticism. For example, the "unmasking" and "debunking" implicit in the concept of latency, so fundamental to many genres of analysis, have themselves been accused of being little more than the "masking" and "bunking" that attend the rise of alternative or emergent forms of "mask" and "bunk". "Society", once viewed as an autonomous and coercive reality, becomes a questionable assumption, one suspected of serving narrow and, more importantly, temporary interests. It is as if society, once our "continent", dissolved leaving an "archipelago" of distinct institutional spheres largely unregulated by any central purpose or universal value. Additionally, the criticism an earlier social science made of the insights of the humanities, a criticism that focused upon the inherent subject-centered biases of its modes of *representing* reality, is now being turned upon social science itself. As R.P. Blackmur noted:

We are condemned ... to act, for the first time in history, out of the strength and weakness of the human imagination alone. It is not that

11

imagination is different, but our relation to it; that we know it to be unreservedly human, immitigably worldly, utterly subject to our own control. We know its smallness.

(Blackmur 1989: 109)

PLURALISM HAPPENS

If any single concept dominates discourse about postmodernism, with the possible exception of "discourse" itself, it is the concept of *pluralism*. What we have been slow to incorporate in our discourses is that pluralism permeates all aspects of life; it is not merely a matter of ideas or intellectual fashions, but a pluralism of human experience. The very tendency of contemporary social science theory has been to create abstract formalisms that obscure this pluralism of experience, as such theories seek to discover transcendent uniformities in the "socio" logics and "psycho" logics of behavior.

Varieties of humans, especially varieties of individual characteristics, abilities, or potentials, have always been present, though perhaps never in such abundance, as the explosive growth of populations provides more of each possible kind and as the growth in the density of circuits of communication makes it more difficult to evade recognition. In *paradigmatic societies*, as described above, ideology and experience coalesce in the reproduction of social life because both derive from the same history of continuing practice; it is as if they are already pretested within histories of usage. It is in such settings that sociological theory should find optimum confirmation; and, for that very reason, individuals in such settings rarely feel required to create their own sociological inquiry.

Paradigmatic social orders take the larger variety of human capacities or histories and transform them into a smaller number of possible outcomes or transform most of existing diversity into non-consequential variations. This production of conformity is largely facilitated by the slowness and fearfulness of change. In contrast, *postparadigmatic* (or postmodern) social orders, where change becomes normalized, operate in reverse, as identical points of origin give rise to many different outcomes and, moreover, where identical outcomes can be recognized as the product of a diversity of origins. The postparadigmatic social experience, even when occasioning identical experiences, seems less capable of inspiring a corresponding sense of solidarity or collective identification. Where reports of patterned behavior persist, such patterns tend to describe aggregates and rarely cohesive groups. In other words, part, but not all, of the pluralism of the postmodern world is the increased significance or empowering of individual differences both genetic and contextual.

The modern world created the conditions that in turn created individuals as significant actors in their own right. Individual narratives are rarely synonymous with the narrative of some larger collectivity. More-over, constraint, even when uniform and widespread, tends to be experi-enced individually rather than collectively. Paradigmatic settings offer us *the self as other*; their version of a self is one fully dominated by tribal or collective identifications. It is a relationship that many disturbed by the experiences of postmodernity seek to simulate as a refuge. In contrast, the experience of the modern world gives rise to *the self for the other*, where even the most fundamental of reciprocities are subject to negotiation, where the individual learns "to give in order to get", where the individual learns to purchase security with conformity. This is typified by Freud's observation that the child approaches significant social development when it learns to "smile when it is not happy". Elias extends Freud's observation to include the possibility of the potential postmodern response within the very experience of the modern.

> Only gradually do the children of internally differentiated societies learn to smile without feeling. And then it seems to human beings that their real self is imprisoned within them and exists without relation at all to other people.
>
> (Elias 1984, cited by Honneth and Joas 1988: 120.)

The postmodern experience, then, occasions *the self for itself*, the response of those who have no choice but to manage the increasing diversity and density of interpersonal and intrapsychic dialogues; where many indivi-duals learn not only to stage their own lives, but to "stage direct" numerous changes of scenes and acts.

Traditional social settings require loyalty as the basis of conformity – the legend of patriarchy in its purest form. Modern societies occasioned the invention of love (of other) – the oedipal family creates bonds of inescap-able paranoia. And, finally, the effect of the postmodern is to have (self-)love consume loyalty; where, in a very significant way, many can be said to have been "born to shop" and "be shopped".[7]

In the modern social world, little is more disturbing than repetitive irregularities for which no comprehensive explanation can be established. The initial charge of social science was to normalize such deviance, to bring it within the dominance or conceptual boundaries of the normal (Cohen 1985). This was a task that grew increasingly difficult as the modern social world tended to increase heterogeneity in the production of conformity, as well as in the production of deviance.

Abstraction in social science theory, as well as in other cultural institu-tions, such as art and architecture, was the dominant response to an ever-increasing individuating and diversifying of what were previously com-mon activities. As abstract art could accommodate diverse and temporary settings or sites, as the international style of building, even with a post-modern facade, could shelter an enormous diversity of activities, social

13

science concepts struggled to achieve an immunity to the specifics of history and locale.[8]

It is possible that individuals adapt to the individuating postmodern experience more easily than the institutions within which they exist. As we often know more than we can express as knowing, we often adapt to complexities we have great difficulty in conceptualizing. This may be particularly true of organized science and its anomic division of labor, which followed increases in the scope of information with an equally substantial increase in the number of available scientific workers. Diversified and isolated spaces of theories and substantive interests increase, and, in time, abstractions from social life become the coercive guides to the study of social life.

This enforced specialization inevitably leads to the treatment of specific attributes or behaviors as if they were "nouns" instead of "adjectives", as specifically situated, contingent attributes become objects of study and subjects of theorizing in their own right. A common interest creates a common self-referencing audience, self-certifying expertise, as well as a shared structure of rewards. Concern for familial relationships gives rise to the pursuit of "the family", concern for race relationships gives rise to the study of "intergroup relationships", concern for sexual behaviors gives rise to "the homosexual" and, mostly as an afterthought, "the heterosexual".

A definition, implicitly a theory, inherently and dangerously essentializes the particular objects of concern. For this there may be no alternative. The nature of language, more than the nature of life, imposes the risk of essentializing upon all efforts at arriving at a shared understanding. This essentializing masks variability in two distinct ways. The first is typified by a quest for a singular cause of all who fall into some common category, as in the recently advertised search for a "gay" gene. The second is an indifference to changing contexts, encouraging us to view such categories of behavior in ways in which they appear to maintain some constant essence, such as assuming that same-gender sexual contacts in Periclean Athens share some essential identity with such behavior occurring today. It is in this fashion that essentializing, in its several meanings, creates the "normal", even where the "normal" is viewed with suspicion.

Once the normal is constructed, its explanation organizes our understanding of all other variations by moving us to conceive of all other outcomes as violations or variations of the logic of the normal. The power of the normal is its ability both to establish "difference" and, then, to disguise "difference" by transforming it either into "variation" or "deviance". In doing so, all instances falling within a category become understandable in terms of the contours of some instances. Differences within a conceptualized category are rarely to be seen as requiring different explanations, but only as variations of an already established "theme".[9] This process of developing explanations is particularly irresistible when we start the process with already defined and differentially evaluated outcomes, that is, when there is a pre-existing commitment to what at the moment is defined as the normal.

The pressures that create the tyranny of the normal are evident in the subsequent creation of the normal deviant, which represent explanations of categories or sub-categories of deviants, conceptually "victimizing" deviants by ordering them in terms of a double homogenization: the inevitable homogenization that accompanies the construction of the normal and then that of the construction of normal deviance. As the post-modernization of social life moves forward, the pluralization of experience and the pluralization of the ways in which specific individuals incorporate experience have a double effect upon the future of social theory. First, the ability of theory-based categories, and the seemingly more concrete variable labels derived from them, to encompass significant homogeneities must diminish. This accounts for the inability of the collective research effort to increase substantially the ability to account for variance, despite decades of investment in talent, money, and the development of increasingly complex analytic techniques. However, this "failure" of accountability is only, in a restrictive sense, a problem of theory or methodologies. Rather it reflects a problem of social life and a problem of social theory in social life.

Second, there is the possibility that challenges posed by the pluralization of experience tend to create different, and possibly new, architectures of the self that are different from those implicit in most inherited theory. The latter possibility suggests that continuity in the development of theory, currently so positively valued, can also be viewed as a dangerous seduction.

In highly pluralized contexts, the very attempt at general theory, even a general theory of relatively specific social phenomena, may be condemned to banal abstraction or limited empirical validity and, in any case, must occasion recognized and unrecognized essentialisms. This is why so much of what appears as postmodern social science, whose very initiating premise is the recognition of the dangers and dangerous uses of essentialistic thinking, appears so negative.

Note, for example, the essentializing characteristics involved in the employment of such terms as "modern" and "postmodern" or "paradigmatic" and "postparadigmatic". Further, even as one invokes the term "postmodern", it is hard not to acknowledge how much of social life – indeed, how much of one's own experience of the contemporary world – is describable in the characteristics of the most traditional of social orders and, if not such characteristics, then the desire for experiences associated with the feel of traditional social orders.

One critical sense of the idea of postmodernism is that history can no longer be seen as an unfolding, but as a constant turning in upon itself. The very term "the history of the present" reminds us that transformations of the present inevitably bring with them corresponding transformations of the past. There may be no immediately available representations that can reflect the image of a fluid, multilayered, pluralized world, one where our heightened awareness of the over-determined character of all social life makes equally apparent its continuing under-determination, its unfinished character.

In this pluralized context, it is not enough that competing versions of social life are available. A pluralization of social theory cannot adequately describe the pluralization of social life. Nor is some common ground they all might share necessarily an insightful source of understanding; the residua of shared agreement that Mannheim (1936) expected, when he held that a "science of politics" could emerge from a residuum of shared agreement occurring among fractional class interests, has yielded little, little beyond the banal. The unresolved dialectics of multiple theories may provide the best context for deepening our understanding of the dialectics of social life *at any one point in time*. Unfortunately, within our current anomic division of labor, this is precisely what so rarely happens, as the adherents of each theoretical perspective seem to occupy their own space, addressing their own audience, while busily aggrandizing available resources in their own narrow self-interest.

The requirement of theory in this postmodern context is not, as has been proposed by the first wave of postmodern critics, the devaluing of empirical methods, but the revaluing of theory or at least an abandonment of formal theory, an abandonment of seeking for the overarching generalization. Methodologies of all types are critical; they are our ways of seeing and occasions for discussion or thinking out loud about the world. They become obstructive when they become occasions for transpiring the specifics of research into wastelands of essentialized concepts of "theoretical relevance".

There is good reason to consider a reversal of the recent practice of perhaps overvaluing a self-conscious link between theory (understanding) and research (description) (Merton 1957) and the encouraging of a greater distancing of the two. While acknowledging that theory and research will inevitably contextualize each other, it may not be desirable that either wholly specify or limit the other. This might preserve the potential of each to simultaneously inspire and embarrass the other. Such distancing provides for encouragement to try to understand what we cannot fully measure, and, perhaps more importantly, to attempt to measure (observe) what we do not wholly understand.

This reciprocal freeing of each kind of effort is itself facilitated by abandoning a kind of pluralized autotelism that science's anomic division of labor has encouraged; an autotelism that encourages us to speak of progress in each branch and sub-specialty of the social sciences as if each

16

provided, by itself, measures of its own significance. It may also require an abandonment of the existing tendency to seek the perfection of both theory and methodology, as is implicit in the establishment of these concerns as distinct and privileged callings. In honoring these as distinct and elevated positions, we recreate and celebrate in our own practice the very alienative, hierarchical and self-exploitative relationships that describe the larger social order where implicit theories, including – or especially – of the sexual, tend to shape practice.[10]

What follows is not a comprehensive survey of sexual behavior. This is not because "the data are not yet in". No such data are likely to appear. Nor is it a comprehensive theory offering explanation of all of sexuality's manifestations or all the behaviors currently recognized as possessing sexual meaning. Perhaps the best that can be offered at present is theory as a conceptual apparatus that confronts its own uncertainties and seeks its unseen biases and shifting parameters as are inevitable in a context of continuing rapid change and heightened pluralization.

Theories are also autobiographical statements, their authors are both witnesses and subjects of change. But the same may be said of you, the reader, and what you will make of these texts.

1

THE POSTMODERNIZATION OF SEX

There are times in life when the question of knowing if one can think differently than one thinks, and perceive differently than one sees, is absolutely necessary if one is going to go on looking and reflecting at all.

(Michel Foucault 1985)

INTRODUCTION

The very use of the term postmodern in application to so many aspects of the contemporary experience and life, as well as the ease with which we have come to accept as blandly descriptive a term that initially sounds oxymoronic, suggests that we are at a point in cultural development that can only be viewed as a major watershed. Across the arts, humanities, and human sciences, one detects a sense of intellectual crisis: in particular, a crisis of paradigms (Lyotard 1984). Indeed, the very term postmodern appears to be descriptive of broad ranging recapitulation, refurbishment, and reordering of our cultural past; collage and pastiche become the basis for the appearance of novelty. Disciplines and sciences alike seem incapable of either consensus, discovery, or consolidation; it is not that there is little that is new, but that there is little suggestive of the freshly innovative.

Despite the advertisement of future shocks and multiple revolutions of little more than a decade ago, of which a sexual revolution had to be among the most widely advertised, the future seems to have turned in upon itself. Modernism, which was for most the promise of an ever-expanding (for some, an ever-threatening) emergence of the new, seems to have ground to a halt; it is as if we had exhausted the possibilities of the new. Not since the Renaissance has the concept of progress been viewed with such suspicion.

In more general terms, the optimism – a broad-ranging optimism that touched virtually all aspects of social life – of two decades ago seems to have given way to the most profound pessimism. For the first time in centuries the Western world appears to be without a vision of tomorrow that is brighter than today; our idealizations almost all seem to derive from

18

images of the past, with none of these attracting wide endorsement. A social world that little more than a decade ago promised the wisdom and technologies to enrich our sexualities, sexualities that would, in turn, enrich our lives, now appears to be offering far less than that. The liberation of the sexual, at the time, was viewed as the abandonment of its bondage to the traditional accompaniments of danger and damnation, and of the requirement that it be allowed only when preconditionally harnessed to very specific uses, most of which had little direct relevance to sexual pleasure.

The 1960s and 1970s, which can be seen as the apotheosis of modernism, were the culmination of a period of change, of optimism and innocence. If we recall, those of us who were present, what predictions were made then about what today's world would look like, it would be the rarest among us who could escape embarrassment: how little those mid-1970s projections of today anticipated the current, massively less encouraging sexual landscape. Indeed, the horizon that once offered competing images of sexual health and joy is now completely dominated by competing images of impending sexual disaster. If anything is to be learned from this dismal failure of our collective prophetic powers, it is that there is little reason to assume that today's pessimism provides any clearer vision; pessimism has its own claims to innocence, its own history of embarrassments.

Two conclusions can be drawn from this brief retrospection. First, the hopeful have as much right as the despairing to distrust the pronouncements of "sexologists". The sexual future in whatever form it is conceived may in fact be brighter than life today encourages us to expect. Second, the future of the sexual is only in the most minimal sense in the control of what presently constitutes the sexual, and possibly still less in the application of what relatively little we already seem to know or are likely to learn in the next few years.

I hope that this current situation might encourage us to broaden our concerns for the sexual, to deny it its traditional position of privileged isolation, and to try to understand how the sexual helps to shape the totality of experience and how the larger context of social life may shape the sexual experience at its most fundamental level.

THE REMOTENESS OF THE RECENT PAST

The scientific study of sex can trace the earliest of its most significant roots almost to the memory of living humanity. But the growth, one might almost say explosion, of scientific attention to the sexual must really be charted from the end of the Second World War. A period of some forty years, half of which was almost entirely dominated by the works of a single group – Alfred Kinsey and his colleagues.[1] However, this explosive growth of scientific attention did not occur in isolation.

A distinct era in the Western experience that culminated in the mid-1970s saw comparable shifts and transformations in most other aspects of our lives and the landscapes that surrounded us. For example, within far less than the span of a single generation our uses of time and space were utterly transformed. The concepts and implicit valuing of modernism seemed all at once to permeate almost all of social life; what for so long had been the major source of assault upon the conventional became the conventional. It was as if, almost without warning, tomorrow finally arrived and, more than being contemplated, had to be lived.

After two decades (1950–1970) of almost unprecedented affluence, an enriched and enlarged North American middle class was pressed hard to demonstrate a talent not merely for success but for living and enjoying that success (Simon and Gagnon 1975). Thus the sexual, which previously had been a source of compensation for the common deprivations and denials of life and a motivational spur to achievement, became something to do more than contemplate. The sexual became proof for many of their capacity to experience life to the fullest. The sexual had come out of the closet.

A quality of affluence also described the condition of both theoretical and applied scientific work in the sexual realm. Moreover, it was not merely financial affluence (dangerous, but not the least dangerous of all the forms of affluence) but an affluence of attention as well. Sex commanded or competed for the center stage, not as innuendo, but as something that appeared larger than life and was available for immediate exploitation.

MODERNISM AS A WAY OF LIFE

Modernism represented a pervasive adherence to the concept of progress, to the idea of constant movement toward the achievement of ever-changing ideals. As modernism in art was to take us ever closer to the purest expressions of the sublime, modern science was charged with bringing us closer to pure truth, final truth – and if not these, then an improved version of truth, one closer to truth than any of the previous versions of the truth, as if changes in truth were synonymous with increases in truth. In more practical terms, the application of science to the realm of the sexual was expected to solve its historic mysteries, to unlock puzzles old and new, until all that was natural yielded up its lawful recipes.

Sexology was born in this modernist tradition. The modernization of sex critically involved the naturalization of sex; the sexual was to be subjected to the perspectives of natural science which, in turn, required the quest for taxonomies, structures, and mechanisms of change that paralleled the vocabulary of the natural sciences as they were applied to all other life forms. A cool detachment or impersonality and a grinding empiricism, more often in rhetoric than practice, justified the license to investigate, to observe, and commit public talk about sex.

While being cloaked in a version of science brought new legitimacies for

20

conducting sex research, it also carried its own burdens. Willingly or unwillingly, all who participated were drafted for continuing debate on the parameters of normality and healthfulness; even those who struggled to expand the definitions of both normality and health, and thereby lessen the exclusion of many of those whose sexual behaviors were distrusted or despised, inevitably gave credence to the very concepts of normality or healthfulness.

MODERNIZATION AS NATURALIZATION

Cultural license was granted to contemplate the sexual, but in an isolation that actually reinforced the continuing exile of the sexual from the rest of social life. The experience of sexual *conduct* was necessarily viewed as translatable into the facts of sexual *behavior* – the idea that the establishing of the physical geography of the sexual orgasm could become the foundation of sexual science at its most transcendent. The naturalization of the sexual required a view of the sexual that was increasingly ahistorical. An ahistoricism, in turn, that produced a concrete abstractness that allowed orgasm to become a thing unto itself, a "hyperreality" with a physiology, chemistry, and neurology all its own. From Kinsey *et al.*'s (1948, 1953) "outlet" to the Masters and Johnson's (1966) graphic representation of *the* stages of *the* orgasm, the new science of sex was complicit in producing an alienated orgasm – one fortunately alienated more in its thinking about orgasm than in most people's experience of orgasm.

This naturalization of sex encouraged, first, the adoption of a preference for taxonomic distinctions that assumed permanent basic differentiations. The Kinsey homosexual–heterosexual continuum often became in its uses discrete categories as if delineating sub-species, describing individuals by the number of their position on this continuum as if some specific position along it was reflective of some basic characterological attribute. And, similarly, much of the continuing quest for origins of homosexuality assumed a singular source, a naive assumption that a homogeneity of acts implied a corresponding homogeneity of actors. In effect, what was little more than an analytically convenient but shallow typology was transformed into an oppressive taxonomy; the multiple meanings of all sexualities were dissolved into global identities that obscured more than they revealed, beyond the social responses they often legitimated.

Involved was a conceptualization of the object of sexual desire so abstract that, when applied to behavior, the issue of sexual desire was almost totally obscured by a preoccupation with the limited issue of the gender of the sexual object. This encouraged a vulgar behaviorism that tended to render invisible the meaning of the larger part of observable behavior and virtually all of non-observable behavior, such as motivation and the intrapsychic landscapes that evoke sexual excitement. This objectification

21

also served the politics of sexual behavior by allowing the issues of inclusion and exclusion to appear to be solidly based upon the biological substrate. Thus, ironically, what were initially attempts to reduce the significance of the homosexual–heterosexual distinction evolved into the raw material for the creation of a homosexual whose difference was inscribed in nature, appearing almost "racial" in character (Epstein 1987; Escoffier 1985).

DRIVE AS TRUTH IN ITSELF

Similarly, the naturalization of sex that accompanied its modernization tended to welcome Freud's drive theory and its corresponding invention of a sexually responsive infant and child, even when much of the other baggage of psychoanalytic theory was rejected. Viewing sexuality as a biologically ordered developmental process allowed for the introduction of a language of sexual behavior that seemed to be independent of the specific meanings necessary for its expression beyond childhood; it defined a sexuality that need not have immediate social or emotional meanings.

The surviving illusions of childhood's essential innocence allowed for scientific discourse on the sexual to occur without involving heavily charged erotic meanings. As a result, an emotional distance was created that gave credibility to the objectification of sexual behavior, which, in turn, could be described as resembling biological systems like the digestive process.

INFORMATION PLEASE: EXPLANATION WITHOUT UNDERSTANDING

The naturalization of sex occurred in the larger context of the application of scientific method to a wide number of human activities, not all of which could equally be subjected to this objectifying approach. A new sexual science was viewed as the accumulation of the exhaustive and precise delineation of the parts constituting the sexuality of the person. The implicit expectation was that once all the essential facts of each part were in hand, the explanation of the phenomenon would be realized, its mysteries revealed. The approach was not unlike that of the eighteenth-century anatomists who were convinced that they would find the secret of life on the dissecting table. Some analogies to this reductionist application of scientific method, frequently a caricature of scientific method, could be found in the German Sexual Hygiene Movement of the 1920s (Haeberle 1983), elements of Wilhelm Reich's concept of bio-energy (1961), as well as many of the applications of technologically fixated "hard science" appearing in our current journals.

Popular images of medicine tended to share this master paradigm. Identifying the specific cause, the specific cure or vaccine for a specific disease was the essential program: a program infused with the language of discovery, discovery of what was waiting in nature to be discovered. For many illnesses or diseases this was and remains a perfectly effective model. Heroic figures became part of popular history in association with the discovery of the source of specific illnesses and specific cures. However, this application of the medical model tends to be effective only for those conditions where the uniformity of the symptom is matched by a comparable uniformity in the underlying "pathology", where description, explanation and understanding are virtually synonymous. But for many other conditions it is clearly not as effective. And perhaps it is least effective in dealing with those "pathologies" that are rooted in the shifting complexities of social and psychological life.

THE FACTUALITY OF SEX

This narrow conception of the application of scientific method found passionate adherence among sexual researchers for the obvious reason that it provided protection and legitimacy. The language of science, its postures, even its costumes, became the conceptual rubber gloves that allowed for the examination of what the larger social world predominantly viewed as "dirty business". Sexual activity could be described in a cool, unexcited language wondrously remote from passionate emotional conflicts or heavy breathing. It also created the illusion of distance that protected researchers from accusations of self-interest beyond the admirable quest for truth and the facilitation of individual and social health. The definition of what constituted health was often unspecified, except as the apparent absence of what conventional wisdom held to be ill-health. By describing subjects in language through which they rarely could recognize themselves, sex researchers also shrouded themselves in a protective suggestion of little direct involvement. Sex researchers, themselves, were to be seen as being beyond sexual failure and anxiety, beyond being moved by sexual fantasies involving the improbable, the unattractive, or the unacceptable. Such objectivity muted concerns about questions of motivation for initiating research and about the possible consequences of a preoccupation with so suspect a topic.

Beyond the work of Stoller (1979, 1985a) and relatively few others, the question of what creates sexual excitement, how it is rooted not in our bodies but in our lives, has only been considered in the most superficial ways. In other words, we have been encouraged to avert our attention from the creation of the erotic, the creation of sexual meanings, sexual motives, and sexual priorities. The naturalization of sex rendered such concerns unnecessary: as an expression of the natural it was alleged to be there at the

23

very beginning – that it came as standard equipment with the body. Postures associated with reproduction, though they might also be little more than shared metaphors capable of many different uses, became a psychobiological bedrock that need be examined only when they appeared in unattractive or undesirable guises.

The functionalism often implicit in the language of the natural sciences unreflexively granted a legitimating utility to these attractive, desirable and generative sexual postures which required scrutiny only when suspicions of taint or failure were raised. The discourses of sexual normality appeared predominantly within the empty spaces of the discourses of sexual abnormality – tapping sources of sexual excitement, sources safely insulated by silence.

HEROIC RESEARCH: MILESTONES AND MILLSTONES

In Paul Robinson's (1976) view, the modernization of sex was associated with the works of Havelock Ellis, Kinsey, and Masters and Johnson. To which I would add the path-breaking work of John Money for having enlarged our attentions to the fullest implications of gender. These are people we associate with works and traditions of work from which we have all been beneficiaries. However, as monumental as such labors justifiably appear, they have also proved to be curiously barren of expanding traditions of exploration or understanding. Working in an oppressive isolation, such pioneers rarely challenged these conditions of isolation: rather than shaping their views of the sexual to meet their beliefs about the nature of the human, they (Kinsey, Masters and Johnson, and Money, more than Ellis) allowed their image of the human to be shaped by their beliefs regarding the sexual.

The Kinsey tradition was the least ambiguous about its commitment to empiricism at its most reductionist. The very titles of the classic works, *Sexual Behavior in the Human Male* (1948) and *Sexual Behavior in the Human Female* (1953), spoke directly to this narrow conception of "scientific" treatment of the sexual. The basic model for the research on sexual behavior was anticipated by Kinsey's prior work on the gall wasp (Robinson 1976: 51–2). This model was the source of his aspiration to finalize his research by completing a hundred thousand sex histories; his assumption was that in doing so he would be able to sample the human experience with sufficient density to reveal all forms of human sexuality in their relative frequency. Being an individual of extraordinary gifts, he often went beyond his own empiricist model, providing us with insights that went well beyond his statistics. But he rarely questioned the model itself.

More than two decades later, Bell and Weinberg (1978) and later Bell *et al.* (1981) did little better and possibly worse. Demonstrating how little they understood the implications of the titles given to their monographs

(*Homosexualities* and *Sexual Preference*), they sought the cause of object preference through a maze of quasi-simulations of reality (path models). Finding no one satisfactory social or psychological explanation of homosexual preference in men and women, from their data they concluded that its source must surely be found elsewhere. Their work culminated in finding a probable explanation of sexual preference in innate attributes that they could not describe, let alone explain or understand. Still conceptually trapped in the simplistic approach of the medical model, the possibility that sexual preference might be the outcome of a complex and highly variable process was not seriously considered. To risk confronting just how contingent our destinies are, as well as the degree to which these destinies are as much rooted in the minutiae of everyday life as they are in its moments of high drama, is consistent with modernism's abstract and ahistorical requirements.

Similarly, Money's unqualified condemnation of all attempts at a social–psychological explanation of human motivation, and his equally unqualified commitment to the ultimate explanatory powers of body chemistry and neurophysiology (Money 1980), can only be described as an act of religious faith, since it does not seem to rest upon reason, theory, or data. Money (1988) may conceptualize the isomorphism of "gender identity" – an intrapsychic experience – with "gender role" – observable behavior – but he does so only by linguistic fiat (see below, page 32). And appropriately so, as these concepts may function only as simplifying metaphors for processes of almost infinite complexity which have themselves been abstracted from processes of still greater complexity. His abstractions ignore the complexity of links between the sexual aspects of self and all other aspects of self and the ways in which gender roles reflect the linking of individual history with that of surrounding social life.

More recently, Lauman and his colleagues have provided us with what will remain for the indefinite future the definitive Kinseyesque survey of patterns of sexual behavior in contemporary North America (Lauman *et al.* 1994). This study's unequaled methodological sophistication probably qualifies it as the apotheosis of the modernist project to comprehensively audit sexual behavior. Moreover, embracing a tamed social constructionist or "scripting approach", the authors remain comfortably within a modernist paradigm by shifting the regulation of the sexual from the laws of nature to the laws of social life. This is accomplished by the employment of "network analysis", a questionable statistical method pretending to be a theory, and an "economic resource approach", which provides for an emotionally eviscerated conception of the sexual actor. Assuming with remarkable naivety that *sexual behavior* is virtually synonymous with *sexuality*, the major and largely ignored finding of the research is its demonstration of how little of sexual behavior is in the direct control of sexuality, as it ignores the profound and complex role that sexuality, in the

25

fullest sense of that word, plays in the dynamics of cultural, social, and personal life and, in particular, in the interplay between these.

The crisis of modernist perspectives seems to have come to the area of human sexuality more understandably than to most other areas: the best of a tradition of research that promised so much appears to have brought us close to a kind of disturbing pause, as if trapped in a sentence that cannot be completed. It should be obvious, except for the most myopic or naively optimistic, that the mere continuing of accumulation of more information, of more data, will not move us forward substantially. We are not dealing with an issue of information – at least, not of information alone; it is not so much a matter of *what* we think about the sexual as it is a matter of *how* we think about the sexual, not a matter of explanation, but one of understanding.

Let me be very careful at this point. It is not that I believe that we currently possess all the information we require or that what we have learned, frequently at very great costs, is without continuing relevance to our practice or our lives. What we have is a crisis of paradigms, one that follows, not because the prior paradigms failed but because they succeeded. As a result, we currently see more than we could have seen prior to the ascendancy of these paradigms. These works have made us aware of the distribution of the experiences of the sexual and of its different meanings; they have also made us aware of how these changed. Such works have themselves directly contributed to a revolution in thinking about the sexual, altered its meanings and prompted changes in realms of experience as well.

POSTMODERNIZATION AS DENATURALIZATION

The issues setting the agenda of postmodernism, simultaneously observable within many contexts, tend to share several elements or perhaps several ways of describing the same fundamental phenomena. The most common of these is an emergent consensus about a seeming absence of consensus. And perhaps this is not so much an absence of consensus as a sense of being forced to an unexpected and often discomforting pluralism. Marxism, neo-Darwinism, and Freudianism all seem to have undergone refurbishing, with no one intellectual tendency appearing to dominate; the marketplace of ideas has come to resemble a surreal carnival midway. More importantly, rarely has the gap between theory and ongoing research been so wide; the more global the aspirations of theory and the more technologically involved the research, the wider the gap appears.

One positive aspect of this new pluralism is the movement towards an abandonment of linear, one-dimensional concepts of intellectual progress, an abandonment of the promise of bringing a contingent and malleable reality into closer harmony with the essential (permanent) principles guiding life. This pluralism has brought with it a corresponding reappraisal of a model of incremental, incorporative progress in science, a concept of science that can be seen as having yielded little beyond coercive and latently ideological banalities when extended to consideration of human sexuality. In the postmodern debate, there is an increased acceptance of the possibility that the broad realm of human behavior creates a relativity that condemns us to what is, in some sense, permanent failure, or at least to an obligatory sense of the provisional. Karen Horney's observation of a half century ago that "there is no such thing as a normal psychology which holds for all [of humanity]" (1937 [1964]: 19) has a kind of renewed currency that lessens the risk of deceiving ourselves regarding the culturally and historically circumscribed aspect of our work. Recent historical research too abundantly reveals that the efforts at framing the "facts" of a specific time and place in the language of the timeless and the universal serves neither science nor society.

THE REALITIES OF THE SEXUAL REVOLUTION

What threatens the recently established, and still disputed, naturalization of the sexual is a growing awareness that not only do the meanings of the sexual change as the sociohistorical context within which it is experienced changes, but also that the very nature of the sexual may change as well. In other words, the possible need for new concepts regarding the sexual does not follow merely from the inadequacies or errors in the older concepts of sexuality but from the fact that sexual realities have undergone and are continuing to undergo substantial change.

The "sexual revolution" may in fact have been just that: a revolution – one that created a temporal compression such that, both within and across cohorts, it becomes difficult to speak of many dominant sexual homogeneities, except at the most overly concrete levels, the level of organs and orifices. It becomes increasingly possible that individuals separated from each other by only a few years or only by small differences in their respective personal histories may experience identical sexual behaviors in vastly different ways and often with vastly different consequences. Behind the deceptive stability of language ("a kiss is just a kiss"), the meaning of experience and the experience of meaning change.

Recognizing the existence of a plurality of homosexualities has been, and remains, a slow process. There may be even greater resistance to recognition of the existence of a plurality of heterosexualities. One major source of the resistance to this recognition has been the naturalization of sex with its commitment to concepts of the sexual as a matter of organs, orifices, and phylogenetic legacies.

27

DIMENSIONS OF THE REVOLUTION

For the puritan tradition, the sexual represented an oppressive presence by the self-consciousness with which its presence was excluded from public life and most of private life as well. In contrast, in less than three decades we have moved to practices that allow for images of the sexual to permeate our entire culture. The current freedom given to the visual, literary, and dramatic representations of the sexual could not have been described by the most prescient of mid-twentieth-century commentators.

The acceptance of premarital sex, the major issue of scandal attending publication of the second of the famous Kinsey publications, has become virtually normative in both terms of statistics and attitudes (Miller and Simon 1980). This ranges from adolescent engagement in coital behavior at ages that suggest sexual acts that are truly pre-premarital, early sexual activity that only in a minority of cases can be described as being motivated by family-forming commitments, to the acceptance of premarital and post-marital cohabitation at virtually all social levels. And, despite a backlash from fundamentalist religious revivals and concerns with AIDS, there have been shifts in the perceptions and conduct of homosexuality of a most profound and equally unanticipated character (Levine 1986, 1992). Homosexuality has become a presence in the everyday order of things.

THE SEXUALITY OF A POSTPARADIGMATIC SOCIETY

The persistence of these trends, or at the least the unlikelihood of a return to the status quo of an earlier period, is assured not merely by the significance of these changes within the sexual realm alone, but by a number of changes that occurred, and continue to occur, in many other sectors of social life; changes that occurred simultaneously and interactively with these and other changes in the sexual realm; changes that make the use of such terms as postindustrial and postmodern convenient. There have been and continue to be shifts in labor force composition, the structure of our communities, patterns of family formation and maintenance, and many more interrelated aspects of social life.

What is at issue is not only that the distribution of behaviors, meanings, and institutional responses has changed but also that, with these and related changes, the very character of the human experience may be in the process of changing as well. Thus, even were a most unlikely return to the sexual patterns of a pre-Kinsey era to occur, the sexual experience, in all but its physical details, would be profoundly different. And while it might appear that the biological substructure and its attendant chemistries would remain constant, it is unlikely that our interpretations of their meanings could remain equally constant.

In relatively stable, largely homogeneous social settings (paradigmatic

28

social orders) the continuity of the self is assured, indeed, mandated, by the continuities of social life. In such settings remarkably few conceive of being anything but what they are. There are abundant exemplars of the individual's past and future in her or his immediate company, and the "community of memory" is experienced as a living presence, one that in being constantly re-enacted is constantly reconfirmed.

In contrast, in large, heterogeneous, complex, and change-prone settings (postparadigmatic social orders), the self, its integration and cohesiveness, becomes as problematic as the meaning of a past that is constantly subject to being viewed from different contexts of experience and, thus, constantly subject to revision. At the same time, the future is called into question, if only by the discontinuity between the present and the past; history ceases to be the legend of origins and becomes instead a chronicle of transformations. In such settings, the self must achieve its continuity by recourse to the reflexive, as even shared experiences often can only be preserved as personal history. The ensuing growth of the responsibilities of the psyche increases the power and claims of psychic realities.

As the behavior styles of different settings evolve different characteristics, the individual increasingly must question who she or he is by remembering where and with whom she or he is. And in contexts where vacations replace community festivals, the community of memory relies more upon the standardized idioms of a personal narration than upon collective myth. The increasing diversity of personal histories has made the sexual an increasingly unstable chemistry of social and personal meanings, making most forms of sexual conduct problematic to some degree.

The major legacy of the naturalization of the sexual can be seen as something analogous to Barthes's view of the deceptions of the photographic image (1977). The sexual, like the photographic image, is often viewed as being just what it appears to be: a fact derived from life, the purest instance of naturalism. However, this is a deception: it is really a complex text that must be coded; a text selectively assembled to affirm, deny, and persuade; a text embroidered with metonymic "micro-dots" of meaning and history (Stoller 1979).

What has been neglected in the naturalization of the sexual is its capacity for and reliance upon a complex text, a script of the erotic. The erotic is often viewed as the expression of sexual desire, when more appropriately it might be seen as the sexualized representation of desire – the costuming and posturing of desire often, but not always, in the culturally available idioms of the sexual.

It is in confronting the distinction between the sexual and the erotic that the limitations of a naturalistic behaviorism become apparent. Even within the context of overtly sexual acts, outside of the visible but indeterminate capacities of orgasm, pleasure or satisfaction is determined in critical ways by sociocultural meanings that occasion the sexual event and by the personal meanings occasioned by that event. The pleasuring capacities of the sexual event are the result of effective performance of the actor's interpersonal script and its embodiment of elements of the actor's intrapsychic script. In the necessary interplay between these two levels of scripting, the derived pleasure most often proves to be complex rather than pure.

A capacity to revise one's own history, including sexual history, is too often required by unexpected destinies; histories change even when the "facts" do not. Further, the meaning of any sexual episode, as anticipation, as an enactment with its own immediate past and future, and as a memory, is subject to multiple uses and revisions. This raises the question, for which of these aspects of sexual behavior is a theory of sexuality responsible? Most typically, concerns have been myopically focused on the overt act itself, as if in itself it contained the explanation of all that is relevant. Such consideration, in turn, raises crucial questions of the validity or value of universal models or theories of sexual behavior, which flourish with such conceptual isolation.

THE DENATURALIZATION OF SEX

The denaturalization of the sexual does not require an abandonment of all we have learned about the stabilities and varieties of the biological substratum, but it does require the effort of going beyond that and examining what can only be understood in terms of individuals situated in specific points of time and social space: individuals with and within history. Moreover, the requirements and variabilities of the human organism, even as experienced at the earliest ages, must of necessity await their destiny in actual experiences; the individual does not come to social life but is created in social life. To use Stoller's language, we might ask: "Are there data to contradict the opinion that [sexual] preference is, in both male and female humans, an accomplishment rather than a given?" (Stoller 1985b: 101). To which might be added, "Is not the very capacity to be sexual similarly an accomplishment?" – one, moreover, that cannot be taken for granted at any level.

In some ways the denaturalization of the sexual might be described as the deconstruction of the sexual. In effect, as already implied, what is involved is a reinterpretation of the predominant biological explanatory concepts as metaphorical illusions that insinuate a legitimacy of sexual practices whose very legitimacy at least partially rests upon an acceptance of such illusions. As a case in point, to see the sexual as essentially taking its present form because of the sexual character of human reproduction creates an interpretive bias that infuses our sense of the meaning of "proper" sexual relationships. Such a bias confuses the nature of the biological and physical apparatus with the naturalizing of the emotions and social meanings that make the sexual experience possible.

Among the greatest and most neglected of the contributions of Freud was his persistent emphasis upon the abundant continuities between what were seen as normal and abnormal. He argued that the psychopathologies of everyday life were reflective of the potentials of the inhabitants of everyday life for still more profound psychopathologies and that the boundaries that separated the everyday from the profound were extraordinarily fragile. This position is echoed in the later work of Stoller when he observes that, "When it comes to the expression of sexual excitement, most people, whatever their preference, often appear to be quite hostile, inept, fragmented, gratified only at considerable price, and deceptive with themselves and their partners" (Stoller 1985a: 97).

The denaturalized approach purposes that the sexual is socially constructed, that the origins of sexual desire can only be found in social life and its variable presence in the lives of specific individuals is predominantly dependent upon their experience in social life. This is a view of sexual desire as the continuously evolving product of human culture, transmitted not through our genes but through language or through the coded behavior of others which, in turn, reflects the impact of language upon their behavior. The difficulty with this position is that it requires that we accept the relatively superficial nature of what many of us experience as emerging from our deepest and sometimes most compelling sense of our own beings.

In a historical context that has over the past several centuries witnessed a persistent erosion of the permanent and the transcendental, such as God, country, family, and community, as well as many of the fixtures of everyday life, this potential abandonment poses a still greater threat of ontological emptiness and alienation from the realm of nature. At best, the claim that the intensity with which many of us experience the sexual is proof of its primary or primitive character represents a very selective description of the universe of encounters with sexual desire, very little of which – at any rate – appears in scientific discourse. Between the opaqueness of the language of drives and the aggressive accounting of sexual events there is an almost complete silence regarding the specific contents of either the desire for sex, the experience of sexual desire, or the different qualities of emotional production associated with either.

THE SEXUAL AS PROBLEMATIC

A hallmark of the sexual in contemporary society is the frequency with which it is accompanied by the problematic at virtually every stage, from anticipation to activity to retrospective contemplation. A second hallmark is the frequency with which the problematic accompanies our attempts to

31

understand the sexuality of others. This is not to suggest that each encounter with the sexual by each individual is necessarily riddled with ambivalence, but only to suggest that its capacity for the problematic should warn against simplistic models that promise universal applicability, particularly those claiming to be predicated upon the universality of the body.

Currently, the enlarged problematizing of the sexual is amplified by the enlarged problematizing of the larger issue of gender. In their reciprocal entanglement, they have been used to reinforce the naturalization of each other. Lessening the apparent biological imperatives associated with each calls into question the naturalization of the other. A major source of the problematizing of gender has been the inconsistent transformation of the application of gender rules to virtually all social roles.

> *Gender Identity Role* (GI/R): Gender Identity is the private experience of gender role, and gender role is public manifestation of gender identity. Gender identity is the sameness, the unity, and persistence of one's individuality as a male, female, or ambivalent, in great or lesser degree, especially as it is experienced in self-awareness and behavior. Gender role is everything that a person says and does to indicate to others or to the self the degree that one is either male or female, or ambivalent. GI/R includes, but is not restricted to sexual arousal and response.
>
> (Money 1985)

Such formulations insist upon assuming precisely what the individuating experience of a postparadigmatic social order increasingly precludes: a direct parallel relationship between social reality and psychic reality. It is the potential difference between the two that makes the sexual and gender into complex and sometimes elusive texts. One might almost assert as a general principle that as social life becomes less predictable and less orderly, behavior becomes more mysterious. And, in proportion, so does our sense of the world.

Some part of this increasing complexity, mandated by the absence of predictability and order in the world surrounding the individual, is subsequently reflected in behavior. Left to our own devices, few of us would have either the courage or the creativity to originate alternatives to what the world of others expects. It is the confusions of that world that create our capacity to desire alternatives and the uncertainty of the world that encourages us to try to get away with it. Having in some measure to bargain with the world, we find it necessary to bargain with ourselves. A corresponding expansion of the capacity for fantasy makes of nearly all potential tricksters – particularly to themselves.

In this context it becomes clear that the sexual can simultaneously be master and servant of desire, though, more often than not, it tends to tilt towards the latter. One must share with Stoller the idea that sexual preference, and all that it might include, is an accomplishment: for some purposes a purchase and for others a form of currency. As W.H. Auden once observed:

The image of myself which I try to create in my own mind in order that I might love myself is very different from the image which I try to create in the minds of others in order that they may love me.
(W.H. Auden, *The Dyer's Hand*, 1963, Hic et Ille)

And while congruence of the two is possible, its chances are diminished by the frequency with which neither the requirements of self-love nor the requirements with which others confront us are typically singular or happily integrated. In a post-Freudian world it should be a commonplace that there are relatively few affirmations of desire that are not at the same time an occasion for renunciation.

Many different others can offer different versions of love to different versions of the self. The coercive power of paradigmatic societies included the fact that they represented a singularity of expectation and judgment. Many modern families made but could not keep such a promise when they assured their children that they and their values represented the permanent judgments of the world. In contrast, the postparadigmatic social world is experienced as a marketplace of expectations with a considerable potential for overlap and reciprocity but not for continuity except for that realized through an exercise of will and a capacity for metaphor.

The sexual becomes problematic, then, to the degree that different aspects or senses of the self make different and possibly conflicting demands upon the sexual; it becomes even more problematic when the same situation comes to describe the others who are relevant to the sexual as either direct participants or members of the many audiences. The problem of the other or others, it must be noted, is most often not merely a problem of recruiting them to and coordinating their participation in a specific sexual event, but also a problem of establishing congruences with the actor's nonsexual identities and involvements.

This problematic finds its counterpart on the intrapsychic level, as individuals must either integrate or isolate their desired identity as a sexual actor from their nonsexual identities (Davis 1983). The issue of the other(s) is reflected in the differences in sexual behavior that frequently occur when individuals are detached from their conventional settings or "free" from the scrutiny of a familiar audience. Similarly, the problem of the management of self-identity may find expression in the tactic of finding anonymity by hiding from oneself by the use of intoxicants or claims of intoxication.

At this point, Auden's observation might be reformulated in more explicit sexual images: the image of myself which I try to create in my mind in order that I might sustain sexual excitement is different than the image which I try to create in the mind of others in order that they may respond to me in ways that I desire. The issue of maintaining sexual excitement comes under the heading of what can be called "intrapsychic scripting", while the problem of eliciting desired responses from others is labeled "interpersonal scripting". A third influential element is "cultural scenarios", i.e. the actions, objects, persons, contexts, and costumes that are defined as having erotic meanings by the surrounding world (see Chapter 2).

The concept of scripting suggests that while the sexual act, more properly the sexual enactment, must be viewed as a very complex, multi-dimensional process, it is not necessarily experienced as complex. It is precisely the reliance upon the scripting process that leads actors through the action, allowing them to experience their sexual desires as powerful native forces capable of the most particularistic preferences that can be instantly recognized without being articulated.

THE OPPRESSIONS OF OBJECT CHOICE

The initial task involved in the denaturalization of the sexual is a critical examination of the categories of the sexual that reinforce the illusion of compelling homogeneities. By far the most important of the categorizations must be and continue to be those based on object choice. The notion of object choice, however rich with meaning it might be, refers, almost without exception, to gender.

Perhaps it is the seeming visibility of gender and, as part of that, gender's direct reference to the reproductive aspect of sexual behavior that established claims for naturalization, for admitting to sexual theory the naive functionalism of general biologies. Even for sexual actors whose object choice and sexual practice appear to circumvent reproductive consequences, this linkage with the phylogenetic provides comfort by establishing a strong, almost independent basis for the assumed strength of sexual desire.

Clearly the powers of sexual instincts are often seen as a better explanation or apology for sexual behavior than preferences that emerge from the vagaries of individual history. Such a view is equally useful to those who would have chastity or adherence to highly restrictive sexual standards elevated to the status of exemplary behavior.

The view of object choice as the expression of a powerful biological mandate frees the observer from the embarrassments created by the plenitude of other attributes that variably and significantly enter into object choice. The seeming simplicity and obviousness of gender create a bright light effect that either obscures other dimensions of object choice or establishes the gender of the object as the encompassing distinction that renders all other attributes subordinate. However, as should be obvious,

34

gender without further specification provides only a neutered mannequin, one with only the most limited potential for eliciting sexual interest. The most one can say about the dominance of gender in eliciting sexual interest or excitement is that it is a minimal precondition for most individuals most of the time, and even then not necessarily for the same reasons. The issues of age, race, physical appearance, social status, quality and history of relationship and the specifics of context, among other attributes, also play roles as compelling, if not more so, than that played by gender. Indeed, gender limited to sheer biological definition may be little more than a signifier whose larger content is totally dependent upon a history of experience and a promise of future uses.

This is not to say that object choice, even when defined exclusively in terms of the gender of the object, is without substantial influence in the shaping of the sexual identity of individuals, as well as their sexual and nonsexual histories. To the contrary, it may be among the most significant determinants of the history of the individual, one that perhaps explains more of the nonsexual aspects of such individual history than it does the intrinsically sexual.

Object choice viewed in its fullness of detail, viewed as a balance of permissions and exclusions, can only be understood as a process of construction and, at times, of negotiation; a process that may differ in critical details not only among individuals but also over time in the history of the same individual. Freud (1905), in focusing our attention on explicitly sexual motives, insisted on a clear distinction between the *object* of sexual interest and *aim* of sexual interest. By making gender the focus and explanation of sexual behavior we have dissolved the enormously complex issue of the aim into an excessively simplified conception of the object, and in doing so, we have created versions of the "normal" heterosexual, the "normal" homosexual, and we are currently in the process of attempting to create the "normal" bisexual (Weinberg *et al.* 1994). We are thus creating versions of a "normality" whose precise appearance in living form may be sufficiently rare to truly earn them representation in museums of natural history.

Object choice is not a simple fact. It is an evolving of sexual scripts, scripts potentially rich with metaphor and metonymy. Sexual scripts, in turn, are not special creations of and are not singularly occasioned by the sexual possibility. Nor are they predominantly products of the compressed preparations of earlier experience (the epigenetic) merely waiting for the internal pressures of biological change or the external shift of interpersonal expectations to make their presence known.

Object choice may properly claim its critical importance not only as an expression of the sexual actor's underlying sexual identity but also because of its relationship to the actor's identity in the broadest terms: from the "I" of personal narration to the "me" responded to by the surrounding social world; from the subject of consciousness to the object embedded in and dependent upon social life. Sexual desire is often seen as requiring the attention of special agencies of control and repression when it should be obvious that the major agencies of control and repression are the weight of nonsexual identifications, commitments, and relationships. The sexual is simultaneously characterological and contingent: sometimes our destiny and sometimes the altering of that destiny.

While the current anomic division of labor describing the human sciences encourages the view of the development of a sexual identity in relative isolation from the formation of identity as a whole and continuous process, a postmodern perspective is compelled to struggle towards the holistic, if only because the sense of the problematic experienced by the individual is itself a reflection of the problematic nature of the self in social life.

Few instances of human experience are more fully reflective of the dialogical character of human existence than is the relationship of object choice to sexual identity and of the relationship of both to social life.

> I am a Y, I must desire an X.
> or
> If I desire an X, I must be a Y.
> If I am a Y, I must desire an X.
> If I want to be a Y, I must desire an X.
> or
> Z wants/expects me to be Y, so I should try to desire X.
> or
> If I am X, I should/have to be $X_1, X_2, X_3, \ldots X_n$, or
> Being X, it is easier to be $X_1, X_2, X_3, \ldots X_n$.

Combinations and propositions, such as these, multiply and increase in importance as the larger society is less able to impose responses or ensure a consistency of response across the different activities of everyday life. As gender rules move from the imperative to the declarative to the conditional and even, in some cases, to the optative, there must be an implicit decline of a coercive social logic, such as the decline of the imperatives of God and tradition, which occasions a rise in the prestige of psycho-logics and socio-logics. Such logics allow individuals to volunteer for standardized identities that organize standardized scripts in order to avoid a crisis of individual cohesion occasioned by a failure of societal integration.

DISCOURSE AND PRACTICE

Despite its implicit posture of describing social life from some transcendent elevation, all social science remains inescapably part of the social world it attempts to describe, explain, and understand. The modernization of sex, as suggested above, was itself an aspect of broad-ranging and continuous changes that in recent years affected virtually every sector of social life. In part, the naturalization of sex that followed was part of a more general trend towards the secularization and objectification of social life.

> Many scientific theories have, for very long periods of time, stood the test of experience until they had to be discarded owing to man's decision, not merely to make other experiments, but to have different experiences.
>
> (Erich Heller, cited by Auden 1970: 332)

The relationship between discourse (science) and practice (social life) is complex and becomes more so as social life becomes ever more heterogeneous and increasingly prone to change. Heterogeneity and change are not unrelated; change is rarely comprehensive and rarely uniform in its effects. Moreover, to speak of evolving forms of social life implies the necessity to speak of evolving forms of human experience and even the need to speak of the very possibility of evolving forms of human character.

Change, seen from the lofty perspective of macro-history, is often that of one form of social order neatly replacing another, with corresponding shifts occurring automatically at the levels of human experience or in the construction of human identities. However, it might be more appropriate to think in terms of shifting distributions of the types of identities constructed and, with such shifts, changes in the ease of accommodation to altered patterns of social life. Not only does the past linger much longer than social theorists would prefer, but invariably the future tends to reside in the midst of the present long before it is recognized as such.

The modernization of the sexual reflected and to some degree influenced the contemporary sexual experience. But such experiences may have really been in place for a relatively long time. A case in point would be the changing conceptions and uses of oral sex (Gagnon and Simon 1987; Simon *et al.* 1990). In other words, in clinging to a self-congratulatory status of pioneers, we have often neglected to observe how quickly change to the contributions of the new sexology have already become conventional wisdom.

The changes that threaten to erode what was so recently snatched from still older traditions of thinking about human sexuality are not merely changes in thinking about the sexual but may also reflect changes in the qualities and distributions of current sexual experience. The most general form of such changes, as discussed above, is a kind of pluralism born of change and individuation on many levels of human development.

The social order no longer imposes consistent coherence upon individuals as they traverse the relevant segments of social life in the course of their everyday lives; as a result, the changed requirements of self-cohesion expand the domain of psychic reality. The metaphors of the personal have a capacity to rival, and sometimes successfully contest with, the social meaning of behavior, which often appears to have lost its singularity.

The social world that once was experienced as compulsively requiring that the several aspects of individual existence make sense. (All doctors are men. Women who would be doctors must become like men.) is experienced increasingly as indifferent. This is the essence of a postparadigmatic society as we have postulated it. The response of a self-conscious post-modernism recognizes that there is a fundamental difference between individuals who live identical or nearly identical lives and who experience that fact and those who live identical or nearly identical lives and do not experience that fact: lives may be patterned and still be experienced as invented.

This is what Barthes was responding to when he noted:

> [T]he opposition of the sexes must not be a law of nature. Therefore the confrontations and the paradigms must be dissolved, both the meanings and the sexes pluralized: meaning will tend toward its multiplication, its dispersion ... and sex will be taken into no typology. There will be, for example, only *homosexualities* whose plural will baffle any constituted, centered discourse.
>
> (Barthes 1977: 69)

This perhaps is what Stoller (1985a) intended when he suggested that "homosexual", or presumably any such label, should never be applied to individuals as a noun, but only as an adjective.

THE PROMISE OF POSTMODERNISM

Our approach does not necessarily imply an abandonment of the research effort or the singular importance of that effort. What it does appear to require is an abandonment of the quest for effective formulas, an abandonment of abstract causal models that are applied to specific human beings, and a profound suspicion of the minimalist categories that the actuarial approach requires and often condemns us to. What a postmodernist perspective requires and promises is the development of a conceptual apparatus that can mirror shared collective and individual experiences in what will necessarily be recognized as imperfect and temporary ways. This is a way of seeing that will move us closer, not to truth as such but to finding broadened explanations for behavior and understanding of its meaning, moving us from an arithmetic of behavior to a literacy of behavior. Promising no final goal, such a perspective provides a vision that might serve until the next difference, if you will, the next mutation, in human experience occurs and reshapes our vision of the past, of the future, and of its temporary present.

What is required more than anything else, if a promise of a postmodern sexuality is to be realized, is a self-conscious effort to free the sexual from the intellectual isolation within which the modernization of sex originally prospered. This, admittedly, is no easy task. At a minimum it requires that we place all sexual behavior in the larger context of the lives lived by those having these experiences and that our "theories" of sexual behavior be made responsible to our sense of the human.

2

SEXUAL SCRIPTS
Permanence and change

INTRODUCTION

Scripts are essentially a metaphor for conceptualizing the production of behavior within social life. Most of social life most of the time operates under the guidance of an operating syntax, much as language, as a shared code, becomes a precondition for speech. The construction of human behavior potentially involves scripting on three distinct levels: cultural scenarios, interpersonal scripts, and intrapsychic scripts.

Cultural scenarios

Cultural scenarios are the instructional guides that exist at the level of collective life. All institutions and institutionalized arrangements can be read as semiotic systems through which the requirements and practices of specific roles are given. Cultural scenarios essentially instruct in the narrative requirements of specific roles. They provide the understandings that make role entry, performance, and/or exit plausible for both self and others; they provide the who and what of past and future without which the present remains anxiously uncertain and fragile. The enactment of virtually all roles reflects either directly or indirectly the contents of appropriate cultural scenarios.

However, to serve entire collectivities over reasonable lengths of time, such scenarios must be too abstractly generic to be mechanically applied in all circumstances. Improvisation or tinkering to some degree conditions almost all social interaction. Even in the most tradition-bound of collectivities, not all requirements of a role can be applied uniformly. Distinctions, for example, must often be made between the sick and the well, the powerful and the powerless, the closely related and the stranger, and those who are age peers and those who are not (Bourdieu 1977). With increased individuation, the uniform applicability of cultural scenarios becomes even more problematic. In such contexts it becomes even more likely that others may not share the same cultural scenarios or share a common understanding of those they acknowledge sharing. The possibility of a failure of a congruence between the necessarily abstract scenario and the concrete interactional situation is resolved at the level of *interpersonal scripting*.

Interpersonal scripting

The very possibility or necessity for creating interpersonal scripts transforms the social actor from being exclusively an actor trained in his or her role(s) by adding to his or her burdens of interaction the task of being a partial scriptwriter or adapter. Actors become involved in shaping the materials of relevant cultural scenarios into scripts for behavior in specific contexts. Often such improvisation may be seen as little more than institutionalized variations of existing scenarios. At other times, improvisation represents efforts at creating an interpersonal consensus, be it ever so temporary or uncertain of acceptance. *Interpersonal scripts represent the mechanism through which appropriate identities are made congruent with desired expectations.*

Intrapsychic scripting

When complexities, conflicts, and ambiguities become endemic at the level of cultural scenarios, much greater demands are placed on the actor than can be met by the adaptive possibilities of interpersonal scripts alone. The need to script one's behavior, as well as the implicit assumption of the scripted nature of the behavior of others, is what engenders a meaningful "internal rehearsal", an internal rehearsal that becomes significant only where significant alternative outcomes are available. *Intrapsychic scripting* becomes an expanding part of the self process in proportion to the range and intensity of the internal dialogue. It is this problematizing of options for behavior that creates fantasy in a very rich sense of that word: the symbolic reorganization of reality in ways that make it complicit in realizing more fully the actor's many-layered wishes.[1]

In social settings where most find it difficult to conceive of themselves as being anything but what they are (a triumph of the traditional model of socialization), the content and significance of the intrapsychic are limited. At best, it accounts for minor variations in performance. However, as human societies come to experience higher levels of differentiation and individuation, a distinct version of the self is created in the practice of asking which of these outcomes does he or she want to be. This imposed reflexivity transforms the surrounding social world from one in which external events or locations occasion desire into a landscape of potential settings for desires, occasioning a seeking out or creating of the events or

41

locations appropriate to "desired" desires. The difference is partly that of reactivity and proactivity.

Another and equally important modification in the self takes place when, as must occur increasingly, that form of the question is applied to the "I" itself: What kind of I am I? What kind of I do I want to be? Such questions create the experience of a self distinct from the roles it may be required to play: the experience of a self autonomous in its interests and, of greater importance, seemingly autonomous in its desires (Simon 1972).

What is being touched upon comes very close to the conditions of increased uncertainty, starting at the Renaissance, that for Trilling (1972) virtually occasioned "a mutation in human nature". The historic development he points to is that where significant numbers of individuals began to cope with what is among the most commonplace experiences for the contemporary world, significant interaction with others who for all practical purposes are strangers. An uncertainty that necessitates questioning the sincerity of others ultimately becomes the condition for the questioning of the self by the self. The subsequent emergence of what was experienced as the imperative claims of an "authentic self", a self that might be represented in any one of its several roles but that need not be fully represented in any, might well be taken as a comparable "mutation" occasioned by the emergence of a "postmodern era". This is an experience described most clearly by Merleau-Ponty when he observed,

> It is incomprehensible that I, who am irreducibly alien to all my roles, feel myself moved by my appearance in the gaze of others and that I in turn reflect an image of them that can affect them, so that there is woven between us an "exchange" ... in which there are never quite two of us and yet one is never alone.
>
> (Merleau-Ponty 1970: 14)

For Trilling, as for others, the conflict between the claims of sincerity and the claims of authenticity is seen as part of the traditional dialectic of the requirements of civilization juxtaposed against the urgencies of nature. What is currently perceived as the unanticipated enlargement of the claims or powers of the authentic self is commonly explained by reference to the weakening of agencies of socialization – in other words, a weakening of the forces of social control that allow the previously subdued residues of biological evolution to be heard with a heightened clarity. Implicit in this view is the argument that civilization may have drifted too far, may have turned against itself by unleashing the very dangerous propensities within the individual that commitments to sincerity emerged to protect against. However unattractive many of the postures and behaviors associated with the claims of authenticity may be, it may be a mistake to view this as a turn that brings us ever closer to our phylogenetic roots.

These same developments can be viewed as part of the continuing mutations that brought into being so much of the appearance of the human that Trilling found to be both attractive and critical to the Western tradition: the significance of the individual. Intrapsychic scripting thus becomes a historical necessity as a private world of wishes and desires, experienced as originating in the deepest recesses of the self, must be bound to social life: the linking of individual desires to social meanings.

Desire, in a critical sense, is not really desire for something or somebody, though it is often experienced that way, but rather what we expect to experience from something or somebody. Desire is not reducible to an appetite, a drive, an instinct. Desire does not create the self; rather it is part of the continuing process of creating the self. "Desire has its origin and prototype in the *experience of satisfaction*" (Laplanche and Pontalis 1973: 317, emphasis in the original). And the experience of satisfaction, once past the earliest months of life, comes to us tainted with symbolic meaning, and it achieves its uncertain legacy for just that reason.

THE PRODUCTION OF THE SCRIPTING SELF

By the end of the nineteenth century, the idea of a "true self" – a self that existed behind the roles that persons performed in their changing daily lives, roles that existed somewhere between the self and the demands and confusions of social life – was in the preliminary stages of intellectual articulation and existential diffusion. Particularly critical to an aspiring urban middle class was a heightened awareness of the need to self-consciously create their own social lives and personal destinies, to become something other than what they were. The presenting symptom of this profound shift was the growing number of individuals experiencing desires seemingly distinct from the materials of existing cultural scenarios or conventional interpersonal scripts. The response frequently was, and still is, the frightening notion that they were exceptional in not being at one with the world. What they could not anticipate was that they were merely the vanguard of entire classes or social groups for whom not being at one with the world would approach being the normal condition.

It is not surprising that much of this distress should be experienced as being part of the domain of the sexual among socially mobile, middle-class groups. During this period, the sexual was probably the most vividly advertised and, more importantly, the most vividly imaginable occupant of what cultural discourse created as the *badlands of desire*, though the sexual was hardly its sole occupant. Nor was the sexual necessarily its most compelling occupant. Thus constituted, the badlands of desire afford rich opportunities for cross-fertilization, in particular the opportunity to provide human sexual behavior with the meaning it otherwise seems to lack. And this might be only one of the several competing claims upon the desires of the sexual.

43

The pivotal misconstruction in Freud's model of the intrapsychic is in his conceptualization of the id as the embodiment of the sexual and, consequently, as the expression of nature. The confusion of the sexual with the natural can be understood easily as being typical of the historical context. The more instructive error, however, is that of misunderstanding the problem of desire and locating it at the boundaries between the id (natural forces), the ego (self-control), and the superego (the internalized version of cultural scenarios). From my perspective, the problem of desire is not that of a conflict between nature and civilization; rather, it is a problem of the emergence of the intrapsychic as an autonomous domain following the experience of living in modern civilizations. The id, then, is the product of the "civilizing" process and not the most archaic, but the most modern of psychic functions.

To use the less emotionally enriched language of Meadian symbolic interactionism, the *impulsive I* (only partially analogous to Freud's id) may become a meaningful possibility only when confronted by alternative and potentially manipulatory versions of the *reflexive me* (loosely analogous to Freud's ego). An *impulsive I,* one that draws many of its powers from the mediating role it plays in managing what often are the conflicting and competing mirroring responses of the others, is clearly a more complex and powerful aspect of the self than that developed by individuals contextualized by highly consensual others. Moreover, the *generalized other* (analogous in the same partial way to Freud's superego) must shift from being an agency of judgment reflecting shared meanings to being one of rationalization in the absence of an overriding community consensus at most primary levels, including the family.

It is this increasing lack of consensus within the social order, as experienced by the individual, that encourages an empowerment of the domain of the intrapsychic. The disorders of social life do not remove the barriers restraining the primal chaos of the inner self, but rather it is the disorder of social life that creates the chaos of inner life. The sexual becomes a thoroughly democratized attribute that can shake the social world, rattle the heavens, and make visible the human soul.

SEXUALITY: THE INCONSTANT UNIVERSAL

The relevance of the three levels of scripting – cultural scenarios, interpersonal scripts, and intrapsychic scripts – is far from identical in all social settings or for all individuals in any given setting. In traditional or paradigmatic settings, cultural scenarios and a limited repertoire of what appear to be ritualized improvisations may be all that is required for understanding by either participants or observers of almost all expected behavior. However, in what I have earlier called *postparadigmatic societies*, such as ours, there is substantially less by way of shared meanings and,

44

possibly of greater significance, often there are profound disjunctures. As a result, the enactment of the same role within different spheres of life or different roles within the same spheres routinely requires different appearances, if not different organizations of the self. In such settings the instructive implications of cultural scenarios become less coercive, as they become optional or given to alternative interpretations and uses.

In the absence of a pervasive and strongly enforced consensus, the diminished powers of cultural scenarios do not occasion a voiding of the social contract, causing an unleashing of pre-social drives, but give rise to anomie in its classic form. The intensity often associated with anomic behavior might be interpreted not as the instinctive drives freed from the ordering constraints of social life but as restorative efforts, often desperate efforts, aimed at effecting a restoration of a more solidary self. In other words, anomie feeds not on some permanent conflict between the organism and social life but on the ultimate dependence upon collective life that describes all human experience.

The consequences of anomie, as envisioned by Durkheim, were collective and individual disaster, the re-establishment of viable scenarios, and an evolutionary transformation of the individual. The latter, which Durkheim saw as a likely outcome, involved a greater growth of psychic functions such that individuals prove capable of providing many of the narrative continuities that previously were the direct product of collective life (Durkheim 1893).[2] As this occurs, the integration of personal motives and social meanings that make social conduct possible should be constrained to enter negotiations of unprecedented complexity. Scripting is a particularly useful metaphor for understanding this process of negotiation.

By way of summarizing, it is difficult to conceive of any behavior, except one that is in fact biologically programmed, that is not, in our sense, scripted. And if nothing else has been established, it should be clear that the term scripted is not merely a synonym or code word for "learned". All behavior, or perhaps one should say all conduct or all action, involves all three levels of scripting, though not all three are of equivalent relevance in all situations or at all levels of concern.

SEXUAL SCRIPTS

The very concept of the scripting of sexual behavior implies a rejection of the idea that the sexual represents a very special, if not unique, quality of motivation. From a "scripting perspective" (Simon and Gagnon 1969), the sexual is not viewed as an intrinsically significant aspect of human behavior; rather, in this perspective the sexual becomes significant when it is defined as significant by collective life (sociogenic significance) or when individual experiences or development assign it a special significance (ontogenic significance). The significance of some behaviors, such as those defined as sexual, is determined less by the frequency with which that behavior occurs than by the amount and intensity of individual and collective attention paid to it (Foucault 1978).

Sociogenic and ontogenic factors are necessarily closely interrelated. Societal settings where the sexual takes on a strong meaning, where successful performance or the avoidance of what is defined as sexual plays a major role in the evaluation of individual competence and worth, would also be settings where sexual meanings play a correspondingly significant role in the intrapsychic lives of individuals. However, even in settings with a high density of external sexual cues, not all individuals need experience an equivalent density of internal cues. Similarly, it is possible for some individuals in settings marked by relatively little overt concern for the sexual to create a set of sexual meanings and referents far more intense than those describing that setting.

The motivation to perceive and respond in sexual terms need not be determined by what is the conventional significance of a given social setting. Individuals may attach sexual meaning and motivation to aspects of the external environment that are not conventionally defined as having a sexual content. However, deviations from prevailing cultural scenarios tend to be limited to a universe largely created by such cultural scenarios, the application of conventional sexual meanings to unconventional sexual objects or the expression of unconventional motives through conventional sexual activities. For example, most forms of sexual deviance in their initial crystallization, like most human adaptations, parsimoniously alter the smallest amounts of relevant attending conventional meaning; the capacity to add substantially to social reality is generally limited to the extraordinary or the accidental. The ideologizing of the sexual most often follows the contours of the prevailing antinomies of sexual desire (Davis 1983). Thus, we can conceive of sex as a source of salvation only after it has been advertised as an invitation to damnation. Moreover, what is frequently the highly stereotypical outcome that is experienced by the individual as an act of self-invention or, more accurately, self-modification, speaks rather dramatically to the powers of the symbolic. The invoking of social symbols by psychic reality, while subjecting such social symbols to an enlarged number of grammars, does not make them totally plastic. It makes them available to the uses of the imaginary but only in terms set by the symbolic (Lacan 1977).

The most basic sources of sociogenic influence are cultural scenarios that deal explicitly with the sexual or those that can implicitly be put to sexual uses. Such cultural scenarios not only specify appropriate objects, aims, and desirable qualities of self–other relations, but also provide instruction in times, places, sequences of gesture and utterance and, among the most important, what the actor and her or his co-participants (real or imagined) are assumed to be feeling – all qualities that the sexual must share with

46

other domains of desire. Such qualities of instruction make most of us far more committed and rehearsed at the time of our initial sexual encounters than we realize. What becomes problematic is the establishment of linkages between cultural meaning and intrapsychic response.

Where there is a congruence between the sexual as it is defined by prevailing cultural scenarios and intrapsychic response, behavior is entirely dependent upon the shared significant meanings of collective life. In such contexts, the sexual often takes a natural air that obscures the fact that virtually all the cues that initiate sexual behavior are embedded in the social routines of the external environment, just as the absence of external cues served to mute desire. It may have been this reliance upon external cues that made long periods during which sexual activities are not accessible more easily managed in most historical settings than contemporary observers might anticipate.

A lack of congruence between these levels of scripting transforms the sexual into more obscurely metaphoric behavior, as it becomes a vehicle for meanings above and beyond conventionally shared meanings: private sexual cultures grow within the very heart of public sexual cultures. It may well have been the growing number of individuals in Western societies experiencing just such a growing lack of congruence that made prevailing eighteenth- and nineteenth-century discourses on the nature of the sexual, which Foucault (1978) describes, so highly effective in gaining widespread adherence to modern Western sexual values and idealized patterns of behavior (see Chapter 3).

Interpersonal scripting, the actor's overt responses, must draw heavily upon cultural scenarios, appropriating symbolic elements expressive of such scenarios. Interpersonal scripts are the representations of self and the implied mirroring of the other that intend to facilitate the occurrence of a sexual exchange. And while such scripts generally imply things about the internal feelings of the participants, only the representation of appropriate feelings need be manifested or confirmed. At one time or other, desire will follow rather than precede behavior; not only do individuals often "fake" their sexual responsiveness, often they must simulate sexual interest in order to invoke authentic sexual excitement.[3] Interpersonal scripting serves to lower uncertainty by heightening a sense of legitimacy for both the other or others as well as the actor herself or himself.

The motives, conscious and unconscious, that underlie what appears to be manifestly sexual behavior vary widely. As might also be said for any significant genre of activity, there must be many more reasons for behaving sexually than there are ways of behaving sexually. A half century after the death of Freud, the quest for the sexual motives informing nonsexual behavior tends to provoke far less anxiety than a quest for the nonsexual motives that upon occasion organize and sustain sexual behavior (Burke 1941). Moreover, to the degree that most current conceptions of sexual behavior imply a potential for sexual excitement, we also require an understanding of the less directly observable dimension of intrapsychic scripting: that which elicits and sustains sexual arousal.

There are social settings where interpersonal scripts represent, at best, minor variations around dominant cultural scenarios and where enacting these interpersonal scripts appears to satisfy the requirements of intrapsychic scripting. Most typically, these settings have sexual patterns that Freud viewed as characterizing the worlds of antiquity, where great emphasis was placed upon the drive and little attention given to the object of the drive (Freud 1905). However, writing as he did in a world of pervasive sexism, Freud failed to observe that this multiple congruence of scripting elements occurs most often where the concerns for sexual arousal and orgasm were the exclusive or nearly exclusive interests of only one participant – a dominant male.

We must keep in mind that part of the historical record of sexism is the fact that women rarely have been "selected" for sexual roles on the basis of their own interest in sexual pleasure. The very idea of female interest in or commitment to sexual pleasure was, and possibly still is, threatening to many men and women. Even Freud, with what is simultaneously an understandable but still shocking display of sexism, casually comments upon the ease with which women, presumably more so than men, accommodate to varied sexual "perversions" once they have been sufficiently exposed to the potential pleasures of the sexual. This is not to say that women in such settings did not have commitment to effectively utilizing or responding to interpersonal sexual scripts but that these commitments rarely tended to be erotically focused on the production of women's orgasms.[4]

In the "modern" era, Freud contrasted, the drive becomes suspect and most emphasis is placed upon the object and on the quality of the relationship to the object. This shift of focus from the drive to the object must inevitably occasion a growth of empathetic concerns. The transformation of the object into a participating other requires the recognition, however limited, of the other as another subject. Sexual actors must not only take cognizance of the behavior of the other, they must also take cognizance of the feelings communicated however uncertainly by that behavior. For both self and other, the eroticized sexual act often represents an act of offering and possession of what can only rarely be wholly offered or ever truly possessed: the intrapsychic experience of another person. "Did you really want it?" "Did you really enjoy it?" These questions are asked repeatedly, if silently.

A social world that requires that we bargain for our identities inevitably trains us to bargain with ourselves. Desire, particularly *the desire for desire*, becomes one of the most pervasive currencies for negotiating cross-domain exchanges in the highly complex moral accountancy often

48

required by contemporary social life. A highly reflexive, executive self appears, but not necessarily always on demand, to manage the commitments to the world and commitments to oneself. The self in becoming a scripted actor becomes its own producer (managing resources, balancing investments in long-term and short-term pleasures) while becoming its own director in the continuous staging of the self. While non-erotic motives frequently organize and lead us through our selection of interpersonal sexual scripts, an increasing emphasis upon erotic competence describes much of contemporary sexual life.

The estrangement of the erotic from the domain of everyday life, so fundamental a legacy of the modern Western tradition, made the erotic a domain where the abstractions of moral discipline could find concrete and persistent illustrations and tests. This empowering of the erotic often occasions a dominance over an intrapsychic realm where the laws and identities governing everyday life could be softened, a domain where the self could be organized in ways that temporarily included within the nuclear self aspects and qualities that everyday life otherwise exiled or expressed through muted disguises and/or contrary employments.

A cultural tradition that advertised the dangers of the sexual made of the sexual a road map where other dimensions of self that were to be excluded from the everyday self or were denied full expression could rally, enriching the erotic and being enriched by the erotic, which is then to be experienced as having a domain, an elaboration of discourses, a license of its own. This erotic license applied to interpersonal scripts, wherein we are licensed to eroticize our ideals, and intrapsychic scripts, wherein we are licensed to idealize the erotic. License for elaboration often made maintenance of self-solidarity more difficult. An example of such a problem would be the common experience of wanting to express a commitment to elements of interpersonal scripting that were consistent with stereotyped gender-role postures, while simultaneously experiencing feelings intensely incongruous with those very gender-role postures; wanting simultaneously to take possession of the object of desire (the male role in predominant cultural scenarios) and to be the object of desire (the female role in such scenarios), to seduce and to be seductive, to conquer and to surrender, to desire and to be desired *and* desirable.

The separation of an erotic identity from an everyday identity is reflected in the disjunctive experience that commonly occurs upon the entry into explicitly sexual acts, an experience of disjuncture that commonly occurs even among individuals who have had an extensive shared sexual history. This is reflected in the traditional and persistent practice of putting out the lights before initiating sexual activity in order not to be seen, not to see, *not to be seen seeing*.[5] The problem of disjunctive identities is also reflected in the questions: "Who am I when I have sex?", "With whom am I having sex?", and "Why?" In seeking answers to such questions, how often is our everyday identity reduced to being a co-conspirator forever pleading its innocence, and, if not its innocence, its reluctant complicity?

Sexual scripts must solve two problems. The first of these is gaining permission from the self to engage in desired forms of sexual behavior. The second problem is that of gaining access to the experiences that the desired behavior is expected to generate. Multiple desires are commonly implicated in any sex act, not all of which are mutually reinforcing or even compatible. More often than not, the continuing social relationship with the other takes precedence over the immediate pursuit of some desires. Typically, this occurs not only because of the potential importance of the relationship but also because of the inevitable links between the other and complex network of shared social relationships upon which the social standing and reputation of the actor at least partially rests (Lauman *et al.* 1994).

Pursuit of desired experiences frequently requires that the experiences of actors become contingent upon what their partners appear to be doing and also upon what their partners appear to be experiencing. And while this empathetic inference derives partly from available cultural scenarios and partly from what is perceived as the actual experience of the other, it also derives from what the actor requires the other to be in order to maintain sexual excitement. Thus, sometimes the actor, in her or his presented guise, merely provides the plausible access to behavior, while the desired experience is to be gained not from but from within the other: the not uncommon experience of the other becoming a metaphor for the self. Such a response was typified by a transsexual who, when asked how she could have fathered several children while she was a he, replied, "There was always a penis there, but it never was mine". Similarly, Edmund White in describing the gay male *clone* – a figure of hyper-masculine costumes and postures – comments, "we've become what we always wanted" (White 1983 [1994]: 149).

What Freud saw as fundamental to the psychological novel can also describe the scripting of the sexual.

> The psychological novel in general probably owes its peculiarities to the tendency of modern writers to split up their ego by self-observation into many component egos, and in this way personify the conflicting trends in their own mental life in many heroes.
>
> (Freud 1907 [1908]: 150)

"Self-observation", of course, points to precisely the process that must follow the fashioning of an interpersonal script out of sometimes incongruous material, often very careful self-observation. And self-observation represents incipient self-control, and self-control becomes synonymous with the staging of the self. The actor ultimately must submit to the authorial I, while both nervously anticipate the responses of overlapping

50

but not always harmonious panels of internal and external critics (Bakhtin 1981).

The sexual script, like fantasy in general, can be seen as "the mise-en-scène of desire" (Laplanche and Pontalis 1973). In this sense, the concept of sexual scripting takes on a more literal meaning: not the creation and performance of a role but the creation and staging of dramas. As we are reminded by virtually all introductory sociology texts, roles are meaningless in themselves and take on meaning only in relationship to the enactment of related roles. What the actor/ego is (including what the actor/ego feels she or he should be feeling) is dependent upon the creation of a cast of others (including what they should be feeling), the others who complete the meaning of the actor. In some cases this requires others who are obliged to experience what the actor cannot or is forbidden to directly experience in her or his own name.

Most typically, these burdens of construction encourage the emergence of slow-changing, rule-bound genre. Few individuals wander far from the formulas of their most predictable sexual successes. Once we evolve interpersonal scripts that work, that occasion the realization of sexual pleasure as well as the realization of sociosexual competence, there is an obvious tendency to fix or para-ritualize that formula. The stabilizing of sexual scripts often confused with the crystallization of a sexual identity, occurs partly because it works by insuring adequate sexual pleasure with a minimum of anxiety or risk. This tendency toward the formulaic occurs because its stabilities represent an effective accommodation with the larger self-process, an accommodation where the experience of sexual practice and sexual identity is only minimally disturbing to the varied components of one's nonsexual identities.

A recently reported finding (Lauman *et al.* 1994) was to the effect that among adults 18 to 59 the highest rates of masturbation were observed among those who were the most active sociosexually. I would see this as suggesting that such individuals, and perhaps many more, operate with different constructions of the sexual self (Lichtenstein 1977) and that differences in behavior are accompanied by scripts organized to reflect changing power relations between the requirements of the interpersonal and those of the intrapsychic. The enactment of masturbation then is unlikely to be substitutive of a sociosexual experience, but may reflect a different act involving a different construction of the sexual actor(s).

This possibility was expressed vividly by the novelist David Guy in his recent work, *The Autobiography of My Body* (1992), which devotes a chapter to a recapitulation of the masturbatory history of the narrator/hero. Guy's hero concludes this celebration of the special pleasures of masturbation by concluding pointedly that "this is why my happiest experiences with masturbation were during the periods I was married".

It is important that the reader be reminded that much of the process of sexual scripting, while appearing in the obscurity of individual behavior, remains in most critical aspects a derivative of the social process. What appears to be the freedom of the individual from the determination of the social process may, in fact, be little (and yet a great deal) more than a reflection of the increased complexity of collective life and the resulting elaboration of intrapsychic discourses (Gergen 1991).

The ritualization of sexual behavior, however, may depend more on the stability of the individual within social life than in any evolved stability of social life within the individual. Changes in the individual's status or context, as Kohut observed, have the capacity to call into question the larger organization of the self: "certain periods of transition which demand of us a reshuffling of the self, its changes, and its rebuilding, constitute emotional situations that reactivate the period of the formation of the self" (Kohut 1978a: 623). A potential crisis of the self-process and the production of sexual and nonsexual scripts is occasioned because the entire ecology of the self has been disturbed. Such a moment often requires renegotiation of aspects of the self directly related to change but also a renegotiation of virtually all aspects of the self that previously required a negotiated outcome. In modern societies there are relatively few individuals for whom the self-process does not involve such negotiated outcomes.

SEXUAL SCRIPTING AND THE LIFE CYCLE

While not always specifying the full range of expected behaviors, no social role is without life-cycle requirements in the double sense of, first, either having entry and exiting requirements that are life-cycle stage-specific or, second, having expectations that systematically vary with life-cycle stage attributions. Some roles are very specific about age requirements: "you cannot until age x", "at age x you must". Similarly, for many roles and activities, particularly those that are universal or nearly universal, standards of evaluation can vary dramatically with the presumed life-cycle stage of the actor. Only the very young and very old are allowed to be sloppy, self-preoccupied ingestors of food. Indeed, the commonplace admonition, "act your age", speaks directly to the pervasive relevance of life-cycle stage conceptions to virtually all behavior. There are few roles or dimensions of identity that are more burdened with life-cycle stage specifications or more troubled by the transformations accompanying life-cycle stage changes than the sexual.

Where there is near-universal respect for life-cycle stage boundaries and expectations, individuals tend to experience little conflict in integrating the several roles an individual occupies. However, highly differentiated societies, such as the industrial and postindustrial countries of the West, have great difficulty in effectively sustaining just this kind of syntagmatic integration of age-specific roles. While undoubtedly much that is involved in the association of age with social status persists, in sexual domains confusions, uncertainties, and flexibilities clearly abound. These persist in a double sense: not only do the contents of age-specific expectations become ambiguously complex but even where there is consensus regarding such expectations, the applicability of such expectations frequently remains vague. What do we expect of the young? What do we expect of the old? Who is young? Who is old? The order in which these questions must be asked differs radically between traditional and modern social orders.

Folk psychologies or common conventions regarding life-cycle stage distinctions and recognitions appear to have become less common and less commonly effective over the past century. Siegal and White (1982) suggest that the very mandating of the study of child development rested upon the need to create statistical norms against which the behaviors of specific children could be evaluated in social settings where traditional expectations lost their generality of application. This loss of stability of expectation occurred at the very point in social history where enlarged proportions of middle-class parents were persuaded to accept responsibility for the social and moral destinies of their children, a development that ironically proceeded in approximate correlation with a growing inability of parents to fully control such destinies.

An expression of this increasing complexity is the sheer number of available life-cycle stage distinctions and points in the life cycle where shifts in observed behavior or expectations require new bases for evaluations and explanation. And shifts, in turn, call for new strategies for scripting our own behavior and the behavior of others, and for anticipating the interpretation that others might bring to our own behavior.

One consequence of increasingly common confusions regarding life-cycle stages is that the process of translating cultural sexual scenarios into interpersonal sexual scripts has the effect of empowering the actor who often is able to practice considerable discretion in invoking specific aspects of the semiotic of the life cycle. This is an empowering, it should be noted, that is shared with others who also have considerable discretion in confirming or disconfirming the actor's representations. Thus an aging "playboy" whose partners, like the *Playboy* centerfold, never age may be simultaneously an object of ridicule and envy. What were once the coercions of "social facts" increasingly become bargaining chips in negotiation with others, as well as in negotiations with the self.

Infancy, childhood, and, until recently, old age were stages where the appearance of sex-seeking behavior was viewed as pathological because those either too young or too old were assumed to be incapable of comprehending or experiencing the full meaning of the behavior. Community outrage at the rape of an elderly woman or a child is often greater than an even more brutal rape of a mature woman, despite, or because of, the inappropriateness of the object which bespeaks its greater pathological origins and often precludes even the suspicion of initial complicity on the part of the victim.

For some individuals the sequence of life-cycle-based cultural scenarios continues to organize interpersonal sexual scripts in ways that facilitate the harmonizing of sexual commitments with other more public role commitments. For such individuals, cultural scenarios covering conventional family careers serve as the organizing principle of sexual careers; for them, family careers, sexual careers, and the definition of life-cycle stages tend happily (or, in some cases, unhappily) to coincide. Suggestive of the expectation of this integration is the fact that for Kinsey, and virtually all others, categories of heterosexual behavior have been organized in terms of marital status. Sexual careers were subsumed under the headings of premarital, marital, extramarital, or postmarital experiences.

Once a congruence of scripts and identities was essentially mandated and enforced by the institutional order. However, for increasing numbers this coincidence fails to occur or, when it occurs, it occurs with the kinds of strain that subsequently undermine self-stability. The fairly dramatic recent changes in patterns of sexual behavior reflect not only a profound change in the requirements of and meanings attached to the sexual but also equally profound changes in the ordering of family careers and, ultimately, in the very definition of the life cycle itself. The relatively simple and coercively linear description of the life cycle provided by Erikson (1950), a description that is little more than four decades old, has required substantial qualification and may have lost a sense of currency, like the world as imaged by Norman Rockwell, a world most of us never knew, one that may not have existed and yet that we feel a need to believe in. Where life-cycle stage conceptions once offered the comfort of appearing to specify behavior, it is commitment to behavior that increasingly advertises, with understandable uncertainty, one's life-cycle stage.

It is quite common to hear references to the confusions engendered by "blurring of life-cycle stage boundaries". This is often accompanied by an admiring appreciation of more traditional societies that appear to have maintained clear and nearly universal application of life-cycle stage distinctions. Not untypically, such social orders are admired for facilitating the journey across the conventional life course by utilization of "rites of passage". The implied comparison is with contemporary societies that often appear to provide very little instruction for individuals in how to manage such transitions, not only failing to provide training in the behaviors associated with a new stage but also failing to provide an unambiguous basis for reciprocal recognitions.

However, what appears as a blurring of boundaries on the collective level is not necessarily fully descriptive of what occurs on the individual level. A highly differentiated society is unlikely to formulate instructive life-cycle scenarios that can simultaneously realize a level of abstraction sufficient to override existing differences and that can, at the same time, become an occasion for evoking powerful feelings. For example, the question of what constitutes minimal sexual maturity varies considerably across time and cultures. It varies rather dramatically across the contemporary social landscape. Where "serious" involvement in sociosexual activities once marked the boundaries between adolescence and adulthood, it increasingly comes to mark the boundaries between childhood and adolescence. Similarly, changing family patterns, conditions of health and nutrition, and altered value given to manifest sexual viability make expectations regarding sexual activities at post-child-rearing ages equally uncertain.

Sexual cultural scenarios persist but can no longer be located within a singular interpretive context. To the contrary, the specifics of person and place effectively compete for legitimating the appropriateness of a specific scenario. Age or life-cycle stage suggests the possibility of sexual activity at the same time that sexual activity affirms our claim to a specific stage of the life cycle; if I do "it", I am either old enough or young enough depending on "where I am coming from". Here we can observe the commitment to the sexual following the essentially non-erotic motive of gaining interpersonal and/or intrapsychic confirmation. Current adolescent sexual patterns speak to this rather eloquently. The fairly dramatic sexualization of early adolescence provides an exemplification of the desire for meaning, in this case commitment to displays of gender competence preceding and shaping a commitment to the meaning of sexual desire (Miller and Simon 1980; Schmidt *et al.* 1994).

This is not to imply that the sexual is entirely organized directly by the press of external requirements. As I've noted, while operative cultural scenarios substantially condition overt behavior, both in behavior and in the anticipation of behavior, internal rehearsals represent the trials or experiments where a multitude of accumulated desires are tested for compatibility with each other, allowing for an initial crystallization of a so-called sexual identity (Laufer 1976). However, sexual identity isn't the only pressing issue of identity, nor is it the exclusive substance of fantasy. The early eroticization of such trials through masturbatory experience may serve to strengthen the claims of the emergent intrapsychic scripts in seeking expression – however muted – in operative interpersonal scripts. Occurring typically during a period of heightened narcissism, such fantasied rehearsals have a capacity to harness social ideals more effectively to mechanisms of sexual arousal than may result from the actual sociosexual experience. While emotionally charged, not all – possibly very few – erotic rehearsals or fantasies are acted out, though many fantasies continue to be acted within. In the sexual moment, dialogue with the other can often bear little by way of resemblance to the ongoing dialogue with the self.

Unfortunately, almost all of our concern with the sexual activities of adolescents centers upon overt behaviors – which indeed have important consequences – while virtually none of this concern focuses upon the imagery informing that behavior. Most adolescents, however, find a negotiated compromise between the requirements of both levels of scripting, though the stability of that negotiated compromise is a matter of considerable uncertainty.

Sheltered by its internality, the imagery of the intrapsychic yields to change far more slowly than the more externally monitored production of interpersonal scripts. With shifts in life-cycle status, from adolescence to adulthood in its varied stages, from being children to being parents, from engaging in violative behavior to engaging in mandated behaviors, the very accommodations effective at one stage become problematic at subsequent stages. The transition from the sexual being a problematic of a relationship to being a conventional aspect of the relationship often occasions a crisis of scripts.

Aside from its own intrinsic requirements, the sexual also shares the burden of demonstrating social, gender, and moral competence and, as a result, the demands placed upon interpersonal scripting often represent distinct influences. Thus, rather than being reciprocally reinforcing, the requirements of interpersonal and intrapsychic scripting of the sexual frequently represent a continuing – and for some a costly – dialectic.

One consequence of this synthetically negotiated sexual repertoire is that it is highly responsive to subsequent narcissistic wounds or threats (Kohut 1978a). The mid-life crisis, for example, often manifests itself in terms of reactivated sexual experiments, though it may represent more of a renewal of the sexual than a failure of previous strategies of sexual repression or containment. This would be renewal in the sense that, had the disturbance not occurred, the individual might well have continued on his or her previous sexual trajectory. In other words, renewed focusing upon the sexual may have roots in a problematic aspect of the self remote from the sexual. The aspects of self that occasion an initial disturbance of the self often link the individual to social life far more critically than any burden the sexual may carry. Typical of these might be the conflicts between the self as child and the self as parent, the crises attending both success and failure in the world of work, and the unpredicted disordering of the social context.

The sexualization of this kind of crisis often has two distinct consequences. First, while appearing initially as a threat to the traditional social order, sexual "acting out" actually lessens the estrangement of the individual by mandating a transformation of the self within the social order and not a transformation of the social order. This is done by moving the individual toward a quality of interpersonal scripting that personalizes discontent and its solutions. For example, much, perhaps most, of the increase in female participation in extramarital sex may not be an expression of a feminist revolution so much as it is a more comfortable alternative to such a revolution.

Second, as a post-adolescent, heightened sexual activity generally follows the eroticization of the sexual and, as such, it utilizes the powers of the intrapsychic to create new metaphors of desire, metaphors of desire that effectively link the "archeology" of desire with new and often unanticipated social destinies. Both the anomie of deprivation and, even more profoundly, the anomie of affluence focus the individual's attention upon available repertoires of gratification in ways that commonly highlight the promise of the erotic (Simon and Gagnon 1976). The enlargement of psychic functions attending the anomic condition is attracted to the promises of erotic experience: promises of intensity, promises of confirmation. As Lichtenstein (1977) observes, the role of sexuality in its most frenzied dominion is in providing confirmation of a very special construction of identity, however temporarily. The sexual act providing a form of pleasure is particularly salient during moments when self-solidarity is itself in question. And despite a traditionally bleak prognosis offered by Durkheimian and psychoanalytic traditions, for some the promises afforded by the sexual moment may be kept and the confirmation sustained.

For all the confusions attending both adolescence and the vaguely defined mid-life crisis or post-adolescent identity crises, it is easier to consider the sexual within such contexts than it is during other segments of the life course. These have become matters of sufficient public concern that speculation on the scripting of the sexual within these contexts becomes possible. Other segments of the life course remain largely uncharted domain. One suspects, however, that even where the journey through the life course appears without trauma or significant episodes of disorder – as it well may be for many – the problems of adapting sexual scripts to changed, even slowly changed, circumstances and conditions are an important if relatively unexamined issue.

The power of sexual scripts, perhaps much of the power of the sexual, is tied to the extra-sexual significance of confirming identities and making them congruent with appropriate relationships. Where identity is for the moment confirmed and relationships stabilized, the meanings and uses of the sexual shift in very basic ways. For many, if not most, there is an inevitable shift from a sexuality feeding off the excitement of uncertainty to a sexuality of reassurance. The stabilizing of identities and relationships tends to stabilize the structuring of interpersonal scripts; even variations and elaborations take on a predictable character, accounting for what for most becomes a declining frequency of sexual activity itself (Lauman *et al.* 1994; Blumstein and Schwartz 1983). It is possible that the sources of sexual interest, if not sexual passion, depend increasingly upon materials drawn from aspects of intrapsychic scripting that can be embedded within the stereotyped interpersonal script. A useful but potentially alienating adaptation that encourages what has always been to varying degrees a potential aspect of sexual exchanges is that we become dumb actors in one another's charades.

The problematic qualities of managing the scripting of the sexual by adults in stable relationships can be seen in two ways. First, the cultural scenarios that dominate the social landscape tend to be drawn almost exclusively from the requirements of adolescence and young adulthood. There are virtually none tied to the issues of subsequent segments of the life course. Indeed, the interpersonal scripts of these early stages, along with the intrapsychic elements they facilitate, may become in part the fantasied components of the intrapsychic at later stages, particularly in their ability to offer the illusion of confirmation of attractiveness and displays of passionate romantic interest. And while this transfer may serve to sustain sexual commitment, it also has the capacity to provide a disenchanting commentary on the observable performances.

Second, the imagery and content of intrapsychic scripts tend to change very slowly because they flourish in the isolation of erotic reality from everyday reality. Drawn from what we once were, as well as from what we were not and still are not allowed to be or express in more explicit form, the intrapsychic in muted form feeds our continuing sexual experiences and, not uncommonly, opportunistically enlarges their claims during moments of crisis, disjuncture, or transition. These are words that to varying degrees describe the traversing of the life course for all of us: transition, disjuncture, and, sometimes, crisis.

3

ADOLESCENCE AND SEXUALITY
Unremembered youth

INTRODUCTION

Adolescence, a concept just a century old, encompasses dramatic variations across time and cultures at almost every level of application.
Adolescence locates an age group at the margins of formal power in ways
that legitimate the creation of a special social status. Like many social
science concepts, adolescence can be assumed to be tainted by its past and
present uses in ongoing discourses of discipline and control. Even those
events or developments that offer the appearance of being controlled by the
biological organism, such as gender, ejaculatory competence, or the onset
of menstruation, must yield a substantial measure of their claims to the
transforming powers of the cultural scripting of interpersonal contexts
(Bourdieu 1993).

The concept of adolescence involves numerous potential users who are
represented by distinct constituencies or markets for the employment of
specific versions of the concept. Among the most visible of such constituencies are the various professionals who specialize in the production and
commodification of knowledge and wisdom regarding adolescents. Another constituency is composed of those who in varying guises are
involved in the parenting or supervision of adolescents, who in both pain
and confusion often look to professionals for guidance and legitimacy. Not
least are those who market services and goods to adolescents. An additional constituency consists of those who are variously subjected to
versions of the concept. Use of the concept so thoroughly permeates social
life that it is not surprising that many adolescents become adept at utilizing
competing versions of what offers to represent them to defend themselves,
not least from themselves. Still another constituency consists of those of us
who have been adolescents, who often still struggle with the consequences
of our experiences, and who, for the most part, still wait for some language
with which and against which we might find some access to the adolescents we were and to a deeper sense of the legacies of that experience.

It is as a member of the first and last of these constituencies that I write

59

this chapter. Much of the abundant literature on adolescence and youth leaves me feeling disconnected; it is as if I were being presented with a description of some alien culture, not a description of something I was supposed to have been. This I am sure is due partly to the dramatic changes that have occurred at all stages of the life course during the past half century. Much of my sense of alienation, however, may also rest upon what is *absent* from the existing discourses surrounding the concept of adolescence. Among these absences is a fuller representation of the experience of adolescent psychosexual development. Adolescent sexuality, ironically, being an almost obsessive societal concern, appears in social science discourses in extremely abstract language. Its language migrates between an almost inarticulate behaviorism and quests for meaning that focus on origins of infancy or childhood or anticipations of adulthood and almost never deals with adolescence as a range of experiences in its own right. As a result, there are very few aspects of the human experience more dependent upon the enriched language of literary writing and pop culture for mirroring representations.

What I shall attempt to do is to focus upon psychosexual development as seen from a traditional psychoanalytic perspective and to engage it deconstructively. The result, the desired result, will be not a new coherent statement of what constitutes adolescent psychosexual development, but merely a heightened sense of what to look for when we think about the lives of specific adolescents in specific contexts.

For whatever reasons it has occurred, the current revival of interest in psychoanalytic thinking is clearly to be welcomed. I can think of no other conceptual approach that offers more by way of sensitizing us to the significance of intrapsychic life and its dependency upon, and the richness of its processing of, the symbolic. At the same time, one despairs of this revival as it gives a renewed prominence to the entire tradition and collection of practitioners who, at best, have only selectively reconsidered and revised basic theoretical assumptions that, like the concept of adolescence, are now almost a century old.

Underlying much psychoanalytic writing on adolescent sexuality is a utopian view of normality that must have excluded all but a minority who, by the very fact of being a minority, may be anything but normal. Such individuals, those achieving the traditional psychoanalytic definition of sexual normality or maturity, may instead be those who are vulnerable to many other kinds of problems. Most psychoanalytic commentators, despite their curious and curiously consistent absence of the most rudimentary empathic understanding of the broadest ranges of sexual experience, do not, I would guess, fall into this select, if suspect, category of normals. Most of them probably come closer to the more uneven and unresolved experiences of the sexual that describe most of us. This means that their ability to maintain this utopian view of what they presume to be the normal experience probably rests upon systematic repressions. And repression, as they have instructed us, not only is called forth to manage anxiety but also becomes a generator of its own and often a magnet for anxieties too embarrassed to speak in their own names.

Among the most original and enduring of the contributions of Sigmund Freud is the concept of infantile sexuality: the idea that sexuality does not begin, as much previous theory held, with the onset of puberty, but that it exists, if only in the most nascent forms, in the earliest experiences of the human. Moreover, according to Freud, most of what post-pubertal sexuality would subsequently become is given both shape (sexual object) and content (sexual aim) in the course of these early experiences.

The present chapter adopts an alternative approach to psychosexual development, one that more than questioning the concept of an innate sex drive, calls into question the concept of a distinct and intrinsically sexual form of desire. Rather, we might consider whether earlier theory may have been correct, even if for the wrong reason: that the desire for sexual experience is acquired – if you will, learned – and is served by, and at the service of, numerous emotions and different configurations of desire. And while the desires that ultimately are attached to the sexual may find their origins in the earliest experiences of the individual, linkage with the overtly sexual tends to occur for most, though surely not all, persons during their adolescent experiences and, for many, at even later ages.

This, it should be clear, is not to reject the idea that *in some instances* early experience has the capacity to narrowly restrict ultimate sexual outcomes, but merely to assert the possibility that for many, if not most, such restrictions of sexual outcomes are sufficiently permissive to make the specific and concrete issues of adolescence as significant in determining sexual outcomes as anything that may have previously occurred.[1] And, moreover, even where early experience results in powerfully restricting psychological insistences, as may often be the case where larger issues such as gender identity are involved, post-childhood sexual outcomes will still be influenced by the contingencies of time and place, including available alternative constructions of the sexual, as well as available alternatives to the sexual. Sexual identity, while expressive of larger issues of personality or character, is also interactive with personality and character. Sexual identity is often the problematic of personality or character; rarely is it their preordained destiny.

While fully recognizing the substantially "overdetermined" character of psychosexual development, that is, the degree to which it is influenced by the totality of the individual's history of development, I shall explore the possibility of an equally profound, if not more profound, "underdetermination" or open-endedness of psychosexual development. I shall consider the degree to which it is influenced by the contingencies of the moment including the contingent factor of the legacies or residues of the developmental past (Castoriades 1987). What is often ignored is that the stability of the organization of the individual's sexual identity, from adolescence on, may be as much in the hands of the individual's unknown social destiny as it is in the hands of the actual history of the individual's development. As the world around the individual changes or the role of the individual within the world unexpectedly changes, the entire ecology of the self may experience disturbances requiring reorganization, including disturbances and reorganizations of the sexual (Kohut 1978a). Such changes, which previously were viewed as changes on the part of the individual, an individual otherwise located in relatively stable social context, are increasingly experienced as reflecting a social world where organizational patterns, institutionalized expectations, and the lives of related others often change in rapid disorder (Simon *et al.* 1993).

I begin by examining Freud's approach to psychosexual development, with a particular interest in his relative lack of concern for the sexual experiences of the adolescent. Our concern with Freud follows not only from the influential character of his approach to psychosexual development, but also from the broader pattern of his treatment of the adolescent experience. I shall then proceed to a consideration of the generally neglected, independent effects upon psychosexual development potentially associated with adolescence.

My primary emphasis will be upon the development of "sexual desire", as distinct from "the desire for sex". While these forms of desire are intimately related, they are far from identical. The latter refers to the desire for sexual behavior, which may be influenced by many kinds of desire, with intrinsically sexual desires, in some instances, playing only a minor, subordinate, and often merely facilitative role. Sexual desire, on the other hand, refers to the initiation and sustaining of sexual excitement, a condition that may, in many instances, be limited to the dimmest thresholds of consciousness (Stoller 1979). In other words, we must recognize that it is possible for there to be sexual behavior with little or no attending sexual excitement and that there may be intense levels of sexual excitement with little or no overtly sexual behavior.

We must also recognize that the explanation of either sexual desire or the desire for sex is rarely fully explanatory of the other. Sometimes sexual desires follow as a by-product of the tactics developed to satisfy still other desires, a situation where sexual desire or its simulacra must be self-consciously evoked. A concern with the desire for sex requires a history of the individual within social life; a concern with sexual desire requires a history of social life within the individual, or with that which places the sexual within the context of the whole person within an increasingly fragmented social world.

FREUD AND SEXUALITY

Perhaps more than anyone else, Freud must be given credit for placing sexuality on the intellectual and scientific agendas of the twentieth century. Within the body of his work there are persistent references to sexual motives and meanings, yet there is actually very little direct discussion of overt sexual behavior or the qualities of sexual experience. This is particularly true of discussions of post-pubertal behaviors. In the entire body of his work one finds only fourteen references to orgasm and slightly fewer than that number of references to "emissions". Words like masturbation and intercourse occur with far greater frequency but almost always in a descriptive isolation that suggests a nervous averting of attention from concrete details.

Nervousness in discussing the sexual on the level of existential experience was something of which Freud was very much aware.

> People are in general not candid over sexual matters. They do not show their sexuality freely, but to conceal it they wear a heavy overcoat woven of a tissue of lies, as though the weather were bad in the world of sexuality. Nor are they mistaken. It is a fact that sun and wind are not favorable to sexual activity in this civilized world of ours; none of us can reveal his eroticism to others .... *Unluckily even doctors are not preferred above other human creatures in their personal relation to questions of sexual life, and many of them are under the spell of the combination of prudery and prurience which governs the attitude of most "civilized people" in matters of sexuality.*
>
> (Freud 1898: 41, italics added)

To say that Freud was more at home within the context of his historical era than is often realized is to raise the most fundamental questions of the interpretation and understanding of his intellectual legacy. The meanings of words and the emotions and associations they evoke are at stake. The language of the sexual, as well as direct sexual experiences, can have many more meanings and associations among present cohorts than among those living at the end of the nineteenth century. The circulating power of the sexual and the power of its representations at opposing ends of this century are so strikingly different that words that seem to be uniformly descriptive of behaviors, such as masturbation or coitus, can only be misleading without self-conscious concerns for contextualizing both individuals and their immediate social landscapes.

Aside from the indication of a curious inattention to development of post-pubertal sexual commitments, this almost studied indifference to historical change in patterns of behavior underscores a common amnesia describing adolescent encounters with the sexual and a general lack of concern with the marked degree to which patterns of sexual development and opportunity for Freud's generation differ from those of contemporary adolescents and youth. Typically, Ernest Jones's biographer notes that Jones was well into his twenties and a medical school student when he ceased being a virgin (Brome 1983). Similarly, the patient called the Rat Man was a cavalry officer and into his twenties at the time of his initial coital act. How different these experiences from the more common initiating experiences and age of experience that describe the current era. The continuing predominance of ahistorical perspectives in current social science practice suggests just how vulnerable to such an error this practice must be.

Among the potentially most significant twentieth-century changes in patterns of sexual behavior, with possible consequences of enormous proportion, is the collapsing of the period between the beginnings of sexual self-consciousness (social puberty) and entry into a broad range of sociosexual activities. Gone or radically diminished are the years of sexual or near-sexual fantasy and anticipation. With or without accompanying masturbatory behavior, this was a period when sexual scripts could be elaborated in ways that reflected the issues of social life without the effective surveillance of social life.

We might ask, for example, did Freud masturbate? Did he masturbate during his adolescence? During the prolonged period of career development that required the postponement of marriage did he masturbate? Did he frequent brothels? How very little we know about Freud's sex life; how little he told us. What is clear is that he gives us little reason to be at ease in the presence of the sexual, and gives us even less reason to assume that he himself was ever fully at ease in its presence.

In an early essay, Freud made an appeal for physicians to abandon what was, and for many still is, their reticence to inquire into the sexual lives of their patients. He pointed with typical eloquence to the requirements of his charge:

> The resistance of a generation of physicians *who can no longer remember their own youth* must be broken down; the pride of fathers, who are unwilling to descend to the level of humanity in their children's eyes, must be overcome; and the unreasonable prudery of mothers must be combated.... But above all, a place must be created in public opinion for the discussions of the problems of sexual life.
>
> (Freud 1898: 278, italics added)

A difficult charge to meet. A charge that should alert us to the consequences of failing to meet it fully. What, for example, might be the possible consequences of Freud himself having failed his own charge? Not for failing to remember his own youth, but for having repressed his experiences in ways that left them free to return in disguised expressions?

SEXUAL DANGER

In this same early essay, Freud deals with two orders of neuroses. In the case of the first of these, psycho-neuroses, he found inquiry into the current sexual practices of patients to be of little value. As early as 1898, Freud believed such psycho-neuroses to be rooted in the experiences of infancy and childhood and repressed beyond recall except for those made accessible through psychoanalytic hermeneutics. The second, however, *neurasthenic* disorders, he believed was a direct result of current sexual practices.

> Neurasthenia [symptoms would include intracranial pressure, proneness to fatigue, dyspepsia, constipation, spinal irritation, etc.] can always be traced back to a condition of the nervous system such as is acquired by excessive masturbation or arises spontaneously from frequent emissions; anxiety neuroses regularly disclose sexual influences which have in common the factor of reservation or of incomplete satisfaction – such as coitus interruptus, abstinence together with a lively libido, so-called unconsummated excitation, and so on. ... [A]nxiety is always libido that has been deflected from its [normal] employment.
>
> (Freud 1898: 268)

The most common of these "pathogenic" forms of sexual expression was masturbation; masturbation, as Freud viewed it, represented a form of addiction as difficult to treat as narcotic addiction, requiring medical supervision preferably within a hospital setting. Indeed, he viewed masturbation as "the primal form of addiction" (Gay 1989: 170). Freud's negative views of masturbation persisted despite a growing number of colleagues who would set the stage for the subsequent normalization of masturbation. In his remarks concluding the 1912 discussions of masturbation held by the Vienna Psychoanalytic Society, Freud points to a "positive" contribution of masturbation as a lesser evil:

> On the basis of my medical experience, I cannot rule out a permanent reduction in potency as one of the results of masturbation. ... This particular result of masturbation, however, cannot be classified unhesitatingly among the injurious ones. Some diminution of male potency and of *the brutal aggressiveness involved in it* is much to the purpose from the point of view of civilization. It facilitates the practice by civilized men of the virtues of sexual moderation and trustworthiness that are incumbent on them. *Virtue accompanied by full potency is usually felt as a hard task.*
>
> (Freud 1912: 252, italics added)

One can find plausible explanations for why the rhetoric surrounding masturbatory prohibitions, which reached its height during the latter part of the nineteenth century, was so readily institutionalized as scientific and conventional wisdom. The widespread endorsement and dissemination of anti-masturbation beliefs undoubtedly served as powerfully personalized metaphors for the regimes of self-discipline required by the emerging urban-industrial societies of Western capitalism. The prevailing concepts of prudential investment within the realm of the economy necessarily found their counterpart in the prudent managing of the realm of emotional life (Weber 1958; Foucault 1978).

I agree with Foucault that the inhibitory discourses about masturbation, the explicit threats of disease, decay, and uncontrollable perversions, tended to encourage much of the prohibited behavior. However, the potency of such discourses rested upon the larger individuating socio-cultural processes, such as those described by Elias (1978) and Trilling (1972), that helped create the modern self and by doing so gave the masturbatory experience meanings not generally known previously. The major condition for this increased significance of masturbation, if not its increased frequency, was the development of an interior self distinct from any of the self's overt appearances; a lack of a consensual, public clarity about the individual's present and future sexual roles; and a dramatization of the sexual as intensely pleasuring, morally significant, and inherently dangerous. There was clearly a waiting audience for the anti-masturbatory rhetoric, an audience with existing anxieties, anxieties in search of explanation.

The theme of regulation, the disciplining of emotional response, is of course one of the major themes in Freud's writings. This is evident in his welcoming of the presumed potency-reducing consequences of masturbation. In a similar vein, Helene Deutsch recalled that in a small seminar Freud stated his opposition to Wilhelm Reich's insistence that sexual activity should begin in adolescence – that is as soon as biological readiness is manifested. Freud regarded the postponement of gratification as *an important element in the process of sublimation and thereby essential to development* (cited by Offer 1969: 215).

One must ask how Freud, having passed safely through his own adolescence, could continue through most of his life to defend the validity of masturbatory prohibitions? Given the intensity of his feelings, it is almost unthinkable that Freud could have found nothing in either the content of his own post-pubertal masturbatory experiences or the tactics for managing that temptation to inform his treatment of the behavior or to interest him in its content and imagery, which appears so uninforming and unconcerned with content and imagery.

If Freud as a practicing physician was capable of believing in the toxic potentials of masturbation, how less informed and more subject to anxiety and panic must have been the sexual encounters of the naive adolescent

Sigmund Freud? Answers to the question of Freud's history of sexual development have been provided recently by Isbister, who indicates that masturbation was not an innovation of Freud's early adulthood:

> It is known for certain, from his own lips, that Freud was not a virgin when he married. . . . Similarly, it is also clear that Freud was engaged in sexual activity during this time but of an autoerotic kind, that is to say, during his engagement Freud found sexual release through masturbation. Masturbation, a solution that he had sought for the frustrations of his calf-love in his teens, was the only solution for Freud at this time.
>
> (Isbister 1985: 87)

Ascertaining that Freud's view of masturbation was in part conditioned by his own experience adds to the significance of what can only be termed his exaggerated views of its pathogenic potentials. Indeed, Isbister suggests that Jones and Bernfeld had information that the fantasies of "gross sexual aggression" reported in Freud's 1899 paper on "Screen Memories" were in fact his own (Isbister 1985: 88). In not fully confronting his own adolescent experience and by displacing it, Freud may have failed to fully appreciate the role of masturbatory experience in psychosexual development or its role in the most general aspects of development.

Of Freud's actual experiences in adolescence, relatively little appears in what presently constitutes the public record. The periods of childhood and youth are covered in less than fifteen pages in the official biography by Ernest Jones, where Freud's adolescence is described as "a calmer development than the majority of youth" (Jones 1953: 20). Klumpner, however, adopts a far less charitable view.

> It seems to me that the Screen Memories paper supports the opposite hypothesis, namely that as late as May, 1899, there is no evidence that he had in any way analyzed his adolescent conflicts. Why would anyone who had mastered his adolescent struggles have to camouflage his materialistic or sexual fantasies from age seventeen behind a screen memory about dandelions and the delicious taste of a big piece of black bread? Rather, the paper on screen memories can be considered as evidence of a continuing defensive struggle with limited, if any, insight into the nature of the underlying conflicts.
>
> (Klumpner 1978: 19)

Though more contemporary psychoanalytic theorists, such as Blos (1962, 1985), Laufer (1976), Laufer and Laufer (1989) and Kaplan (1988), adopt a somewhat more balanced view than Freud, without exception they view the contributory consequences of masturbation as a necessary risk, one fraught with the familiar dangers of regression and fixation. Virtually without exception they view the positive consequences of masturbation in terms of an unmodified commitment to a concept of genital maturity that carries its own time-line. For them, genital intercourse and its desired "discharges" remain truly "the real thing". The risks that concern them involve the revitalizing of the longings for infantile forepleasures or pregenitality that inevitably attract attention away from the more authentic meaning of true genital engagement.

The dangers are the legacies of earlier development, while healthfulness involves the fulfilling conventional social expectations of some point in the distant future. With the exception of concerns for physical transformations, few of the existential challenges of adolescence are viewed as having significant influence. It is apparent that these contemporary theorists are largely indifferent to the evident changes across the century in the erotic content of the surrounding social landscape or to the changed patterns of sociosexual behavior, which begins for many during the early and middle adolescent years.

REMEMBERING THE UNREMEMBERED

From Freud we received some of our first insights into how the experiences of infancy and childhood influence all subsequent stages of development. The question raised at this point must be to what degree did Freud's possible "failure" to come to terms with his own adolescent experience influence his view of childhood sexuality? To what degree, like the patients described by Lampl-de Groot, was Freud compelled to address what possibly was so painful to him (and painful to many of us as well) in idioms and images that made it more tolerable: the idioms and images of childhood? As Lampl-de Groot observed:

> The adult looking back on his life history feels more responsible for his adolescent than for his infantile behavior; he feels more guilty and more ashamed about his adolescent conflicts, disharmonies, and oddities. As he usually remembers the factual events of his adolescence, he tries to escape the revival of the accompanying guilt- and shame-burdened emotions, either by suppressing and denying every emotion of that period or *by retreating to infantile experiences*.
>
> (Lampl-de Groot 1961: 97–8, italics added)

This *adolescent amnesia* or use of infantile experience as a screen memory has also been considered by others, notably Klumpner (1978). Lampl-de Groot suggests that much of this reconceptualization of the narrative of the self is encouraged by the unintended complicity of clinicians. Of considerable importance may be the psychoanalysts' unwillingness to reopen the issues of their own adolescence and its potential agenda of unfinished business. Freud may have been *ordinarily* effective in repressing the behavior of adolescence or *ordinarily* effective in repressing a concrete sense of the experiences he was unable to repress fully, ordinarily in the sense that Freud, not as doctor, but as the bearer of a symptom, may have done little more than most have done. As a result, it is likely that such repressions may have produced their disguised subtexts of meaning in Freud's theoretical productions, just as such "secrets" fed and ordered the symptoms of his patients, layering them with powerful, if not easily legible, condensates of meaning and significance. *The repressed can return through the representations of childhood as well as from the experiences of childhood.*

The possibility to be considered is that Freud, who bravely confronted and reported upon his childhood sexual lusts, may have adopted this very discourse as a disguise for the guilt and anxieties of the ordinary adolescent Sigmund. His observation that most of us would more willingly confess our "misdeeds than tell anyone [our] fantasies" (1907: 145) applies to Freud himself, as it applies to virtually all who followed in the traditions of both psychoanalysis and the sexual sciences. An issue to be examined is the degree to which, in this case, Freud's confession of the "sexual sins" of the infant and child were in fact the productions of the fantasies of the adolescent or the degree to which the penetration of childhood amnesia was, in fact, a last-ditch defense of adolescent amnesia, an adolescent amnesia that successive cohorts of behavioral scientists and clinicians might have found equally comfortable, equally seductive, equally self-protective.

STAGING THE EROTIC

Where societies provide a tight, coercive, yet seemingly frictionless integration of sexual roles with all other roles, the need for the self-conscious management of a specifically sexual identity, one that accommodates both cultural meanings and intrapsychic response, is minimal. In such relatively stable, well-integrated cultural settings, "sexual habits" can be understood in much the same way in which one might seek an understanding of eating habits and preferences. Both eating and sexual behavior in such contexts appear seamlessly attached to related behaviors and beliefs. Indeed, in such social settings, sexual "disorders" or sexual "deviance" would be no more common than eating "disorders" or eating "deviance". Moreover, sexual behavior in such settings requires little by way of empathy; cultural scenarios that articulate the specification of appropriate objects, locations, and occasions provide effective, predictable guides. As a result there is little need to fashion a sexual identity experimentally; sexual preference, like food preference for most, is a cultural given.

Where this is not the case, as in contemporary society, where heightened heterogeneity and heightened choice produce problematic, alternative, and sometimes conflicting versions of the good life, the testing and creation of links between sexual desires and the requirements of the larger self process may be one of the major dynamics shaping individual versions of the erotic. It may be that it is the uncertainties and ambiguities implicit in social life that foster the widespread salience of the erotic in modern Western societies. As the individual loses a sense of transparency, not necessarily being what she or he appears to be, each individual must learn to offer herself or himself for reading by others just as that individual learns to read the presentations of self offered by others. In such contexts, cultural scenarios become suggestions or options, but not road maps, and inter-personal competence becomes more important. The enlarged role of the empathic requires explanation and understanding beyond the questions of behavior and extends to qualities of consciousness, the dimensions of consciousness that constitute the dimensions of self.

The most general contextualizing aspects along which the construction of the self varies are complexity, pluralism and choice.

> Choice is like a river; it broadens as it comes down through history – though there are always banks – and the wider it becomes the more persons drown in it. Stronger and stronger swimming is required, and types of character that lack vigor and self-reliance are more and more likely to go under.
>
> (Cooley 1902: 39)

We fail to observe that the response to the challenges of choice (uncertainty) may be met in relatively unspectacular ways by ordinary persons living ordinary lives.

What Cooley's remark speaks to is a necessary empowerment of individual psychology, of the domain of psychic reality, where the ordering of the self is not merely the reflection of social life, but is occasioned by problematic, choice-laden encounters within social life. "Problematic, choice-laden encounters" more commonly describes the ways in which most adolescents encounter the sexual than it does for any other segment of the population, when they encounter the sexual at either interpersonal or intrapsychic levels. In recognition of this sexual problematic, a great deal of attention has been focused upon the patterns of sexual behavior of adolescents. Relatively little has been paid to the flowering of sexual activities on the level of the intrapsychic. Despite all differences from the now remote experiences of an adolescent, which may be considerable, as well as its continuing similarities, which also may be considerable, youth remains safely unremembered.

4

ADOLESCENCE AND SEXUALITY
Almost remembered youth

Though the sexual may appear as a universal aspect of all social life, the timing of its formal recognition and consequent influence upon other aspects of individual development is far from being equally universal. On the societal level, some form of heterosexual genital intercourse is virtually universal; while not all members of a society need practice heterosexual intercourse or any form of sexual behavior, such intercourse has to occur with sufficient frequency to insure group survival. However, *sexuality*, the meaning and significance of what is defined as sexual behavior, manifestly varies in dramatic ways. Sexuality varies not merely as culturally inscribed meanings change, but also when change occurs in what might be termed the psychological architecture of the individual (Castoriades 1987; Elias 1978). As Elias noted with reference to the evolution of Western societies:

> [Sexual] functions are gradually charged with sociogenetic shame and embarrassment, so that the mere mention of them in society is increasingly restricted by a multitude of controls and prohibitions.... [W]ith the advance of civilization the lives of human beings are increasingly split between an intimate and a public sphere, between secret and public behavior. And this split is taken so much for granted, becomes so compulsive a habit, that it is hardly perceived in consciousness.... In conjunction with this growing division of behavior into what is and what is not publicly permitted, *the personality structure is also transformed. The prohibitions supported by social sanctions are reproduced in the individual as self-controls*. The pressure to restrain his impulses and the sociogenetic shame surrounding them – these are turned so completely into habits that we cannot resist them *even* when alone, in the intimate sphere.
>
> (Elias 1978: 190, italics added)

In contemporary Western societies, it is this privatizing of sexual experience that gives adolescence its significance in the construction of sexual careers and the attending issues of sexual identity. Adolescence is a time when many must begin the fashioning of their intrapsychic sexual scripts, fashioning them out of diverse and often conflicting materials. Adolescents must construct representations of the self and the other(s) that signify sexual possibilities, including the emotions the individual and the other(s) are required to experience in order for erotic arousal to occur. As the philosopher Robert Nozick noted:

> Sex is not simply a matter of frictional force. The excitement comes largely in how we interpret the situation and how we perceive the connection to the other. Even in masturbatory fantasy, people dwell upon their actions with others; they do not get excited by thinking of themselves or of themselves masturbating while thinking of themselves. What is exciting is interpersonal: how the other views you, what attitude the actions evidence.
>
> (Nozick 1989: 62)

PUBERTY: PSYCHOLOGICAL AND SOCIAL

The sexual possibility is placed upon the agenda of the adolescent by both the concerns of relevant adults and the expectations of significant peers (Miller and Simon 1980). In contemporary society, not all adolescents will be sexually active, but very few will be inattentive. An *initial* effort at consolidation of a sexual subject during adolescence is virtually mandated by a social order that treats the management of the sexual as if it were a direct barometer of current collective moral and mental health. Early in adolescence, many for whom internal sexualization has barely begun will still engage in various sexual postures because they are valorized in current coinages of social competence, particularly with age-specific competencies regarding the issues of gender and morality.

The complexity of motivations to engage in sexual behavior reminds us that the desire for sex is rarely, if ever, in the exclusive control of "sexual desire". This fact points directly to one of the major confusions in the development of theories of sexuality, theories that have traditionally been held responsible for accounting for what sexuality may influence but cannot control. In part, this confusion has been a legacy of an over-sampling of clinically based "research" that sustains images of an imperial sexuality, images that rarely correspond to the experiences of larger segments of populations for whom the sexual may have far less salience.

For a small proportion of men and relatively larger proportion of women the route to the development of a sexual identity and the capacity to experience and desire sexual excitement may take totally different paths as a function of the idiosyncrasies of individual development (Stoller 1985b). Many females may experience the eroticizing of desire much later in the developmental process than is typical for males and, as a consequence, it may occur within the context of a different ecology of the self. For some individuals the sexual will always remain a mystery ("Have I missed something?"), for some it will be most of the poetry or mystery they will ever know, for some a passing or occasionally recurring fever, and for relatively few the dominant obsession of their lives. This possibility may shed some light on a significant number of individuals who exhibit little or only minimal sexual desires, outcomes that need not be pre-emptively dismissed by an unreflective recourse to the language of dysfunction, repression or sublimation.

A costly misconception, particularly noteworthy in Freud (1905), is the idea that it is the biological transformation that occasions the transformation at the level of social expectation and social attributions. Puberty as a biological transformation occasions much of this heightened sense of the sexual. The imagery of an innate hormonal time-release mechanism tends to dominate explanation of a marked increase in sexual preoccupations. However, this association describes the relationship between a disorderly biological transformation and what has been termed "social puberty", the point at which individuals are recognized as having reached some minimal sexual maturity. The application of social puberty will precede biological puberty for some individuals; for others it may lag behind.

It is understandably comforting to find the origins of gender role capacities and commitments in something as stable and universal as hormonal chemistry; such biological explanations provide both a legitimizing of the normal and a normalizing of the legitimate. However, regularities in the sexual behavior of most adolescents will reflect meanings implicit in social puberty far more consistently than any meanings attributable to the biological process.

It is by being socially defined as an adolescent that she or he is assumed to have become a self-motivated sexual actor, even if she or he is not aware of that. Adolescence, then, becomes an occasion for negotiation and experimentation involving an expanding portfolio of desires, desires that often contest with each other for access to representation in the scripting of sexual behavior. Though most adolescents have already experienced the need to negotiate between conflicting and ambiguous expectations, the sexual, with all of its confusing applications, often occasions a new order of negotiation, one vastly more diffuse in its implications, if only because of the intensity of emotion that is evoked by its presence. *Experiments in the management of sexual possibilities may have a more lasting effect in shaping the individual's still uncertain sexual and general future than any specific sexual event.* Some, like Laufer (1976), view such experiments as occasioning the crystallization of a final sexual identity. I suspect that they might better be viewed as constituting *initial* efforts at consolidation of a sexual identity, an identity that forecasts subsequent sexual possibilities in only the most general way.

Adolescence for many may be the point at which the individuals, for the first time, experience themselves as sexual subjects who, more than experiencing excitement for the sexual, can experience sexual excitement. In part, this is what accords masturbation (or the construction of fantasies with explicit sexual implications) its significance. Masturbation occasions a series of experimental "trials" where desires, behaviors, and scripted versions of contextual contingencies can be tested for reciprocal compatibilities (Kaplan 1988; Laufer 1976; Hillman 1975; Gagnon and Simon 1973). The circumstances that legitimate both feelings and behaviors must be "scripted" within the domain of the self, a self that must sustain an illusion of self-plausibility while sustaining a minimally accommodative relationship to ongoing social life. This entails a dialectic that goes far beyond the relative simplicities of a pleasure principle vying with the requirements of the reality principle.

Adolescence, too often described exclusively in terms of its significance for subsequent adult behavior, is experienced by the adolescent not merely as a transitional development, but as a response to a living present with its own compelling agenda of immediate issues. Representations associated with sexual excitement do not magically appear; they must evolve out of successive experiences not unlike the trial and error patterns that accompany the most diffuse ranges of social learning where there is little by way of formal instruction. What *can* be included within an operative sexual script, what *must* be included, what *can* be excluded, what *must* be excluded, and what *can* be included only when carefully disguised – all these issues must be examined. While this process of definition and redefinition extends across the life span, for most people substantial responses are critically formulated during adolescence.

THE ADOLESCENT AS AUTEUR

Even granting Freud's questionable assumption that fantasy might reach its peak during adolescence, it can hardly be said to begin with puberty.[1] Though new contents and new issues are posed by entry into adolescence, in the evolution of fantasy, as in most aspects of human existence, there are powerful strains toward the preservation of continuities. Newly sexualized fantasies undoubtedly reach out and incorporate materials from prior and current nonsexual (or presexual) fantasies. Many of these desires may claim a kind of seniority, with origins in early childhood, and the most significant are themselves layered by residues of intervening uses and pleasures.

Latency, virtually all now agree, is not a period during which the sexual conveniently lies dormant, but is one in which an increasing store of sexual meanings and social uses is accumulated and refined. Of particular significance will be the continuing encounters and experiments with gender commitments, which will constitute most of the framework for subsequent sexual consolidations (Sarnoff 1976; Thorne and Luria 1986).

74

As a result, there is an increase in the amount of dialogue in requisite internal rehearsals, rehearsals undertaken with increasing skill and self-consciousness, even if this training is unevenly manifested in overt behaviors. The self must be explained to the self more often than before. These explanations require the self of others to be explained as well. The adolescent is also expected to enact many of the dramas of life with more coherence than before. The bland language of development disguises what are often experienced as difficult, sometimes precarious, sometimes terrifying accomplishments.

A common diagnosis of the "normal" problems associated with the experience of adolescence in contemporary North America is the relative absence of formal rites of passage, rites that might give recognition to a critical transformation of status in ways that affirm the solidarity of the larger community as such and with the adolescent. However, given the unevenness and irregularity with which adolescence is experienced and the profound uncertainty surrounding its conclusion, a more self-focused exercise in managing an increasingly diversified holding of commitments and pieties may better prepare the adolescent for the decentering qualities common to postmodern social landscapes. Where public rites of passage enhance social solidarity, the skills of scripting and re-scripting models of behavior acquired in producing fantasies serve to enhance the development of effective rituals of self-solidarity.

Prevailing *cultural scenarios* dealing with the sexual undoubtedly introduce new settings, characters, and gestures, though many of these will not be totally new to most adolescents. The potential sexual implications of what were previously experienced as nonsexual scenarios also tend to become more visible. This greater visibility involves not merely the direct and indirect re-creation of the wishes of remote childhood infused with the powers of newly eroticized images, but the restaging of the fantasies reflective of current aspirations and current frustrations. For example, students learn to add strategies for handling the enlarged category of extra-familial authority figures, such as teachers. This learning in turn shapes images and uses of parental figures just as parental images infuse attitudes toward other authority figures.

The predominant cultural scenarios newly available to adolescents are those involving adults or near-adults engaging in adult behavior. Even those rare instances that acknowledge that adolescents are engaged in explicitly sexual behavior are strongly colored with the *proto-adult* character of the moment. However, the continuing expansion of the youth market, as constituted by the enormity of youth audiences as well as the marketing of images of the young to audiences of those no longer young, may be altering distinctions between the pre-adult and the fully adult rather rapidly. Definition of age-status distinctions becomes increasingly unclear, with a lack of clarity that extends to generational distinctions.

What have been termed oedipal issues, as a result, do not disappear but must be played out in a more chaotic field with previously unseen overlaps and cross-generational parallels. It is questionable whether the adult figures in this fantasied realm are, as conventional Freudian theory would have it, direct representations of parents or fed by experiences of witnessing "the primal scene" (Kaplan 1988). If, in fact, parental identifications are implicit in eroticized images of self and other(s), they must compete for inclusion with other equally competitive sources in the rich imagery of the cultural media and those valorized by proximate peer culture. Where parental figures play significant roles in evolving erotic capacities, their most significant role may be as an occasion for elaborating capacities for constructing images that either exclude or disguise direct references to them.

Adolescents commonly experience new and sometimes conflicting demands and desires, but also demands and desires with new and sometimes conflicting claims upon the loyalties of the past or the promises of the future. The purchase price of a promised future is often an undisguisable disloyalty to earlier commitments – disloyalty to friends, toys, and sacred promises made previously by the self to the self. This sacrifice of the past is particularly endemic in future-oriented modern societies, where a future is promised with urgency but with few specified details and those rarely guaranteed. Desires, both old and new, become capital to be used in bargaining with and for the future. Despite the assumption of most psychoanalytic theory that the major task of adolescence is to "divest pregenital drives of their independent aims and progressively subjugate them to genitality" (Blos 1962: 160), the most substantial pre-latency legacies are probably those which in muted form continue to influence the fantasies of later childhood. Moreover, it is likely that the staging of the sexual fantasy focuses upon narrative fragments that endow genitality with social and psychological significance rather than the relatively inarticulate fact of genitality itself.

The residuum of such sexual fantasy materials plays a critical role in the sexual scripts employed during adult years. This later use of fantasy materials may flow from the capacity of all stages of postpubertal life to generate the risks of both imposing and being subjected to injury, humiliation, and violation with their corresponding dreams of survival and retaliation. Additionally, this original legacy of sexual fantasy constitutes a repertoire of intrapsychic sexual drama capable of sustaining excitement within the security and predictability of behaviors embedded within the interpersonal routines of everyday life (Stoller 1985a).

The sexualization of desire, which cannot be taken for granted, involves the establishment of links between definitions of the situation and sexual response, a process through which the actor experiencing desire either initiates the direct beginnings of sexual excitement or initiates or tries to

76

initiate an explicit exclusion of sexual excitement. Sustained excitement typically requires a reordering of identity themes describing self and other. It requires not only the establishment of positive presences but positive absences as well. Some aspects of self or other must be there; others must just as insistently not be present in *recognizable* form. Sexual scripts, both intrapsychic and interpersonal, emerge to transform a complex evolved negotiation into what appears as only minimally self-reflexive behavior. There are obvious parallels with Stoller's useful concept of "the microdot", which assumes that sexual excitement is sustained when the actor can perceive the other as possessing some attribute or combination of attributes that functions as a metonymic reduction of a complex narrative of justifications, potentially containing other microdots or micro-microdots.

> Sexual excitement is a microdot. Microdots are fantasies; the term "microdot" is useful because it suggests certain functions and purposes of fantasies, efficiency above all. "Microdot", more than "fantasy", implies all at the same instance; an ability to condense masses of data; to be retrieved instantly into consciousness for actions, affects, and inspiration; to be moved around weightlessly and slipped into situations in which it brings about desired results. It is efficient. But the conscious experience of instantaneousness hides logical, motivated (even if unconscious) planning.
>
> (Stoller 1979: 166)

THE ADOLESCENT PSYCHOSEXUAL AGENDA

Most of the issues described by Freud as constituting infantile and childhood sexuality appear (or reappear) during adolescence. The issues of masturbation, bisexuality, sadomasochism, castration anxiety, penis envy, and oedipal involvement can all be expected to make their appearance during adolescence. However, unlike their sequential appearance for the infant and child, for the adolescent they make their appearances simultaneously, as the experience of an increasingly more self-conscious and knowing organism. It is important, moreover, that these appearances be considered as psychic phenomena that partially claim roots in adolescence independent of other legacies or residues that also influence them.[2]

OEDIPAL ISSUES

The oedipal family was a theoretical necessity for Freud. However, this focus on the family reflected a more general trend in social science discourse, a discourse that emerged in a period when a multitude of disciplinary problems was becoming apparent, problems for which the "nuclear" family, despite its increasing privacy and anonymity, was used as a plausible source of explanation of attractive and unattractive out-comes.[3] The family became a dominant explanation through which our destinies and the destinies of others were made legible to ourselves and others. Destinies for growing numbers seemed to require explanation in ways not previously known. Other efforts at theorizing the family included Mead, Dewey, Cooley, and Burgess.

The family is still commonly viewed in much of social science discourse as the nexus through which effective agents of socialization (parents) are assigned primary responsibility for both socialization successes (confor-mity) and failures (deviance). Somewhat ironically, to an unprecedented degree, the family was burdened with responsibility for its children's social and moral destinies at precisely the point in history when most families were losing control of their children's social and moral destinies.

The interior space of the family was to be policed by a volunteer force of dedicated care-givers. However, the very discourses that focused what was to become a near-puritan zeal in pursuing investment in children also introduced the taint of corrupt self-interest. To see the potential adult in the child required that the legacy of the child, in the form of unreasoned desires and normal misperceptions, be found in the adult. All who might parent would be children first and could be expected to carry forward their own histories of focused and unfocused desires.

Issues of adolescent psychosexual development, as we have been trained to think about them, such as masturbation, penis envy, castration anxiety, bisexuality, and sadomasochism, implicitly assume a context resembling the emotionally dense and sexually hypersensitive oedipal family. An enriched vocabulary of sexual possibilities was both distanced and naturalized by being seen as having been initiated before personal responsibility could be an issue. Even as the inherent dangers of the sexual were being advertised, the healthfulness of these concerns was sheltered by a well-ordered if incoherently understood narrative of development. The inner beast in all of us need not be denied; normal development was the civilizing of the beast, its proper harnessing to socially useful ends.

Despite our eagerness to anchor the complex and variable character of the human to stable foundations, the assumed universality of infancy and childhood may not continue to serve that function; a universalized infancy tends to sustain mythologies of the origins of human personality in much the same way that an assumption of a state of nature sustained theories of the origins of human societies. It is as if these points of origin harbored some ultimate, if mysterious, truth of continuing relevance (Levin 1992).

The oedipal family, in many regards the ideal-typical urban, upper-middle class family at mid-century, gave an ordering, a coherence, almost an organic quality to a rich psychosexual brew. The corrupting governesses or servants of Freud become the anxiously seductive parents of Erikson who are active in the purchasing of love in much the same way that Freud's anxious child purchased security – at inflated prices (Riesman 1952). In a social setting permeated with Freudian convictions regarding parental influence, the discourses of the family gave rise to the rhetoric, and in a considerable measure the practice, of *the child-centered family*. The architecture of the family dwelling, and its very location among other aspects of family business, increasingly reflected the powers of children. The imperial child on the interpersonal level may have moved closer to parity with the imperial child at the intrapsychic level than most expected.

Three relevant features of current social conditions contextualize the contemporary family: pervasive change in almost all aspects of social life; unprecedented permeation of the total society by centralized, yet diversified media systems; and high levels of individuation. These tend to make a single model or comprehensive view of the role of the family in psychosexual development difficult to the point of danger. We must now speak of the family as a thoroughly pluralized institution whose many forms exist within equally pluralized contexts. The legacy of early emotional attachment that emerges in different family settings, and the experiences of childhood through which these are reworked and to some extent transformed, must also be considered in terms of the specific social contexts within which their claims upon individual behavior and affect are to be realized. Evolving child–parent relations reflect not only changes in what it is to be a child but also, not uncommonly, changes in parents and in generally accepted conceptions of parenting roles. Even the home, the basic stage upon which the family drama unfolds, has changed in virtually all regards, from its architecture to its political system and economy.

Increasingly the family is experienced as being less permanent physically, socially, and psychologically. In other words, we have too exclusively focused on the adolescent as a transitional figure, while assuming the parent and the surrounding context as such are unchanging, finished products. However, the literature on the mid-life crisis, and more appropriately the patterns of behavior that give a semblance of plausibility to such a literature, suggest that many adolescents may be experiencing their initial adolescence while their parents (or other proximate adults who resemble parents) may be experiencing substantial crises of identity that can be too easily mistaken for a second adolescence – in some instances we might be tempted to say "an additional adolescence".

The normal pathologies of adolescence, as well as its lesser irritations, are conventionally seen as the inevitabilities attending the multiple transitions occurring during this period. Young adulthood to the end of middle age, the longest block in conventional views of the life cycle, years covering parenting behaviors, too often was described exclusively in terms of stabilities and gentle slopes of change. Discontinuities during this stage of "full" adulthood were treated as deviance and attention was focused upon finding restorative treatments and effective preventatives. More recently, we have come to accept these as the normal pathologies of transitions, transitions that are as likely to be imposed by collective history as they are prompted by the events of individual biography.

It is reasonable to assume that sexual development will of necessity reflect the surrounding context. The family obviously plays an important and for some a key role in the achievement of sexual identities and patterns of sexual behavior. (The two are far from being identical or always stable in their reciprocal relations.) The role the family plays in these developments, however, may be no more or no less than the role the family plays in other socially significant developments.

At the neonate level there are aspects of developmental transformation that are universal or close to it. However, what is universal in such experiences can have the significance of that universality diminished by the increasingly variable experiences within modern and postmodern cultures (Kagan 1985). Critical qualities of parenting have changed since Freud, as they were changing dramatically while he lived. Perhaps, more accurately, we might say that the distribution of parenting styles has changed dramatically over this past century while the cultural contexts within which the parenting occurred have been changing even more rapidly. Among these changes is the increasing dominance of mass media that provide hyperreal images of alternative styles of family life (a pluralism of styles of family life sharing primarily a view of family life as organized around anticipated manipulations, attempts at manipulation, and the tactics of counter-manipulation). As the world of opera furnished the family romances of the early part of the century, more current versions of family romances have the capacity to play as alternating components of multi-screen, electronic collages.

Current relationships between adolescents and parental figures may be as significant as those found in the archaeological survivals of the psychic experiences of early childhood. Rather than viewing the development of a sexual identity as the delayed flowering of earlier commitments, I would propose that the achievement of a sexual identity for most of us is a continuing act of *bricolage*, a process of assembly that joins the past and present, a process where the value of all personal history must risk fluctuation in significance.

Achievement of an initial version of one's sexual identity relatively early in adolescence may be of greater importance today than ever before. Contemporary adolescents experience themselves within societies that advertise a pluralized sexual culture more explicitly than before. They also face heightened probabilities that they themselves, and many around them, will be initiating and concluding significant kinds of sociosexual relationships.

Given the virtual normalization of pre-premarital sex, combined with the continuing trend toward delaying the age of first marriages, recent

80

cohorts come to their first marriages with significantly more sexual experience than any prior cohorts. Even those adolescents whose socio-sexual experience remains limited do so within a climate that increasingly assumes and normalizes such experience. A small measure of this change can be found in current public debate on providing condoms in public high schools, where significance is to be found in the very fact that such a debate occurs in the first place.

One consequence of this trend, one that will probably have enormous ramifications, is the collapsing into a brief period – some might say too brief – of the time between an initial sense of oneself as a sexually significant person and the point at which regular sociosexual involvement occurs. This period is one where the dimensions of an intrapsychic erotic culture are elaborated, in the relative freedom of an inner space where the regulations of actual social and physical limitations need be observed in only the most flexible ways and where the passions and injuries of the moment can compete with their earlier incarnations. This would suggest that the balance of relations between intrapsychic sexual scripting (making the exciting acceptable) and interpersonal sexual scripting (making the acceptable exciting) may be in the process of being altered. As the practice of fantasy and the practice of behavior meet earlier, the sexualization of desire is more available to the issues of the present moment and, correspondingly, more remote from the archaic toxic waste of the legacy of childhood's lusts, hurts, and misperceptions. Such legacies must now compete with the enforcement of group norms, which are commonly experienced as being equally unreasoned and equally cruel.

Most adolescents, then, find themselves within richly sexualized sub-cultures where there are modes of acting in sexually significant ways that are not necessarily genital in uses of language and costume, as well as pluralized definitions of relationships in which they are expected to be sexually involved. There is probably more social support for adolescent sexual activity by peers and others than has been known previously in modern Western experience (Kallen and Stephenson 1982). The greater visibility of the sexual, including the greater visibility of the sexuality of all family members down to the youngest, like the presence of sexualized language, becomes a near constant. The primal scene, as performed by bodies not unlike parental figures, is available in a constant flow of mass-media images.

I am not sure anyone presently understands fully the implications of these shifts in age and relationship to courtship. One possibility that seems reasonable is that a greater visibility of sexual activity will lead to an increased empowering of the process of interpersonal scripting, a greater employment of the sexual in the service of what is on the immediate surface of social life. This, in turn, opens the possibility of the formation of sexual identities that are less the servant of compacted semi-permanent simulations, less the obsessions of deep character than the opportunistic affectations of the moment. Previously, the involvement of adolescents in sexual relations was associated with separation from parental control. The larger part of premarital sexual experience, particularly for females, occurred in the context of courtship. Currently, for most adolescents it occurs without leaving the parental household, though boyfriends or girlfriends often become quasi-family members. This earlier entry into sociosexual activities creates a powerful, but far from exclusive, claim on peership with parents and other adults that can only further the continuing transformation of the politics of the family. A peership particularly for those adolescents whose parents were the initial vanguard of the sexual revolution, parents who themselves were familiar with both extensive premarital sex and the use of recreational drugs. The traditional erotic farce that commonly plays off a confusion of generations, with parents and children encountering each other in questionable circumstances, finds extensive material in all segments of the contemporary scene.

Undeniably, the family remains an environment of great significance in the process of adolescent psychosexual development. However, the effective penetration of the family by pluralized media and the powers of peer attachments make it difficult, in many cases, to point to singular and *direct* effects of the family that retain the burdens of responsibility for their children's social and moral destinies. The secrets of our sexual behavior and the employments of our sexuality will reflect changing family histories and evolving family romances, the latter moving in tides of public visibility from comforting romantic idealizations to a return to gothic horror stories of sexual abuse presided over by hypersexual parents.

The current, if still muted, sexual climate of the family can alter the interplay of guilt and anger that infused the oedipal family and enriched the erotic for so very long. The interplay of guilt and anger is reflected in the surrounding society's changing concerns for the sexual vulnerabilities of children. Traditional concerns with protecting the young from premature discovery of the sexual created an atmosphere that cast a nervous furtiveness about adolescent sexual activities, concerns that succeeded in generating strong feelings of guilt. More recent concerns with abuse encourage paranoia as a mask for anger. Let me be very specific. I am not referring to those who have been abused, for whom both guilt and anger are not uncommon, but to a much larger group – those who grow up in climates that broadly advertise and instruct in the possibility.

Where once children were medically examined and psychologically inquisited in a search to uncover the vice of "self-abuse" (i.e. masturbation), they now experience the same procedures in the scrutiny for evidence of sexual abuse. Likewise the induction of anxiety to protect the child from self-abuse has been replaced by the induction of anxiety to protect them from the sexual danger posed by others. The adult gaze on the sexuality of the child still renders them "subjects of study" and/or "objects of concern", and the sexuality of the child is still reconstituted from adult confession. Adult tales of the resultant damage of childhood masturbation have been replaced by adult tales of the resultant damage of childhood sexual abuse.

(Rogers and Rogers 1992: 166)

This partial shift from a focus on masturbation, which is essentially guilt producing, to a focus on abuse, which tends to produce anger, points to even more dramatic change in the psychological, as well as social, structure of the family.

Parents, particularly the parents of the opposite sex for those experiencing themselves as moving towards heterosexuality, will obviously have many of the attributes that the adolescent is expected to recognize and respond to as being sexual. This connection becomes particularly significant when the parents are seen by the child as being sexually active, sometimes increasingly evident particularly to those adolescents who have witnessed parents returning to the dating and mating game. The stereotypical notion of Victorian reticence and prudery clearly create a different set of conditions for managing the problems of inclusion and exclusion than would be true for most of the varieties of contemporary middle-class North American families – even where the family remains intact. The same may be said about changing patterns of authority within the family and the changing division of labor within the household.

MASTURBATION

While masturbation by adolescents is now routinely acknowledged as a common, "phase-appropriate behavior", curiously it is rarely scrutinized for either its contents or its dynamics. Where masturbation has been directly addressed, as in Blos (1962), Laufer (1976) or Kaplan (1988), it is viewed as necessary, useful, and risk-laden. It is necessary, as Laufer points out, because it serves "as a way of testing which sexual thoughts, feelings, or gratifications are acceptable to the superego, and which of these are unacceptable and therefore must not be allowed to participate in the establishment of the final sexual organization" (Laufer 1976: 30).

The major risk to proper development, as traditional psychoanalytic theory views it, is that the substantive images and associated emotions of masturbatory behavior are preponderantly regressive. Kaplan, who is more responsive to the thoroughly gendered nature of individuals than most psychoanalytically oriented theorists, still finds the adolescent encounter burdened with developmental responsibilities and threats.

A chance phrase, a fleeting odor, might overcome her resistance to masturbating. Such unpredictable upsurges of desire are totally devastating to the adolescent's self-esteem, because they represent a challenge to her sense of control over her body and her destiny.

(Kaplan 1988: 186)

This negative idea of regression and threat to development is largely sustained by unexamined assumptions about the sexual history of infancy and childhood and an absence of information about masturbatory experiences of non-clinical adolescents and adults.

A notable exception to the general narrowness of the theorizing about masturbation is the work of James Hillman (1975), a neo-Jungian. Aside from providing a broad and informing history of the masturbation prohibition, Hillman offers a singular conceptualization of the nature of masturbation and its role in both specifically sexual and more general forms of psychological development. His essay is one of the very few in the relevant literatures that consider the role of masturbation in the sexual life of the adult. Of special importance is Hillman's suggestion that masturbation by adolescents and adults is not merely substitutive but has a line of development and developmental correlates of its own. This is a concept given heightened credibility by the finding of a recent major study (Lauman *et al.* 1994) that those who tended to be among the sexually most active also tended to be among those who currently were masturbating most often.

Hillman suggests that an aspect of the masturbatory experience is linked to the development of creative imagination, as it provides occasions for learning to invest symbols with emotional significance and deriving gratification from the imaginative manipulation of symbols. However, competencies in manipulating and responding to symbolic representation may vary as other aspects of psychological development vary. One significant dimension along which such variations commonly occur is socioeconomic status. What comes to mind is Bernstein's distinction between developing a capacity for "elaborative coding", as against the more limited and limiting capacity for "restrictive coding", which describes social class differences in language socialization, with obvious implications for other aspects of cognitive and affective development (Bernstein 1972).

Masturbation may represent an illustration of the ability of sexual experience to differentially characterize specific categories of persons and patterns of developmental outcomes. This is suggested in the differential patterns of masturbatory behavior among individuals at different social class levels, with higher masturbation levels at all stages of the life course positively relating to socioeconomic status. Similarly, females who engage in adolescent masturbation at any level beyond the minimal tend to be more sexually focused, more orgasmically competent. They also tend to be more academically and career oriented. In that sense, their sexual atypicality is associated with other aspects of gender atypicality in ways that are probably significantly interactive (Gagnon and Simon 1973; Lauman *et al.* 1994).

Masturbation, Hillman notes, serves moral development by occasioning an urgency for elaborating effective rationalizations. The enactment of sexual behavior within the theater of the mind, either in masturbatory activity or quite commonly in association with sociosexual activities, is no less circumscribed by moral constraint than it is in overt behavior (Simon and Simon 1958). The difference is merely that the organization of psychic realities allows for a complexity of rationalization that is rarely afforded by "real life" experience.

My most critical quarrel with Hillman involves his uncritical acceptance of drive theory and, consistent with his Jungian perspectives, his tendency to universalize the meanings of behavior. As a result, he postulates an endopsychological emergence of both the impulse to masturbate and an inhibitory predisposition, a process that gives rise to "secrecy, guilt, and fantasy" or, in other words, "a sexual impetus to psychological or internal culture" (Hillman 1975: 116). I would argue the reverse: that it is the experiences of the individual in social life that create the impetus for the development of a capacity for secrecy, guilt, and fantasy, the impetus for the creation of an enlarged and empowered intrapsychic domain, and that it is this development, when or for whom it occurs, that creates a compelling source of sexual desire for which masturbation represents a very special mode of expression.

MASTURBATION RECONCEPTUALIZED

While infant and childhood masturbation may in fact be among the most universal of human experiences, the meanings and consequences of such activity are varied. Like most of the dimensions of infantile sexuality, the understanding of the content of infantile and childhood masturbation rests upon borrowed words and thoughts, words and thoughts borrowed from an as-yet-unlived future. The difference between infant and child masturbation and adolescent masturbation from Freud's view was not new content but heightened hormone-based imperatives and additional mandates for the reworking of these initial issues. Such reworking involved the partial repression of all that had flowered during pregenital stages, in order that entry into the social as well as the sexual relationships of "responsible" adulthood become possible. In other words, the past, with its lingering dreams of *unreasoned* desires, and the future, marked by the near final consolidation of renunciations, totally obscure the experience of adolescence itself, seemingly obscuring the experience of adolescence for all except the adolescent.

The complicated role that masturbation plays during adolescence is something Freud understood. He viewed it as a way of having access to a half-way region interpolated between life in accordance with the pleasure principle and life in accordance with the reality principle. However, while masturbation made it possible to bring about sexual developments and sublimations in fantasy, these were also seen not as advances but as "injurious compromises". Though, as Stekel noted, these same compromises render severe perverse inclinations harmless and avert the worst consequences of abstinence (1912: 252). The absence of visible indicators of adolescent turmoil (Offer 1982), often described as a normal aspect of adolescent development, may be partly explained by this early version of a lightning-rod approach to masturbation. From this perspective, turmoil is acted out safely (at least for the moment) within the arena of fantasy, acted out passionately, excessively and, for the moment, with finality. This latter concern should cue us to the more contemporary meanings and uses of renewed sadomasochistic fantasies.

Despite its autoerotic appearance, the post-childhood masturbatory act is an intensely sociosexual act. The deceptively obvious link between masturbation and narcissism is supported by the image of the individual seeking pleasure in a manner that appears independent of social life, as if it were possible to describe the individual in any but a relative sense as being independent of social life. Masturbation's more significant link with narcissism may rest in its command of intrapsychically generated idealizations of the self in social life.

Post-coital *tristesse*, like post-coital *jouissance*, is known only to the human animal and occurs as orgasm most often signals the end of immediate sexual excitement, if not the end of the pursuit of further sexual pleasure. At such moments, the pleasures of orgasm may only partially compensate for the probable requirement of the abandonment of the images that generate sexual excitement. Such images have only rarely been examined in social and intellectual realms, realms where the prohibitions regarding talk about the sources of sexual excitement may have significantly outlasted the prohibitions surrounding sexual behavior itself. This is particularly true of masturbation.

SCRIPTING MASTURBATION

Much of the anxiety and guilt that must have permeated the masturbatory act for Freud's generation, as for members of following generations, may not have been engendered only by fears about masturbation per se, which given the folk psychologies of the day were considerable, but by the still greater anxieties and guilt about what was being done within the realm of the imagination. It is the content of the masturbatory act, the specific and sometimes imagined cast of characters, scenic references, gestures, utterances, costumes, and explanations, that has been ignored.

The physical act of masturbation may be less a desire for an object or act than a quest for the construction of a self, however provisional, that is appropriate to such desires (Burke 1941). Among the pleasures sought in masturbation may be that of experiencing oneself within a context of scripted social action where a version of the self is experienced as more free from conflict or ambivalence than may ever be achieved in real life. In this sense, the pursuit of orgasm through masturbation or other forms of sexual activity may be less a primary end than a means of experiencing a construction of the self different than that required by the established identities of every-day life (Lichtenstein 1977; Davis 1983; Simon and Simon 1958).

The masturbatory fantasy most commonly involves a scripting of social life that makes possible a nearly perfect balance of desire, honor, and justice. *However unpleasant or self-punishing such a fantasied realm sometimes appears to be, it has a wholeness that often compensates for its lack of reality, while reality rarely affords compensation for its frequent lack of wholeness.* Freud argued that one of the dangers implicit in masturbation was that in the fantasies accompanying masturbation "the sexual object is elevated to a degree of excellence which is not easily found again in reality" (1908: 200). "The degree of excellence" to which Freud refers is clearly not necessarily the same as that of the idealizations of the sexual as portrayed in prevailing cultural scenarios. This excellence can also refer to the intensity of sexual excitement generated when the fantasy is more in the control of the individual's psychic reality than is usually the case when the "wish" is compromised by the pragmatic interactional constraints of social life.

The realm of fantasy is a realm where there are no secrets; the motives and experiences of the other or others are fully, if inarticulately, available. As Ferenczi noted, "[t]he onanist feels (a) alternatively the emotions of two people, (b) finally of both at the same time" (1931 [1980]: 266). Such empathic projections speak directly to the interpersonal, and possibly intersubjective, character of all forms of erotic activity. This neglected aspect of the empathic component implicit in masturbation, and possibly all sexual behavior, should remind us that no form of behavior is more subject to the constraints of the dialogical than is the sexual, where all gestures are both a response and the anticipation of a response, where the presence of an other is an absolute necessity (Bakhtin 1981). From this perspective, masturbation must be seen not as an act but as an enactment, a fully dramatized representation of the self. It is in this context of the intrapsychic that so many dimensions of sexual possibility are enacted with new meaning and within a consciousness far more knowing than could possibly describe most prepubescent children.

It is within the dramaturgically enriched arena of masturbation that the other dimensions of psychosexual development most generally initi-ally occur, if only in the guise of an internal rehearsal. They do not in specific overt acts, but in interpretations and projections that range from obsessively ritualized performances compacting meanings often lost to the untutored observer, something akin to Stollar's "microdots", to minimalist collages that can claim no surface coherence beyond the shifting intensities of sexual arousal.

The qualities of sexual enactment implicit in the experience of masturbation – except for those who believe that it can be done with thinking about what is being done – may well have their origins in the unarticulated panics and possessions of childhood. However, their subsequent articulation in the idioms and costumes of a time and place is a critical moment of the sexualization and desire the effects of which may endure at least as compellingly as any in the continuing production of semiotic chains of desire.

BISEXUALITY

Gender, a complex of anticipations and instructions, is an essential hermeneutic of virtually all social experience and all responses to experience. To the degree that a polarized gender system provides a major framework within which clues to identity are sorted, and within which individual erotic interests are elaborated, a complexity of responses should be an increasing by-product of the contemporary Western experience. To the degree that gender distinctions are mutually exclusive, individuals must often choose between very specific desires that generally announce their presence with highly restrictive gender distinctions as well as their implications for larger senses of gender identity.

The significance of gender in the development and maintenance of self-identity may actually have increased in recent decades as it becomes one of the few remaining aspects of identity that colors virtually all aspects of our lives. It approaches constituting a master status imposed upon all.

Gender identity, too often described as a simple, unidimensional aspect of the self, must increasingly be understood to be a complex dynamic and highly contingent process, a process that includes, among other aspects, the individual's recognition of *its* inclusion in a universe of seemingly uncompromising bimorphs, or what in this sense can be termed *gender identification*. Another aspect is the degree of comfort the individual experiences in effectively executing the behaviors attached to gender-significant roles, the contents and requirements of which are in the control of the individual in only the most marginal of ways, or what we can term *core gender identity*. And, lastly, there is the internalized judgment of others, often disguised as the self's most authentic voice, or what can be called *ideal gender role expectations*.

The latter two (*core gender identity* and *ideal gender role expectations*) are clearly given to varied vicissitudes in the course of the individual's history of development within the developments of history. However, such transformations are rarely without surviving residues of earlier

88

constructions of gender. To the degree that these two present incongru-
ence, if not conflict, gender-significant behavior must of necessity reflect
how such incongruities are resolved and, moreover, the overt quality of
performance rarely articulates with precision specific experiences at the
"core" of identity.

In recent considerations of the history of the psyche, there is a notable
tendency toward conceiving of the evolution of a more abstract self
(Gergen 1991; Zurcher 1977), a self whose gendering is closer to the surface,
less tied to "primitive beliefs" (Rockeach 1968) regarding identity and, as a
result, more responsive to changing social expectations. This position is a
consistent implication of much current constructionist, deconstructionist,
and feminist re-evaluations of current conventions regarding the gendering of both behavior and feeling. Indeed, gender may emerge as a
problematic only in sociocultural settings where many individuals are
required to create and sustain the cohesiveness of the self, settings where
individuals must achieve integration of their several social roles in contexts
of considerable ambiguity ("What is it that I should desire to be?") and
uncertainty ("Am I really one?" "Will I ever become one?"), as against
contexts where the existing integration of social roles creates the appearance of a constant self. It is in this sense that, as Freud observed, even when
individuals fantasize themselves as appearing as members of the opposite
sex, this does not necessarily mean that they desire to be that gender, but
merely that they desire the experience, including the experience of an
emotion, that is commonly associated with that gender (Nunberg and
Federn 1965–72).

This is not the occasion for a full examination of how common bisexual
experience is or all of its possible consequences. What is important at this
point is that common to many *contemporary* versions of adolescence is a
fantasied bisexual experience and that it occurs at ages when it is accompanied by a well-developed sense of the social meanings of such an
experience. *Contemporary* must be specified because it is possible that this
developmentally significant experience is not in many critical regards a
universal occurrence.

Among the major sources of anxieties involving gender among adolescents is the often visible discomfort of adults with what is often yet to be
decoded by the adolescent. An already pronounced self-consciousness is
further inflated by the ambiguities of child–adolescent distinctions that
often contain opposing permissions and a seeming arbitrariness in how
they are applied. What is casually permitted in childhood is often
accorded great significance in adolescence. This is particularly characteristic of physical contacts between males, as well as those between males
and females. This self-forming heightening of self-consciousness attaches
to the sexual in both dimensions of significance: the larger and more
diffuse issues of gender and, within gender, the character of the erotic.

Such self-scrutiny must include a nervous monitoring of one's own intrapsychic responses and the perceived, often imagined, attributions of a growing number of significant others for whom the individual's gender competence and sexuality are of concern.

Past puberty there can be few wholly autoerotic sexual acts; almost all sexual acts, particularly those enacted within the realm of the imagination, are conditioned by an awareness of the meanings such acts have for all whose presence is invoked by the enactment. Sexual fantasy requires that the actor author the behaviors and the emotional experiences of all participants. The individual in staging and role-playing the activities of all participants must risk knowing the emotions of all participants. It may have been this aspect that marked the role of the sexual in the creation of the modern self and accounted for the ease with which it occasioned a moral panic of remarkable duration.

The ecology of desires (the meaning of or response to behavior) that creates and sustains sexual excitement and the possibility of sexualized pleasure is drawn from the experiences of *all* who play a role, however slight, in the enactment of the sexual script. *This includes deriving pleasure or heightened excitement not from but through the feelings attributed to the other.* This aspect of bisexuality is associated with the adolescent masturbatory experience and extends to erotically involved fantasizing or daydreaming. This was precisely what Ferenczi saw as one of the most debilitating aspects of masturbatory practice. A concern echoed later by Blos (1962: 168) and what Kubie (1972) termed "the drive to be both sexes", or the psychic participation in the experience of both or all participants in the sexual performance.[4]

The more explicitly heterosexual the fantasy, the more inevitable is the bisexual nature of the experience. For some there will be the pleasure of feeling different emotions and different pleasures when acting in the guise of the other gender within the realm of psychic reality, while it is the other who is experienced as experiencing the feelings that the subject desires and, for whatever reasons, may only be able to experience vicariously. In any case, the fantasied feelings and confirming mirroring of both parties become a source of satisfaction.

At this point a distinction must be drawn between the degree of development of a bisexual capacity at the intrapsychic level and the capacity to develop a bisexual capacity at the interpersonal level (Herdt and Boxer 1995). The former speaks to a capacity to experience sexual excitement, however latently, through cross-gender identifications, where some part of the chemistry of sexual pleasure is dependent on subjects experiencing themselves as acting sexually toward or being sexually acted on by others of the same gender. The latter speaks to the capacity to overtly experience desire for both cross- and same-gender sexual contacts.

Intrapsychic bisexuality, I think, might be occurring among increasing numbers of successive cohorts of adolescents and with heightened claims upon consciousness and desire. Several interactive developments sustain this speculation. One such factor is the dramatic lessening of homophobia that tends to make both homosexual possibilities and expressions of continuing, if embattled, homophobia more visible.

Moreover, more general cultural trends encourage heightened andro-gyny, or what has come to be known as "gender blending". As the modern novel invites its readers to empathically share the consciousness of many kinds of social and psychological others, more recent electronic texts make such cross-gender, empathic identifications even more com-monplace. It was more than two decades ago that the gendered nature of the gaze first informed film theory (Mulvey 1975). The camera's gaze is fully gendered, often recruiting the viewer to the subjective point of view of the other gender.

Clearly present across our current landscapes are numerous instances of what an only slightly older era would term gender reversals or radical revision of the gender typing of social roles. Many of these instances, while often shocking in initial encounters, have all too quickly become the unrecognized familiars of everyday life. The major of these is the entry by large numbers of females into occupations and professions once limited to males.

The significance of increases in capacities for a bisexual response extends well beyond the gendering of the object of sexual desire. What also may be implicit is the possibility that the same conditioning factors that potentiate heightened levels of bisexual response will contribute to a revision of the very privileged status of the sexual as an act of extraordinary intimacy to be properly performed only within the most intimate of relationships.

Lastly, as the changing gender rules and conduct continue, responses remain conditioned by the gender residues of given roles or situations. The surgeon and police person are still emotionally perceived as male, the nurturer as female. The power of the phallus cannot but enrich the meaning of the penis. Similarly, the mock phallus, once viewed as the exclusive product of male pornography, appears as a regular feature of some part of lesbian pornography. Concepts of penis envy and castration anxiety, which in some regards are opposite sides of the same coin, must acquire new dimensions of meaning in such a context.

PENIS ENVY

Adolescence is a period of mandated reassessment of the body, with a particular emphasis upon those parts of the body and body contacts that the larger society defines as having erotic significance. The cultural certification of sexual significance is especially true for the genitalia and other parts of the body that are described as having sexual uses. Regardless of whether the individual, at the time, experiences such aspects of the body as associated with sexual excitement, they command increasing attention. Such cultural certification dictates not only the rules of exclusion and inclusion – how, where, and by whom can contact be viewed as sexual – but also establishes a linkage with a special vocabulary and correlated expected emotional responses. We must *learn* what the one touching and the one touched are expected to feel (Gagnon 1973). In this context, the genitals take on additional metaphoric significance, where the genitals become a problematic of erotic status, concepts like penis envy and castration anxiety also take on additional meanings.

It is hard to conceive of any aspect of Freud's thinking that is more burdened by the markings of time and place than is the attribution of "penis envy" to females. At its very core, the concept, perpetuated by Kohlberg's more recent (1969) application of a Piagetian model, assumes that the perception of gender differences is the legacy of childhood's naive eye. The misperception of the vagina as a wound that transforms a body part into an accusatory metaphor requires continued acceptance of the idea of the imperial child as the core of all subsequent erotic response.

The behavior of adolescent females that can be termed "penis envy" must also be explored in terms of its potential origins in the current moment. Penis envy may, in fact, represent conflict and rage at what is currently experienced as powerfully mandated demands for the surrender of ambitions that are inconsistent with conventional gender role expectations at the broadest levels. Ambitions that were literally unthinkable in many sociohistorical settings become what growing numbers of young girls are encouraged to incorporate within their projected futures. The pervasive ambiguities of social responses to the gender typing of social roles must become a potential for troubling ambivalences for most females regardless of the direction – traditional or innovative – of their ambitions.

In Freud's era, most adolescent females had to cope not only with a near total absence of legitimacy for expressing their discontents, but also with the most minimal language and relatively few models. Knowledge about the constructions of gender identity can be misleading in understanding the adolescent unless there is a continuing understanding of the history of subsequent encounters with changing or growing meanings of gender identity (Harry 1982; Herdt and Boxer 1995). This is not only a process where new meanings and emotions are added or merged in complex ways, but also a process where commitments to the expression of that identity are tested and become imperatives of the self.

During adolescence there is commonly an increased elaboration and testing of the appropriateness and coherence of specific desires and commitments with these identities. Many of these desires and commitments must be modified and still others abandoned. For many this is an occasion for continuing conflict, resentment, and often sheer rage. Moreover, given

92

the possibility that much of the conflict and rage is centered upon the denial of desires that for the most part are fairly remote to the erotic, we might more accurately term this phenomenon "phallus envy", acknowledging that many sexual representations often serve as sublimations of angers far more dangerous in their subversive implications. Most available metaphors for such abandoned desires are typically exiled to "the badlands of desire", a psychic zone where the sexual comes to occupy an increasingly central place.

MALE PENIS ENVY

Often neglected is the significance of the penis and of "penis envy" among male adolescents. This is an expression of envy, not only of the greater or seemingly greater competence and ease in signature male accomplishments of other male reference figures, but also one of more literal significance, an envy of the penises of other males. The presumed hypnotizing powers of the penis, seen in male-produced and male-consumed erotica, speak to this quality of male penis envy. Concern about inadequate penis size was one of the most common inquiries sent to the *Playboy* Adviser.

Sexual excitement generated by the ambiguities and tensions of status differences has long fed all levels of cultural production. The issue of penis envy for females, as an expression of sexual politics or, more accurately, politicized sexuality, focuses on the alternative valances associated with penetration, with being the penetrated and with being the penetrator. The politics of sexual penetration, raising, as they do, the gestures of dominance and submission, the postures of control and permission, make of sexual engagement an optimally accessible staging area for both licit and illicit, both probable and improbable enactments of the politics of interpersonal relationships. The realm of the Phallus is the realm of social power.

CASTRATION ANXIETY

For many males, entry into adolescence occasions conflicts over varied behaviors and relationships experienced during masturbation as well as over the possibility of failed or embarrassing sexual encounters. Both tend to encourage an objectification of the penis. The projection of hostility towards one's own penis must be a common response. The most common of these must center upon fears that one's penis will betray the individual by undesired tumescence or a failure to sustain tumescence. The penis also serves as the objectification of desires that, even when they must be rejected, cannot be fully renounced.

Few words carry as much metaphoric richness as does "castration". Its associations are as complex as its range of applications. The connection between sexuality and human reproduction accounts for much of this metaphoric power and, as a result, it is not unusual that an erotic residue attaches to instances of the application of the term castration, even instances that may initially appear remote to the explicitly sexual. Varied forms of emotional and political castration come to mind, this is typified in description of the Jim Crow racial code as serving to socially castrate African-American men or in the description of women who are seen as aggressively competitive. Whatever the referent, there is an immediacy of connection with an *assertive denial of power, potency,* and *generativity,* on the one hand, and an association with concepts such as *permanent immaturity* and *flagrant passivity* on the other. Sexual castration becomes an attractive metaphor with many uses, both admonitory and optative. This was exemplified in Ovesey's (1969) concept of "pseudo-homosexuality", where homoerotic imagery becomes a metaphor for conflicted relations with authority figures.[5]

The articulation of castration anxieties, then, can often be understood as being powerfully focused but insincere statements expressive of a desire to end ambivalence, conflict, and the abandonments that accompany almost all individual development. Among other things, such anxieties can also serve as a defense against one's hostility towards one's own penis, as a metaphor for a complex array of anxieties regarding shifting expectations and uncertain futures, and also as a desire to retain the comforts of one's penis while shedding the expectations and responsibilities imposed by identification with the Phallus.

Conflicting desires more than the simple repression of desires often can be found behind imagery of castration anxieties. One can only wonder how many grow up to be wholly what they are at the level of what is experienced as primary identity. The cross-pressured, history-burdened interests of *ego ideal* and *ideal ego* feed a reflexively enhanced internal critic. The dark side of individual achievement is often abandonment; current mythologies of success ritualize the near inevitability of having to purchase success with the betrayal of others and the greater inevitability of self-betrayal. It is not surprising that masochism is often a "vice" preferred by men of apparent success. Perhaps those habituated to failure usually put masochism to more practical uses.

Castration anxiety is understandably linked to assumptions regarding sexual rivalries experienced during childhood, when the image or concept of castration serves as an immunization against impulses to resist pater-nalistic imperatives and as an advertisement for resistance. In adolescents' staging of their dream of desire, the threatening oedipal father often plays his historic role of intimidation and chastisement, even though he may be called on stage for reasons of a more contemporary origin, such as when fathers, or those occupying the father's role, are experienced as offering tests of the ideals of masculinity that the adolescent experiences as problematic.

94

SADOMASOCHISM

In traditional psychoanalytic theory, a form of sadism is one of the earliest of instinctive drives to make an appearance, becoming manifest as the second phase of the oral stage (Laplanche and Pontalis 1973). Its appearance is associated with "instinctual ambivalence", suggesting its inextricable connection to dialectic, to conflict, to choice. (Is it Ernst Kris who suggested that comfort generates object relations, while it is conflict that generates character?) However, it is important to keep in mind that *infantile* sadism, if this term is at all appropriate, stands in much the same relationship to postpubertal forms of sadomasochism as that in which childhood masturbation stands in relation to adolescent masturbation. Even where similar emotions are involved, the different capacities for self-reflexivity are profound.

The limited part of the clinical literature that has dealt with adolescent sexual fantasy notes the common occurrence of sadomasochistic elements in such fantasies. It is not surprising that this content is predominantly seen as related to the disturbances that bring the adolescent to the clinical setting in the first place. What is missing in this limited literature, and possibly forgotten as part of our own unremembered youth, is the role such sadomasochistic fantasies may have played in the adolescent experiences and psychosexual development of many of us.

Adolescence is commonly seen as a time of enlarged preoccupation with the issues of justice. By the time development reaches a point when justice is a major concern, it tends to occur within the enlarged appreciation of the multiple appearances of hierarchy and uses of both formal and informal power. The heightened salience of justice, hierarchy, and power also coincides with restrictions regarding the direct expressions of anger and promises of retaliation. Further complicating the life of the contemporary adolescent are the seemingly endless ambiguities of expectation and response that often make everyday life a minefield of potential unearned injury, humiliation, and intended and unintended violation.

For some, a preoccupation with justice may reflect an already developed erotic agenda, as in the case where preadolescents are drawn into sexual vocabularies that sufficiently load sexual referents with strong moral connotations such that they become insults of aggressive devaluation even when used in what are patently nonsexual moments. These connotations do endure and enrich the subsequent elaboration of sexual scripts. However, it is more likely that the preoccupation with justice will influence sexual scripts. In the Western experience, the sexual always appears burdened with moral significance, burdened with the possibility of transgression.

In fantasy, sadomasochism rarely depicts explicit images of consensual sadomasochism. Characteristically, sadomasochistic fantasies center on behaviors that are coercive, non-voluntary, and at times brutal. But implicitly transgressivity is not a rejection of justice in the name of the power of unconstrained passion; to the contrary, such fantasy themes are almost always scripted to establish the exercise of personal passion as an instrument of justice. The behaviors represented are acknowledged violations, but always "earned" or, if you will, justified violations. The justifying coinage takes the form of compensatory pleasures, where excesses of pleasure can become forms of abuse, or where deserved punishment and earned retribution become just deserts.

Sadomasochistic images may be rooted in angers and hostilities, focused by and upon the self, not fixed entities but complex and varied responses and reactions. Consistent with this development is the increased appearance of aggressive acts of penetration, including the use of dildos and anal and vaginal "fisting", in recent lesbian erotica. The gestural potentials of penetration, given the layered history of uses of the sexual, permeates contemporary sexual codes. Much of this focus upon penetration explicitly adopts the language and costumes of sadomasochism, but in most instances it will be sadomasochism in the service of giving dramatic impetus to sexual desires rather than sexual gestures in the service of sadomasochistic commitments (Samois 1982).

The Romantic tradition encouraged a view of the ideal sexual act as a merger of identities. Much of this tradition continues to find expression in prevailing cultural scenarios and the conscious preferences of numerous individuals. However, processes of individuation, dramatically heightened during the past century, correspondingly find expression in the expanding realm of intrapsychic scripts. This trend has been reflected in and shaped by the relative democratization of the right to orgasm, which tended to move master sexual scripts from idealizations of simultaneity and similarity of experience to idealizations of reciprocal attentions that individualize the encounter. Critical to contemporary expressions of sadomasochism is their ability to frame sexual interaction strongly from each separate participant's perspective; the dominant role contains the appearance of the command and control of gestures and their meaning, while the submissive role remains the center of attention; the former serves as the *instrument* of justice, while the latter becomes the *subject* of justice.

At the same time, sadomasochism has the capacity to draw upon the tensions of everyday life in giving renewed meaning to practiced gestures. The residua of such sexual fantasy materials may play a critical role in subsequent adult sexual scripts or, more accurately, the sexual scripts employed during adult years. This later invoking of fantasy materials flows from the capacity of all stages of postpubertal life to generate the risks of injury, humiliation, and violation with their corresponding dreams of survival and retaliation. Additionally, such fantasy materials constitute a repertoire of sexual drama capable of sustaining excitement within the security and predictability of the sexual embedded within the routines of everyday life.

Stoller's (1979, 1985a) observations on the role of hostility in generating sexual excitement point to hostility masochistically directed towards the self. Sadism is more often the servant than the master of masochism; it is the illusion of the authenticity of the sadist that serves as the source of authenticity for the masochist.

. ACTS AND ORGASMS

The "centering" of desire, especially the desire for meaning, within the organism is essential to the view of the human as active participant in even its earliest phases of development. This may be among Freud's most generative contributions. My quarrel is not with this concept. Rather it is the taking for granted of the specific content of desire and the meanings to which desire becomes attached that is at issue. Nowhere is this more significant than in the taking of the sexual for granted, viewing it as a primary given that requires explanation only of its expressions and transformations but not of its origins or meanings. It is this assumption that allowed the very tradition of thinking that argued for the centrality of the sexual in human motivation to protect the sexual from critical scrutiny. In other words, the unexamined assumption of innate sexual desire made unnecessary a careful examination of the processes through which desire becomes sexualized.

In adopting a perspective that views the full development of the human in terms of repetitions of initial, primitive meanings expressed in varied metaphors, psychoanalytic theory became locked into archaeological rather than genealogical perspectives. This is what made necessary the "discovery" of the unconscious as the site that contained the critical determinants of subsequent behaviors, a site whose contents could only be observed indirectly. This discovery, I would submit, was required to obscure the increasing presence of the conscious – a strategy not unlike hiding adolescent (conscious) eroticism behind the screen of infantile (unconscious) eroticism. The discourse of the unconscious allowed for charting a wide menu of transgressions to which most could plead "no contest", without admitting current guilt.

At its most basic, the acknowledgment of the unconscious was the acknowledgment of a person's *negotiating* with herself or himself behind her or his own back. And it is the increasingly experienced need for this kind of negotiation that shapes and, in some sense, creates the modern self – including its capacity for generating chronic conflict and confusion. More enduring than the discovery of the unconscious is what it represented at the most general level: recognition of the inevitability of the divided self, as a normal condition.

The sexual can no more serve theorists of human development as the illusion of continuity within the lives of individuals than it can as an illusion of continuity across the human record. The origins of sexuality, as with the origins of all that is part of the human, remain of considerable significance, but we must be prepared to recognize that the very significance of such origins may change as their culmination – the living, active self – changes: an inevitable uncertainty regarding the future constantly threatens the past with promises of critical revision and the present a decline of the likely. Time and change tend to require and produce new visions of the future, just as they require and produce new constructions of the past. Such a perspective must come with heightened ease among expanding numbers from those recent cohorts who have been condemned to live their own futures to almost unprecedented degrees.

Our histories, both individual and collective, are significant conditioners of the present moment, but only in the way that they can be: as a history of histories. And these histories, more than a shadowy existence in the fluid territories of the unconscious, are for increasing numbers the scripts that both manage and mirror the complexities on the frontiers of psychological life, part of the continuing production and reproduction of the self. Concepts like sublimation remain rooted in a commitment to a predetermined direction of influence in the continuing construction of the self. Nonsexual activities are often examined for their latent sexual meaning, without considering the ways in which explicitly sexual performances may in fact be an expression of nonsexual motives (Burke 1941). This privileging of the sexual is sustained by its assumed developmental priority and, consequently, its central role in the agenda of the intrapsychic. What is lost from view are the alternative psychic rewards afforded by the issues of the present moment, issues reflective of ongoing interpersonal possibilities remote or indifferent to the sexual. It is as if by overvaluing and overdramatizing the sexual, seeing its presence in many more places than it can be found in, we blind ourselves to the details of what for now are some of its compellingly inelegant idioms as we blind ourselves to the variable role sexuality plays in our equally variable ecologies of desire.

As this is written a fresh cohort has entered their adolescence in the context of a social landscape profoundly different in innumerable regards from that which contextualized the entry into adolescence of the author. Moreover, many of the individuals whose lives have documented available social science literatures had experiences – at least in proportion and coloration – significantly unlike those of the author and those of the latest recruits to adolescence as well. New meanings and experiences of gender and sex may not only produce new patterns of sexual behavior but also provide mute witness to changed qualities of experience among those engaging in conventional patterns of sexual behavior.

5

ADOLESCENCE IN RETROSPECTION

Movies, men and myths

The very idea of myth, a story exemplifying aspects of the belief system of a time and place, commonly evokes a sense of the past, most often a dead and alien past; it is often accompanied by a sense of the primitive. Myths are offered us as part of the archeology of peoples distant in time and culture, occasionally to be elevated to relevance to literature, history, and philosophy in much the same way as primitive artifacts are often elevated to the special realm of art; an archeology of cultures most typically not burdened with the concepts of archeology, art, or myth. Appearing in the guise of cultural crustacean, myth is often a text that reveals something about "them" and "their ways" and is applicable to our own situation only by the sophisticated application of metaphor and metonymy; much, for example, as *Oedipus Rex* becomes a metaphor for the psychic experiences of the contemporary versions of the human.

Under the best of circumstances, our knowledge of the conditions surrounding the production of myths remains far greater than our knowledge of the conditions surrounding the consumption of myths. It is hard to imagine what pleasures were realized, what emotions were amplified or elevated, what tensions were exploited, or what conflicts, if any, resolved for members of their initial audiences. Yet without this appreciation much of the significance of the mythic is lost to us, for myths are not merely a form of instruction in a social order's paradigmatic identities and the attendant dramas of their paradigmatic interrelationships, more critically they are an *enactment* of such identities and interrelationships.[1]

The inaccessibility of these vital intrapsychic components as they occurred in the distant past must be accepted as a given despite the consoling promises of psychohistorians, who often fail to understand that the residues left by the intrapsychic tend to be provocatively suggestive rather than articulate. However, as we approach the contemporary moment – where the functions of the myth remain as profound as ever, though its appearances and uses may be more complex – consideration of the intrapsychic response can neither be ignored nor taken for granted. Indeed, it is the probable lack of an isomorphic relationship between cultural convention and intrapsychic response that makes "a theory of the audience" a significant if still neglected issue in the fields of cultural criticism, a neglect that is difficult to defend when our concerns are with current or near current cultural forms. Under such conditions, we have not only the observations of the text but also the experience of the text, if only we are prepared to read that and ourselves as well (Barthes 1973).

The significance of the intrapsychic conflict takes on a critical aspect in modern conventions of the dramatic, a form that Freud (1906) saw as focusing on a conflict *within* the hero, a conflict of contradictory wishes, of which the hero may not be fully conscious. The pertinent insight offered by Freud with reference to this form of the psychological drama is that such dramatic representations become an effective basis for identification of the moving emotions only when to some degree the audience shares elements of the same unconscious conflicts, elements of the same psychopathology.

It is with this perspective in mind that I want to examine aspects of films treating the American West as a dramatic rendering of culturally shared psychopathologies. In more concrete terms, I propose to examine a well-known Western film as a re-enactment and re-experiencing of the "normal" pathologies attending the American male adolescence and its continuing residues in the lives of American men. I shall examine the use of the mythologized West as an expression of aspects of the character of the American man that are often not directly acknowledged or given expression in contexts closer to our everyday realities.

The specific "case" for analysis is John Ford's 1962 film, *The Man Who Shot Liberty Valance*, a film that ranks high in the amount of critical attention it has received – a curious fact, given how very conventional it initially appears. It might almost be described as regressive. Visually it is not particularly exciting; it was filmed entirely in the studio and on the "back lot". The appeals of the film are almost entirely thematic rather than visual. Even its major surface text appears regressive as it takes us back to a familiar plot: the taming of the frontier or, if you will, the entry of the lusty frontier (the realm of societal adolescence) into a more respectable, if unexciting, maturity.[2]

The more subtle thematic attraction of *Liberty Valance* is essentially its enactment of the most common, culturally promoted inner conflicts experienced by men in many social contexts. This archetypicality is reinforced by the fact that it is acted by three actors who in their film careers have come themselves to epitomize the archetypal characters required by that thematic structure. The three are so closely associated with the qualities of their specific roles in this movie that, with the exception of Lee Marvin in the role of Liberty Valance, we can use their more familiar public names.

Marvin, as we have seen him so often, is an expression of what can be termed "narcissistic grandiosity" – wholly the idealization of personal ambitions, the dark side of over-masculinized individualism. Liberty Valance reflects a reluctance to surrender male adolescent values to the practical demands of an everyday world. John Wayne (Tom Doniphin), in contrast, serves as the personification of "narcissistic honor" – a precarious balancing of personal ambition and social ideals that increasingly narrows options for behavior. He apparently has begun to mature along with the frontier as marked by a desire to marry, however inarticulately expressed, while at the same time manifestly having difficulty abandoning the "heroic" postures so antagonistic to the life of domesticity. Lastly, Jimmy Stewart (Ransome Stoddard) serves as the typification of "social honor" – our best sense of what we ought to desire, an "oughtness" virtually in complete control of behavior, an inevitable relabeling that transforms many of the most craven betrayals of the adolescent nerd into the sacrificing heroism of the conforming adult.[3]

A critical aspect of male adolescent development is the tendency for the conflicting dimensions of the self to be drawn to and acted out in the newly opened frontiers of the erotic. The erotic is presented to most adolescents as the "badlands of desire". For many young men, the intensive and prolonged use of masturbation provides an imaginary erotic landscape within which conflicts between rage (sadomasochism), honor (the tentative promise of an acceptable explanation), and the acceptance of social reality's conventions can be tested totally within the domain of the self.

The basic plot is relatively simple and can be summarized very quickly. Stewart comes to the frontier bringing the law and the dominance of the community. His first encounter is with Valance, in an almost dream-like sequence, during a hold-up of a stagecoach outside Shinbone. It is as if Valance immediately recognizes Stewart as his special nemesis; it is as if they had met before. Valance attacks Stewart ferociously, and strips him of what is most essential to his identity – his books (the law) and his ability to protect women. Finding Stewart unconscious, it is Wayne who brings him to the community (Shinbone) and to Hallie (played by Vera Miles) for nursing.

Hallie is at this point assumed by all to be Wayne's woman, the woman for whom he is about to abandon his frontier (adolescent or pre-adult) ways, symbolized by his building of a house/home for her. In a sense, it may be an ambivalent Wayne who unconsciously summons Stewart to the unsettled community, as in Freudian imagery ego summons forth the power of superego in order to manage the threats posed by the forces of the id. Hallie nurses Stewart back to health. Seen almost exclusively in the kitchen of her restaurant, where she exercises control over her immigrant parents, she is the consummate oedipal solution, with demonstrable capacities for being both a wife and a mother, though ultimately she will prove to be only one of these.

The difference between the three in their use of women is significant. For

101

Valance women represent two aspects of interpersonal relations. On the one hand, they symbolize the order and discipline that comes with home-steading and, for that very reason, are the enemy of the persistent adolescent homosociality of the frontier. On the other hand, women are temporary sex objects serving to confirm his masculinity directly, as well as being the occasion for demonstrating dominance over other men. Valance's sexual style approximates one that Freud (1905) saw as characterizing the worlds of antiquity where major significance attached to the drive, with little significance given to the object. Valance has little direct interaction with Hallie. Little is necessary; in only one encounter, he need only leer at Hallie to remind us of what uses he would make of her but for the presence of the others.

Wayne requires her for the fulfillment of the classic patriarchal pattern; he requires her as property – it is hard to say whether he is building a house for her or pursuing her because he has begun to invest in a house. She would replace Pompey, the Tonto-like former black slave, as trusted companion and domestic. The homoerotic potential of adolescence will give way to a homosocially infused heterosexuality, a sexuality focused on women in ways that can only be appreciated by other men. She will be the vehicle of his final confirmation of true patriarchal status: entry into fatherhood. (In this context, it is interesting that though she finally marries Stewart, it is clear that it has been and will remain a childless marriage.)

Lastly, for Stewart, she is the partner necessary to complete the require-ments of community, family, and career expectations. He will teach her to read, an act that Wayne bitterly resents. It is as if Wayne intuitively understands that, once exposed to the possibility of achieving even marginal subjectivity, she can never happily be his final and permanent adornment.

A unique aspect of this otherwise stereotyped scenario is that it is perhaps the only time in his career in film when John Wayne will grossly violate the Code of the West, the unwritten code of narcissistic honor: he will virtually shoot someone in the back by shooting Valance while Valance is preoccupied with "gunning down" Stewart, whom he has finally provoked into a classic "showdown".

The unbalanced showdown between Liberty and Stewart is provoked by Liberty's violent assault on the figure who serves as Stewart's oedipal father, a previously weak, alcoholic newspaper editor. The accessibility of the Freudian retelling of the Oedipal Myth has produced a curious simplification of interpretations of representations of the father. More common than patricide is the elimination of the father as either an obstacle or threat by structuring a role reversal wherein the son becomes the rescuer and rehabilitator of the father – themes reoccurring in such recent films as *Back to the Future, Peggy-Sue Gets Married*, and *Terminator*. Perhaps, in a mark of the distance we have traveled since Sophocles, it is as protector and avenger of the father figure that the son, Stewart, leaves the kitchen, still wearing the apron that signified his previous yet to be certified masculinity, and takes possession of the gun.

John Wayne's betrayal of the Code of the West not only rids the community of the threat of Valance, it creates Wayne's fatal anomie by destroying his claim for narcissistic honor, a claim for personal honor that could only have substance when set off against the still more dangerously grandiose and increasingly inappropriate challenges of a Valance. Wayne's killing of Valance is simultaneously a homicide and a suicide. Unprotected from his own narcissistic rage, Wayne will burn his own house and with it all claims for post-oedipal happiness. Wayne's uncelebrated death occasions the retelling of the saga and by doing so he returns to unburden Stewart of his (and our) guilt at having achieved full maturity by a narcissistic lapse – allowing the beating of the newspaper editor/father figure moving him to adopt the gun. Such a lapse is shared by many at the level of fantasy, and still leaves a residual and sometimes eruptive taste for desires better left to fantasy.

Stewart initially experiences the shooting of Liberty Valance as his own achievement, and, as a result, becomes a winner – getting Hallie, community recognition, statehood for the previously dependent territory, and, becoming a Senator, is allowed to go off to Washington, the home of the Great White Father. At the same time, however, he is exiled from the desires and fantasies of childhood and adolescence by his very success in the affairs of adults.

The possibility of conflicts between the self as a history of desires and the requirements of civilization with its varied anticipations of maturity is hardly unique to adolescence. Adolescence may properly dominate discourse on the state of the management of such conflicts because for most it is the earliest stage of the life cycle when there is pressure to experience such conflicts as conflict and to urgently resolve or stabilize those conflicts. Such conflicts, it must be noted, need not be located in some Hobbesian conflict between nature and nurture, but can be conceptualized more interestingly as the result of the conflicts of culture with itself. Against the conventional image of human beings, particularly men, as creatures of nature struggling to find contentment within the constraints and civilities of community and family life, Stewart offers us the image of men who are essentially timid creatures whose most successful uses of violence take the form of symbolic violence – which is what his confrontation with Valance was.

Socialization is the learning of the rules of social life, much as we learn the rules of a series of games – rules and meanings of conduct for which nature in most cases does extraordinarily little to prepare us. It involves the training for games where the criteria for success or failure are largely in the hands of others and where the tokens of success are dramatically valorized precisely because they are tokens of success (Simon and Gagnon 1975).

At the threshold of adolescence, much of what is the individual is the consequence of a history of training in such rules of the game, a history of performance, as well as the beginnings of commitment to and experience with many of the current tokens of success. That such games are really more than just games is most often a sustaining ideology for those who have learned the art of winning, the art of appearing to have won, or, failing all else, the art of appearing not to have lost.

This training becomes critical for the adolescent. One reason is clearly the increasing pressures to be (or appear to be) morally responsible to others, the community, and to the self. The latter requires responsibility for what is the least existential and least immediately recognizable form of the self: the self preparing for its own future. Moreover, the requirement is that the adolescent become morally responsible but in ways that are, at the same time, "realistic" and "practical". This potential contradiction between the moral and the realistic becomes the seedbed where the second dimension, narcissistic honor, emerges. Honor can only appear where there is a potential conflict between alternative forms of desire.

Liberty Valance is cruel, sadistic, vicious, the last legacy of childhood: grandiosity wondrously unfettered by the slightest empathic awareness of the consequences for such seemingly abstract realities as the family, community, civilization, or the future. This is perhaps why vengeance may be the first form of justice in which we become schooled and why, in the childhood of most American men, Liberty Valance may have organized our fantasies as often as he haunted our nightmares. Liberty Valance's villainy (if that is what it is) rests largely upon his demand that the games that constitute social life be organized around those rules of behavior that provide a context within which he is sure of winning. In most other versions of the game, particularly those representing the most conventional expectations for adolescent development, he is condemned to being a loser.

Honor also appears as a compelling theme for Liberty Valance, but it is a conception of honor totally subordinated to the defense of his basic grandiosity, a grandiosity often driven to burning rage, appeased only by sadism, and consoled only by vengeance. He is so pure an expression of grandiosity that very little can be effected by compromise and probably less by the promise of future rewards. For Liberty the game must be rigged because the only alternative to winning is death. In contrast, the commitment to honor (as the effective basis for self-acceptance) by the other two characters – John Wayne personifying "narcissistic honor" and James Stewart personifying "social honor" – indicates that they share a common aspect of honor that requires them to play out the game even when they know that it is stacked against them. It is precisely this quality that makes both, each in his own way, the "friend" of the social order in much the same way that Liberty Valance is its enemy. For them losing is both plausible, i.e.

consistent with character, and honorable, i.e. a testimony of virtue, and as a result they are under no pressure to question or leave the larger game itself even when they lose.

In Liberty Valance we can see many of the aspects of self that must be repressed or disguised in order to be a winner by conventional standards. His ability to act impulsively upon his immediate desires, his willingness to invest otherwise trivial gestures with great significance, his willingness to run exorbitant risks for trivial gains, and, above all else, his unwillingness to surrender to the middle ground where compromise flourishes are the postures that make him the instantly recognized enemy of civilization and maturity, or, at the very least, the most common enemy of (self-)regulation and (self-)discipline.

Most young men are prepared to abandon their grandiosity, their chance to play Liberty Valance; others are eager; and still others are given little choice. This abandonment – involving repression, sublimated expression, or retreat to the sanctuary of fantasy – is rarely total, rarely immediate, and still more rarely without compromise and residual ambivalence. The mechanism most typically effecting that compromise is a flowering of concerns for honor. But it is essentially "narcissistic honor" that tends to appear first: honor that is based upon a predominance of personal book-keeping, rather than social book-keeping. It is frequently the only basis upon which new commitments to self-regulation and self-discipline can be assimilated without experiencing an overwhelming threat to self-cohesion, without experiencing a disturbing sense of disloyalty to what one has been and has dreamed of becoming.[4]

The behavior of both Valance and Wayne is significantly referential to honor. For Valance, however, honor is totally at the disposal of his own grandiosity, while for Wayne it is clearly the most effective available constraint on grandiosity, a commitment to constraint that will have a developmental logic of its own. The distinction should closely parallel Kohut's distinctions between the negative and positive forms of narcissism (Kohut 1978a). John Wayne, in both *Liberty Valance* and his general persona, epitomizes this quality of narcissistic honor. It is for the most part an inarticulate honor, one that, while expressed through public acts, can be made meaningful only through being made referential to the actor and his or her purposes, i.e. where the actor provides the interpretive context for the act. Thus, both Liberty Valance and Wayne share an equal commitment to "the law of the gun", differing only in their application of that law. In contrast, social honor, personified by Stewart, is typically an act of conscience, never more unambiguous than when it risks being misunderstood.

The fact that the townspeople of Shinbone, where the action of the film occurs, initially show no great enthusiasm for the social values voiced by Stewart does not make his commitment to honor less social in nature. He epitomizes social honor because his behavior is organized not around the reality of any specific community, but by his commitment to an abstract idea of community life. Stewart can remain secure in his honor because it is within the jurisdiction of an objectified ideal, a realm where the act provides the interpretive context for the actor.

This film, then, can be seen as a parable, where the story of how a community achieves legitimacy provides the imagery for reawakening the psychological archeology of the American male, providing an opportunity to re-experience the vicissitudes attending the journey from the impulsive grandiosity of childhood to an acceptance of the somber and restrained joys of maturity. For many men this kind of scenario is attractive because it re-creates for them not merely the chronology of their negotiated self but also the emotional richness of that negotiation. That the conclusion is known in advance does not discourage us; indeed, that may be a requirement of being allowed to recapture the emotions of almost all parties to the negotiated self without calling into question the wisdom of that negotiation.

Our identifications, as Freud (1908) understood, are rarely exhausted by an exclusive attachment to a single character, but may be distributed among all the significant players: a diffusion of identifications and empathic projections. Men come to the film not merely to survive as Jimmy Stewart nor merely to have themselves mourned as John Wayne, but also to live, however briefly, with Liberty Valance – to live with him and to be reassured that he was properly killed and that the costs involved were worth it.

There is a particular episode that highlights just this. It is Saturday night in Shinbone and all the players are in town. Hallie's restaurant is full. Valance and some of his cronies enter. He approaches a table where three cowboys are about to start their dinner. He looks down at them and says, "These steaks look done just right for us. You cowboys are in no hurry to eat, are you?" They mumble an obsequious agreement and back off. At that moment it is the rarest of men who is not Liberty Valance. To enter a room and have men of unqualified masculinity make way for you as an involuntary gesture of respect has to be among the most universal of male fantasies.

At that moment Stewart appears as a waiter, that is, in what is clearly a feminine role. The timing is perfect; many men will react with the uneasiness that often accompanies our identification with Valance, particularly when *his* acts of narcissistic grandiosity are performed without provocation and with undisguised malice. Too often we have been or feared being his victim. Stewart's entrance in a feminine posture moves us from villainy to the more familiar postures of the victim. Swiftly we are allowed to atone masochistically for our identification with aggression by risking a humiliation that almost all of us must have often feared and many have experienced at one time or another. Stewart is tripped by Valance; he falls to the floor and the steak he is carrying is sent flying across the room. The threat (and experience of the threat) of humiliation becomes real. This is observed not only by Hallie and her parents, but also by the alcoholic newspaper editor and John Wayne, who observe this from a shared table where they posture a relaxed masculinity, the oedipal father and the preferred son as instantly recognized by almost every son who was or dreamed of being the preferred son.

And yet we will survive this, not only because we know how this must ultimately end, but because Wayne, the image of almost all the men we've admired, will protect us, but without the sissifying required by Hallie's maternal protection. And he will do so in a way that thoroughly protects his own masculinity – earning our admiration and, finally, our identification as we have the rare opportunity of being a protective best buddy to ourselves. He will do this carefully, without admitting to sentimentality by claiming a personal piece of the action. "That's my steak," he says, pointing to the steak on the floor.

This time it is Liberty himself who will be threatened with humiliation and we can rejoice in that. Wayne will require that Valance stoop to pick up the steak. However, Valance will be spared the actual humiliation by Stewart, who grabs the steak off the floor and shouts, "Here is the piece of meat you're prepared to kill each other for! Is everybody crazy around here?"

What a round of emotions. We are provided with an extraordinarily rapid shifting of identities and emotions without the slightest disturbance to the rigid structure of pieties that so coercively orchestrates the scene. Nowhere in the film is the contrast between the requirements of the two kinds of honor drawn more effectively. Both Liberty Valance and Wayne enter a game where the rules are fixed, a game that only acknowledges individuals and sees them all as equal, regardless of all manner of otherwise pertinent differences. Wayne and Valance engage in a few swift movements, each of which is blocked with equal swiftness, like long-time players of checkers. And the game must be played by the operative rules until the drawing of guns or a display of submission.

In this case, however, the game and its assumptions are called into question by Stewart. These differences in style of response come very close to paralleling the distinctions observed by Gilligan (1982) in styles of moral reasoning that tend to differentiate women and men. Women, she notes, are more likely to give greater priority in moral reasoning to intentions and consequences, while men are more likely to define morality in terms of the establishment of, and conformity to, given rules. In this, Liberty Valance and John Wayne stand together; for them, Stewart's social honor is a form of capitulation to the world of women, a world from which they have long

107

been exiled, a world whose very essences constitute the negative pole of many of their most important claims upon an identity.

Wayne's anger in the episodes following the shooting of Valance is understandable. Part of it has to do with the realization of his loss of Hallie to Stewart. As suggested earlier, the shooting of Valance is both homicide and suicide. Wayne has lost both honor and potency. Following the shooting of Valance, Wayne enters Hallie's kitchen to find her attending Stewart's wound. Little has to be said. Wayne cannot admit to having been the one who did the shooting nor call into question the honor and admiration that Stewart has undeservedly won. Neither winning nor losing, he has become irrelevant.

Immediately following his surrender of claims to Hallie, Wayne encounters Liberty Valance's two sidekicks. Their behavior by the once operative rules provides more than ample justification for the drawing of guns, but instead Wayne disarms them and hands them over to the once ridiculously unheroic town marshal. Justice is now the property of no person, but belongs to the community. Wayne then leaves the bar-room; his disgust for the surviving residues of Valance is small compared to his disgust with himself. He has surrendered his guns and with them the rules that give narrative plausibility to his behavior and the illusion of cohesiveness to his identity. Narcissistic honor is dependent on being framed by the threat of narcissistic rage.

At the very beginning of the film, before the telling of the "real" story, Stewart, in viewing Wayne laid out in a coffin, asks that his boots, spurs, and guns be buried with him. The guns are clearly an act of restitution, one made when it is too late to be anything but safe. The now aged, former town marshal indicates that there were none; Wayne, he notes, hadn't worn guns for years. The surrender of the guns does in fact become a dangerous surrender of a sense of self. Perhaps far more anxiety-generating than Freud's imagery of fear of literal castration is the fear of symbolic castration implicit in the loss of critical metaphors of identity – our guns, jobs and wisdom that only men can possess, the right of men to appear responsible for women. The gesture of restitution attempts to protect us from the fear of losing what we might never have had or never have been. By this point in the film, the title has ceased to be wholly a hero's accolade and becomes something of an indictment.

Indeed, the retelling of the story is an expiatory effort, one that essentially fails. Stewart and Hallie have returned to Shinbone from lives of success elsewhere. His career as governor, senator, and ambassador has taken them to many places and honors, with the promise of substantially much more to come – a national vice-presidency is mentioned. Yet neither appear fully realized nor in any way free from their ghosts. Hallie describes it as having been cut off from their – really her – roots. Stewart, remember, came to Shinbone rooted only in his idealizations of social honor.

Hallie has paid for this with an abandonment of claims to romantic fulfillment. Her act of attempted retribution is to place on Wayne's coffin a cactus rose. Much earlier, Wayne had expressed his love for her with expected inarticulateness by giving her such a rose, one to be planted in the earth. At that time, Stewart, in what might have been his most explicit effort at romantic rivalry, asks whether she has ever seen a *real* rose. By which, of course, he means a cultivated rose, a civilized rose, one bred to fulfill the ideal conception of a rose. They have lived, as it were, a life of roses, without its replacing the more primitive cactus rose or providing what the cactus rose promised. The sense of loss, however, need not be Hallie's alone. In a somewhat self-defeating way, John Wayne represents the capacity for romantic passion. Perhaps for both men and women, romantic passion can only feed off narcissism, dying where it becomes the fulfillment of the everyday obligations of social honor.

In old age both Hallie and Stewart appear to have taken on a kind of asexual quality. There is no mention of their having had any children. In our kind of society, commitments to parenting increasingly depend upon narcissistic responses and less and less upon commitments to social honor alone. Stewart, as the train takes them from Shinbone, says that possibly they will return to live there again, but only after he has secured passage of legislation encouraging irrigation, which promises to bring a still thwarted fertility to the surrounding deserts. Whether they return or not, which remains problematic, it is clear that the waters will have come too late for Hallie and Ştewart. Both are condemned to exile.

In telling a version of the truth, Stewart has not earned his right to return to the truths of his childhood and adolescence, if in fact he can claim one. This is the meaning of the drama's second significant act (second after the shooting of Liberty Valance). The newspaper editor, after hearing the *real* story of who shot Liberty Valance, to Stewart's amazement rejects the confession – "This is the West," he says destroying his notes, "when the legend becomes fact you print the legend." His exile (our exile) from his own history is permanent. The bargain made with maturity is irrevocable. Or so it seemed at one time. The rewards of more mature achievement and their attendant pleasure need no longer leave us with feelings of guilt. We come to recognize that we must continue to pay for them by the continued surrender of so much of our childhood and early adolescent idealizations of the self.

Liberty Valance, like all viable mythic figures, continues to live. He continues to live if only to be repeatedly killed, as the male audience is afforded frequent opportunities to relive the experience of their own renunciations of narcissistic grandiosity. Between episodes he will be exiled to the badlands of desire where he will continue to pick at our consciousness, proposing complicity in acts always to be committed by others.

109

John Wayne, the personification of narcissistic honor, will continue to inform many of the emptier and more pretentious of male postures. Available for many causes, this sense of self is especially available for the moral indignation of threatened identities that almost always accompanies totalitarian causes. His major use, and why we call upon him so often, is because he serves best in those moments when the duties to which we are called don't appear to make much sense. Social honor has to articulate its rationale; narcissistic honor, in its present, masculinized postures, need only recite and obey the rules.

However, it is the posture of social honor that remains predictive of what most men will see themselves as being most of the time. Gray and unattractive in its reality or unbelievably two-dimensional when formally celebrated, it is to be found in a vast, mid-point plane between the symbolic and the imaginary, sometimes mistakenly called the real, where most of life is lived most of the time for most of us. The burdens of social honor can be shifted from what appear sometimes as meaningless burdens to identity-confirming trials, such as the important things that "a real man" must do and the ways in which he must do them. But often this involves a projection of Liberty Valance waiting in many of the darker places and moments of everyday life to transform the performance of the pedestrian into the hard-won triumph of the moral spirit: that uniquely human ability to dream our discontents with civilization in ways that simultaneously enact our enduring commitment to it.

AFTERWORD

Some comment upon the entirely male perspective of this essay is necessary. In part this derives from one of the major research tools of the author, empathic introspection. Another, more compelling reason for this narrowing of perspectives is the feminist commitment of the author. Understandably, the major focus of feminist criticism has been the representation of women in the discourses of the larger society based upon patriarchal assumptions and uses. The implicit assumption of this criticism has been that men are adequately or usefully represented by such understandings. That is not true. To say that society and its cultural legacy are permeated with sexist conceptions is *not* to say that the experiences of all men are happily contained in what appears to be the protection of those structures of dominance.

It is important to understand that virtually all men, to varying degrees, are influenced by conventional cultural values that are inevitably infused with the legacy of a pervasive sexism.[5] *Liberty Valance* is clearly regressive if only in the sense that it plays off some of the most traditional masculine postures. That increasing numbers of men are alienated from or unsatisfied by current employments of such a legacy does not derive from their discovery of some truer consciousness of gender. Rather, it derives from the experiences of social life and particularly from the changing ways in which women are experienced.

It is, however, equally important to understand that to a considerable extent the same is true for most females, the same legacy of sexist concepts and values, to varying degrees, permeates the consciousness of women. Consciousness raising is not synonymous with consciousness purification, as one might replace one file with another on a hard disk. Many women continue to be pleasured by being the subject that is the object of another's desire. The experience of being desired, not unknown to men, can be as pleasuring and confirming as any other configuration of sexual desire.

Though Hallie is not always visible she is a constant presence, if only as the establishing common denominator for the three male archetypes. For Liberty Valance she is the rejecting mother who fills him with reasoned rage; he never gets to eat in her kitchen. For Tom Doniphin she is the consummate audience for a code of honor that need never speak its name. This is why he is helpless in clarifying the question of who in fact shot Liberty Valance earlier; her response to the wounded Ransome Stoddard is so purely an expression of her being that perfect audience that Doniphin cannot speak. (One cannot help but wonder about Hallie: What did she really know? When did she know it?) And, lastly, for Stoddard, Hallie is the Cinderella of populist mythology: the re-invigorating of the civilized but effete WASP from the East as he encounters the challenges of the frontier by winning the hand, if not wholly the heart, of a woman with the practical intelligence of worthy immigrant stock and a weakness for language and cultivated roses.

For each of the three, there are complementary gestures by Hallie, though gestures that signify differently for her. What for Valance is the rejecting mother is for Hallie an expression of a determination to take charge of her own life, as she has already taken charge of the lives of her immigrant parents and even to ordering the apron-wearing Ransome Stoddard into the encounter over who was going to get, as it were, Hallie's steak.[6] It is her very strength of character that takes Hallie to the limits of conventional female roles, a potential transgression that highlights her ultimate submission to a male worthy of her strengths. The significant choice between John Wayne and Jimmy Stewart, a choice between the gun and the book, the desert rose and the cultivated rose, is inadequately resolved with the illusion that Stewart, in appearing to have killed Liberty Valance, can claim possession of both gun and book, of both nature and civilization.

The choice for women is different, but not vastly different than choices of men. Though trained to different configurations of desire, the choice between the passionate and the prudent is imposed upon both as part of the logic of social life. Long before his public confession, Stoddard must

111

have made it known to Hallie that the gun he possessed was an unused and unusable one. If males viewing *Liberty Valance* are pleasured by a reliving and reconfirming of earlier choices that have left residues of ambivalence and suggestions of self-betrayal, so are many women viewers. In many ways the ambivalence must run deeper for women. The mythic idealizations for men were rehearsed in what were essentially games of make-believe, while for women they were rehearsals for life.

Perhaps it is in the very nature of myths, as representations of a social order's important idealizations, that they offer more than most can or should realize in everyday social life. Their capacity for pleasure may rest in allowing us to affirm what we are not, cannot be, and in many instances do not really want to become. Myth is more often a consoling apology than the blueprint for some social imperative.

6

DEVIANCE AS HISTORY
The future of perversion

INTRODUCTION

The task of understanding sexual deviance, and those forms of it referred to as "perversion", is twofold. First, we must attempt to understand why and under what conditions certain behaviors are proscribed. Second, there must be an understanding of the motivation that encourages individuals to engage in or identify with such behaviors. These two levels of concern are related, but rarely in ways that are either simple or direct.

Attempts at answering these two questions are often the meeting point of naive functionalisms, psychobiologisms, or mechanistic behaviorisms. Functionalist and psychobiological perspectives tend to assume that the reproductive consequences of heterosexual intercourse are the manifestation of evolved drives associated with species survival (Symons 1979). When confronted with the reality of sexual practices that have little or no direct relation to reproduction, these approaches attempt to locate the specific experiences of individuals that alter or divert this essential, phylogenetic predisposition. This is consistent with the nineteenth-century conception of perversion as a pathology of sexual appetites that alter nature's initial intent (Stoller 1975; Kaplan 1986).

My own view, in contrast, rests comfortably within *social constructionist* perspectives, where considerations of sexual behaviors, like most other behaviors, must be viewed in terms of their origins within the sociohistorical process and their derivation of legitimacy from the cultural practices of their time and place. This *constructionist* perspective views the emergence of definitions of sexual normality and deviance within the context of the evolving discursive practices of social life. Correspondingly, constructionists view individual motivation not as the adaptations of unchanging human organisms to changing circumstances, but as occasioning fundamental changes in the capacity of individuals to experience and act upon sexual desires (Foucault 1978; Simon and Gagnon 1986; Irvine 1990).

Sexual deviance also presents embarrassing problems for social constructionists who, like adherents to all other social learning approaches, are

113

often embarrassed by the appearance of sexual behaviors that persistently violate powerfully held social expectations. The failure of "oversocialized" conceptions of human behavior, those that see the individual as merely being "stuffed" with cultural meanings, is not that they fail to deal with the imperatives and varieties of biological requirements. This is the position taken by Wrong (1961). Wrong's position continues the legacy of the Romantic Tradition in its unexamined acceptance of an inevitable, fundamental and tragically unresolvable conflict between the individual as a creature of "nature" and the individual as critically dependent upon social life. In part, the inability of social orders to produce universal conformity may lie in their inability to consistently chart character-shaping adaptations at the individual level, where practices of individuation in social life and variations in genetic endowment, under all circumstances, have a potential for generating deviance. This is present in conditions of anomie where the issues of the fairness of collective justice must compete, often on less than equal terms, with the issues of the fairness of what is experienced as personal justice (Durkheim 1893).

The embarrassments of having substantial numbers of persons display effective resistance to powerfully held social norms need not only be explained by approaches that locate the origins of deviance or perversion in hormonal variations or the direct consequences of infant/child experiences that are remote to societal influence. Rather, it is possible to view such outcomes as derivative of numerous developmental contingencies that, at many points of development, could have produced a markedly different outcome. The profoundly contingent nature of human development is clearly reflected at all levels of that development, physical and psychological. As Luria observed with reference to biological evolution:

> What exists is the almost accidental product of a purposeless historical process. A given visual system or a given device for gene regulation is but an exceptional sample of all visual systems or gene regulatory devices that could have come into being .... The organisms that actually exist are like a group of islands that are but the peaks of a submerged mountain chain. The species and organ systems that we currently see are the adaptive peaks of an ever changing profile. It is the diversity and uniqueness of biological types and devices that make them phenomenologically significant.
>
> (Luria 1975: 359)

The same note of contingency describing all biological life forms that occur over time, as against those that are designed, must apply to the species of human being to a degree unmatched by any other species. Moreover, with increased population size and diversity of experiences, what were once inconsequential differences at the level of the individual become significant determinants of behaviors and patterns of behavior.

114

While sensitive to the factors that might differentiate the deviant from the non-deviant, this constructionist approach requires that individual differences be understood in the context of what is inevitably a greater abundance of common endowments and shared experiences. A common source of misapprehension is the tendency to seek a singular origin or cause for seemingly uniform outcomes. Another equally influential source of misapprehension is the questionable assumption that what are viewed as dramatic effects must require equally dramatic causes. It is also important to acknowledge the possibility that relatively small differences might account for the display of both conforming and deviant sexual behavior. The "normal" or "typical" sexual deviant may be as rare a phenomenon as the "normal" or "typical" sexual conformist.

THE SELF IN ALTERNATIVE REALITIES

It may be something of an irony that human sexuality, frequently viewed as constant across the human record, is actually among the forms of behavior most dependent upon contextualizing contingencies. Modern societies represent an unprecedented point in social evolution where sexual desire and cultural expectations increasingly cease to mirror one another closely (Simon and Gagnon 1986).

Elias (1978) and Foucault (1978) suggest that concepts of privacy, the modern self, and the flourishing of the erotic as a widely distributed personal motive all tended to coincide as a distinctive aspect of the modern Western experience. Privacy has several dimensions. One dimension speaks to solitude, containing, as relatively distinct sub-dimensions, isolation and insulation, both having separate physical and psychological references. A second dimension speaks to the degree to which the management of the appearance of the self is required or controlled. The modern self appears with a profoundly enlarged capacity or necessity to be insincere and to deceive others as an aspect of normal human development. It is Elias (1978) who reminds us of the transformation in socialization that gives rise to the modern self, a self exemplified by a shift from the prototype of the warrior, who must be socialized to be what he appears to be – a killer, to the prototype of the courtier, who must be trained not to be necessarily what he appears to be, as well as to cope with others who may not be what they appear to be.

The sexual, in such contexts, becomes an occasion for enlarged internal dialogues as private thoughts must mesh with public behaviors that have profound social implications (Simon and Gagnon 1987; Freud 1915; Trilling 1972; Goffman 1959; Plummer 1975; Weinberg 1983). One consequence of this is that conventionalized interpersonal scripts, nonsexual and sexual, tend to be shaped by their ability to give permission for realizing subjective desires that are often not necessarily manifest in what is conventionally seen as implicit in such scripts, as metaphor links the public and private in what are often mysterious ways – mysterious even to the individual actor.

The enlargement of the scope of the erotic, as well as the amount of the social landscape it is allowed to stake a claim in, has been a major but far from exclusive source of the empowering of psychic reality. Within such enlarged interior spaces, a self may have been in the process of discovering ways of relating to the external social world that previously may have been the experience of only an exceptional minority and for which there was little by way of shared explanation that might have "normalized" the experience.

Theories of "normal" development are invariably implicit in all explanations of "deviance" and serve, even retrospectively, to facilitate control. One of the major "tasks" of theories of deviance is to protect the legitimacy of theories of normality (Cohen 1987).

SEXUAL DESIRE AND ITS REPRESENTATION

Among the most revolutionary aspects of Freud's conceptualization of sexual development was one that he himself did not fully appreciate nor effectively work into his theoretical constructions. This was his almost casual observation that the object of the sexual drives was not an extension of those drives, not their natural mode of expression, but that the object was "soldered" onto the drives. Freud's formulation encourages us to treat the sexual object not as the *expression* of desire but as a *representation* of desire, a view that conceptualizes the sexual not as an ultimate reality but as metaphoric text (Davidson 1987). The current preoccupation with how the sexual is represented must give way to the more challenging question of what the sexual represents.

This formulation occasions the familiar but largely unemployed idea that sexual behavior is the expression of a wide variety of desires that are not intrinsically sexual and, by the same token, that to speak of "hidden" or "latent" sexual motives is not to speak of desire's ultimate meaning, but to refer to a complex history of meanings (Merleau-Ponty 1962). Individuals acting in virtually identical ways may be doing so as a result of different configurations of desire and they may find themselves experiencing the act in different ways. Similarly, individuals experiencing what are virtually identical configurations of sexual desire, given the specific contingencies of their lives, may find themselves engaging in vastly different activities. To the continuing frustration of conventional behaviorists, individual behavior increasingly must be viewed not as the text of a fact but as a complex outcome for which no one defining label can have assured universal meaning. Clearly, there are more reasons for being sexual than ways of being sexual.

Contrary to the legacy of Freud, for the very reason that there may be no

116

desire that cannot be sexualized, there may be no desire that is intrinsically sexual. The possibility of hidden agendas becomes the commonplace of human encounters in modern and postmodern worlds, agendas hidden from others, and often simultaneously hidden from the self. As never before, more than finding the origins of the sexuality of individuals in the history of their culture, we must seek these origins in the varied histories of individuals within their cultures.

THE EROTICIZED SELF

The transparency of the self in traditional societies, where individuals are assumed to be what they appear to be, gives way in modern settings to the emergence of the more opaque strategies of the narrating subject. Objects of sexual desire, being representations of what is experienced as coming from within the self, as well as a statement to the external world, are the projections of an enlarged and empowered complex intrapsychic reality. While thumb-sucking ultimately gives way to its inability to provide nourishment, the same cannot be said of the numerous objects and experiences that nourish the psyche, which has a more enduring ability to feed upon its own creations. It is in this empowerment of the intra-psychic that the modern world's capacity to democratize eroticism rests, as well as its capacity – albeit a diminishing capacity – to transform sexual desire into specific types of persons.

DEFINING DEVIANCE AND PERVERSION

By definition, what constitutes sexual deviance and what constitutes sexual perversion relate to larger categories of social practice than those that are specifically sexual. This leads us to a useful distinction between sexual deviance and sexual perversion. *Sexual deviance might be defined as the inappropriate or flawed performance of conventionally understood sexual practices.* Rape, for example, is an act of sexual deviance that is rarely defined as an act of perversion. Rape becomes perverse only when performed on an individual whose inclusion in a sexual act goes beyond the limits of generally conceivable sexual practice or is performed in ways that go beyond the limits of generally conceivable sexual practice. Though we may deplore the behavior, it is possible to comprehend, and even empathically reconstruct, the experience of the rapist or his victim. In the language of the pathologists, such behaviors can be termed a *disease of control*.

As the character of sexual practice changes over time, so do the boundaries of the definitions of deviance. An excellent case in point is the increasing incorporation of oral sex in the scripting of conventional sexual scenarios. Although the behavior as a matter of organs and orifices remains unaltered, its collective meanings and uses for specific individuals

117

demonstrably have been undergoing profound change (Gagnon and Simon 1987; Simon *et al.* 1990; Lauman *et al.* 1994).

Perversions, in contrast, tend to be forms of desire too mysterious and sometimes too threatening to the most elementary definitions of desire and satisfaction to be tolerated. *Perversion can be thought of as a disease of desire, not only in the sense that it appears to violate the sexual practices of a time and place, but also because it constitutes a violation of common understandings that render current sexual practice plausible.* The behavior of the "pervert" is disturbing because, at the level of folk psychology, we have difficulty understanding why someone "might want to do something like that". Consistent with this approach was Krafft-Ebing's use of the term perversion as cited by Davidson (1987). In Krafft-Ebing's *Psychopathia Sexualis* (1876) there is a discussion of anomalies of appetite such as hyperorexia (increases), anorexia (lessening) and of perversions such as "a true impulse to eat spiders, toads, worms, human blood, etc." Perversions of appetite thus involve not only the desire to eat the unthinkable, but also the desire to eat for unthinkable reasons. The same might be said of "perversions" of the sexual.

As in the case of deviance, what is considered a perversion is also subject to revision as what constitutes the thinkable changes. Many forms of what for the contemporary world constitute acts of sexual deviance tend not to occur in other social settings not because they are repressed, but merely because they are literally unthinkable. Moreover, the processes through which behavior becomes "thinkable" for a collectivity are not identical to the processes through which behavior becomes "thinkable" to the individual.

The logic that links motive and behavior is the complex, almost magical logic of representation, a logic of metaphor and metonymy that meshes personal history with social history. Concerns for the role of the symbolic in the interaction of individuals often obscure the importance of the interaction between, and even within, symbols. A homogeneity of sexual preferences inevitably masks a heterogeneity of desired emotional productions, and this perhaps is the level at which, to some extent, we may all be perverts, as even the most conventional may find their sources of sexual excitement fueled by the slightest "whiff" of the unthinkable (Stoller 1979, 1985a).

Theories that describe the causes of behavior already presuppose the problematizing of that behavior. It is not theory that renders social practice problematic, but the emergence of the problematic in experience that gives rise to the requirement for theory, as well as the potential for its ability to find a responsive audience. In other words, theories of behavior are themselves behavior and, as such, have essentially the same basic requirements: first, they must be thinkable; second they must be plausible, that is, made either legitimate or explainable in terms of what is held to be legitimizing. In this sense I agree with Canguilhem (1989) when he notes: "[I]t is not paradoxical to say that the abnormal, while logically second, is existentially first. "

SEXUAL DESIRE AND ITS "DISEASES"

Sexual "deviates" are . . . an enigma, and it is the future of culture that they are challenging us to decipher through their obsessions.

(Sylvere Lotringer 1988)

MASTURBATION: FROM PERVERSION TO NORMALITY

Within the Western tradition, masturbation was the first "disease" of sexual desire to become a matter of continuing public preoccupation. From the eighteenth century forward, though known to be a common temptation, masturbation was conceived as a major source of sexual perversions. The speed and intensity with which the masturbatory prohibition was adopted, its capacity to endure for almost two centuries, as well as its continuing capacity to generate powerful feelings of guilt and anxiety, cannot be explained simply by the ideological functions the prohibition might have initially served. The Foucaultian hypothesis (1978) that the widely broadcast masturbatory prohibitions introduced in the mid-eighteenth century actually served to advertise and dramatically valorize the significance of the sexual and make the body itself give testimony to the deployment of power may be only partially valid. It is possible that in the changing patterns of individual development from the mid-seventeenth century on, there were conditions that were already in the process of increasing the actual number of individuals engaged in masturbation and, at the same time, altering the psychic content of the masturbatory experience. What remain unclear are the experiences that might have lent credibility to such horrific conceptions.

Involved in the elevation of the significance of masturbation may have been simultaneous experience of conflicting desires within the self, an experience that may have terrified individuals as often as they enchanted them. In other words, the plausibility of the fear of masturbation did not necessarily rest exclusively upon its "visible" consequences for others, but in the fear of what initially were invisible possibilities within the experiences of the very architects and theoreticians of the masturbatory prohibition, such as Kant and Freud themselves. Masturbation was in all likelihood not an experience that was totally alien to them, which requires that we ask, however rhetorically, what was it about their experience that confirmed their fears regarding the experience? And the answer can only be anxieties generated by the imagery of desires enacted or merely suggested within the reality of the imagination. Neither the capacity for nor the content of fantasy is a constant; they both necessarily vary between cultural settings and individual histories. As a result, it would be a mistake to chart the history of sexual behavior without a corresponding history of the self.

The experience of internally generated desires that reference the external world without being subject to the immediate surveillance of the external world understandably generates collective anxieties. As dramatization of the fullest experience of desire, masturbation might well have been a critical, enhancing developmental experience that is most essential to many post-Freudian models of the human: the divided self, the primacy of the wish, and the centrality of symbolic processes (Weeks 1985; Gagnon and Simon 1973; Hillman 1975, 1979). It must be understood that masturbation could have such character-altering consequences only because of the kind of personalities that were evolving in the changing circumstances of emerging modern Western social life. Unfortunately, the evolution of attitudes towards masturbation to its present status as a danger-laden but normal, age-specific development has largely occurred without examining the kinds of sexual actors and actions that were being evoked or with any substantial attention to its uses beyond adolescence.

There is no reason to believe that the sexual is universally a major part of the narrative of the self. For many it may achieve this status at only certain limited moments in their lives and, though such moments may have significant consequences for individuals, the occasioning element need not be immediately sexual. This occurs mostly in individuating social contexts, where the future of the self is recognized and experienced as uncertain. Sexuality is most likely to become a significant problematic in social contexts where individuals need not always be what they are, which is also one in which individuals need not always be what they appear to be. Fantasy, sexual and nonsexual, becomes significant only in circumstances where individuals can fantasize being something other than the statuses into which they were born. In such contexts, individuals must not only bargain with the world for what they desire to be, but must also bargain with themselves for who they are. Such a world encourages a shift in the narrative of the self for many from self-stability to self-similarity, much as a changing social order learns to exchange similarity for stability.

HOMOSEXUALITY: FROM PERVERSION TO THE SUBURBS OF NORMALITY

The invention of the concept of the homosexual, the major focus of concerns for perversion in the late nineteenth century, made the sexual significant by making it a powerfully signifying aspect of character. While homosexuality took center stage in a heightened scrutiny of the sexual as emblematic of basic character types, it was also an admission of the problematic nature of sexuality in all guises. As a result of this enhanced role of sexuality, modern homosexuals may be as different from previous generations engaging in same-gender sexual behavior as contemporary heterosexuals are different from previous generations of individuals engaging in heterosexual acts (Halperin 1990; Katz 1990).

Underlying the reconceptualization of the sexual during the nineteenth century was the fact that sexuality had become, in many ways, more a problem of desire than a problem of behavior. Not all who desire behave congruently with that desire, just as behavior is not necessarily immediately congruent with desire. Social requirements, by themselves, cannot create desire; still less can social requirements, by themselves, create the capacity to experience any desire as an endogenous force. Social repression, to be sure, is the attempt to regulate behavior socially, to regulate it not merely by discouraging "deviant" expressions of sexual desire but by channeling as many as possible of the inevitable deviant expressions into forms that conformed to, and thereby validated, still more important discursive practices surrounding the sexual.

Sexual behavior comes to be viewed as an ultimate signified at the end of a signifying chain; desire would be seen as a desire for a kind of sex (homosexual or heterosexual) and there need be no, or very little, concern for what these kinds of sex might *additionally* represent. Sexual desire is never merely a desire for a specific gender. Similarly, sexual desire is rarely, if ever, just for sex.

Homosexuality and heterosexuality necessarily share an ability to allow the issue of gender to dominate all competing explanations of sexual desire. This, in turn, gives rise to two powerfully signifying, if deceptive, homogeneities. Specific desires attached to the sexual compromise, often happily, with the desire to be part of a larger normality. The pleasures experienced by the validation of gender competence that accompanies evidence of heterosexual competence provided "obligatory" heterosexuality with its encouragements, while institutionalized homophobia provided restraints. The shared plausibility of homosexuality and heterosexuality was their ability to allow a major social significance of the object of desire, i.e. gender, to obscure and dominate other more intrapsychically dependent aims of desire. This is what Freud almost understood when he observed with reference to dreams:

> Symbolism does not attach great importance to the sexual difference. If the male or female principle is represented by a symbol of the opposite sex, there is no proof whatsoever of the utilization of the symbol in a specific sexual sense. It is dream representation – that is, the dream wants to express something quite specific.
>
> (Nunberg and Federn 1965–72: 157)

And it is Freud, perhaps more than anyone else, who taught us how much of the reality of desire is expressed in dreams and, of equal importance, just how much of reality is lived as if in a dream. To which one might add, the social meanings of desire, as we learn them, are already products of gender coding. Beyond childhood, it is therefore hard to experience a desire without acknowledging its conventional gender coding and significance. As a result, both homosexuality and heterosexuality serve to enhance the primacy of concepts of gender and the patchwork quilt of discursive practices that, in part, rests upon them.

Freud appeared to have understood this far more clearly than many who followed.

> [P]erhaps the sexual instinct itself may be no simple thing, but put together from components which have come apart again in the perversions. If this is so, the clinical observation of these abnormalities will have drawn our attention to amalgamations which have been lost to view in the uniform behavior of normal people.
>
> (Freud 1905: 162)

If the "fact" of homosexuality created the preconditions for recognition of heterosexuality, the ideologizing of homosexuality also ideologized heterosexuality, but more importantly it reflected a transformation of the role of the sexual in the lives of many, something that, in turn, reflected a transformation in the very nature of those living those lives. The creation of a sovereign individual within the West, while transforming political, religious, and familial behavior, was also impacting upon the sexual on the level of both discourse and experience. Modern homosexuals were different from previous generations of "sodomites" to the same degree that many practicing heterosexuals were different from previous generations of individuals engaging in heterosexual acts.

By the middle of the present century, homosexuality had effectively lost its status as a perversion, especially in the sense we have used it. In recent years, ironically encouraged by the information and imagery attending the current HIV epidemic, it can be said to have lost its status as a significant deviance (Simon 1994). And there is little reason to anticipate a change in the direction of this trend. Beyond the gender of the desired partner, the specific behaviors associated with homosexuals, oral and anal contact, have become the common practice of large numbers of heterosexuals. Still more importantly, with heightened expectations of reciprocity in sexual exchanges, it has become more difficult to assign specific gender significance to modes of participation in sexual acts. (Being "active" and "passive" widely become alternative and reciprocal modalities rather than consistent postures (Bell and Weinberg 1978; Blumstein and Schwartz 1983).

The diminishing of the perceived deviance of homosexuality does not necessarily imply a corresponding erosion of the viability of homosexual identities. It should be understood that the explosive emergence of gay liberation, mostly contained within the last twenty-five years, rested upon a number of contributing factors, not least of which was the changed role of the sexual in integrating the narrative of the self that occurs precisely when the individual is burdened with greater responsibility for sustaining this integration than was previously the case.

The emergence of the homosexual as a type from homosexual behavior places many engaged in such behavior still more completely in the control of social life. It is a process that creates the "good homosexual", the "responsible homosexual", the "community-oriented homosexual", and so on. From some perspectives, gay liberation resembles nothing so much as an escape from the isolation wing of a prison into the larger prison. Though the achievements of the goals of homosexual liberation need not culminate in the disappearance of the homosexual identity, it would be more than naive to assume that it will remain unaffected (Browning 1994).

SEXUAL DEVIANCE TODAY

Sex is dirty to the extent that erotic reality threatens to undermine the cosmic categories that organize the rest of social life. This is the source of the fears that surround sex, but also the source of its fascination. If sex did not disintegrate the cosmos to some extent, human beings would want to copulate only so much as animals, which are less preoccupied with sex. Those who desire to wash the dirt from sex ... are polishing away the very impurities that make it worth doing, that allow sex to rise above mere biological process into an existential act.

(Davis 1983: 245–6)

The confusions and uncertainties that attend massive social change, particularly those that are massive without being immediately catastrophic, change that almost imperceptibly invades and alters our social worlds, are reflected in concerns focusing upon the sexually deviant and the sexually conforming. Not only do the changes manifested in the social responses to conformity and deviances contextualize each other, but both must bear the effects of changes in related, broader social practices in the domains of work, family life, and community.

Much of what has shaped current sexual patterns is still very much in place, even if undergoing continuing revision. These forces involve virtually every aspect of social life, from the technologies influencing the worlds of work to those that have transformed our most intimate living spaces. What only a few decades ago represented hard-won understandings of the intermeshing of biological time and social time in comprehensive models of the life cycle (Erikson 1950) appear to be less universal in their application and less usable as a basis for creating guides to personal and social wellbeing.

The relationship between behavior and desire has been dominated by the need to establish firm limits on the expression or confession of desires.

123

Much of current commentary on contemporary sexual patterns speaks of excessive change (the sexual revolution) and of returns to normality or, at the very least, of a backing off from current patterns with a renewal of older standards and constraints (the sexual counter-revolution). Even many secular observers viewed the appearance of sexually transmitted diseases, such as AIDS or genital herpes, as manifestations of some natural sanction against "excessive" or "unnatural" sexual behavior. Similarly, the swiftness of the construction of a new psychiatric disorder, "sexual addiction", gives further evidence of what is commonly described as "a retreat from permissiveness" (Levine and Troiden 1988).

The postmodern experience may begin to reverse this as the claims of many desires are heard more emphatically. The *hyperreality*, the attempt to re-create in social life what was never there, that Baudrillard (1983) finds intrinsic to postmodern culture may find its analog in the hyperreality already to be found in modern versions of sexual desire. In this case, hyperreality represents the ascendancy of the "simulacra" or "dream of desire" over the enactment of desire, which sustains the repetitions that are fueled by the quest for what does not, and by its very nature cannot, exist. This would be consistent with the Lacanian (1977) notion of a circularity of desire, where desire presses upon behavior, not seeking satisfaction alone but also seeking confirmation of itself. Sexual hyperrealities press even more strongly upon the conventional, allowing the narrating self to reach, if only briefly, toward an experience of the self that compensates for an accumulating legacy of compromise of sexual pleasure with the requirements of other, more consistently public aspects of social life (Lichtenstein 1977).

We might also speak of the decentering of the sexual in recent years in recognition of its increasing detachment from the family as an institution, which was once its nearly exclusive legitimate social address. This partial abandonment of the familial near monopoly on legitimate sexual expression involved not only changes in sexual practices but also the changing practices describing other aspects of the family. The implications of this sociocultural shift for the immediate present and future of the sexual in our lives are numerous.[1]

Given the ability of the sexual to represent a layered history of desires and associations, different dimensions of sexual desire can be evoked on the level of the intrapsychic than are being performed, often simultaneously, at the level of the interpersonal. The sexual has the capacity to be productive of the confusions associated with "semiotic excess", to become the bearer of multiple meanings and associations (Barthes 1968). Thus, the sexual scripting of tenderness can accompany feelings of disdain and a retelling of a myth of love can be accompanied by displays of aggression. The distinction between the *intrapsychic* dimensions and the *interpersonal* dimensions of the sexual becomes critical: *the logic of the intrapsychic script is organized to make desire possible, whereas the logic of the interpersonal script is organized to make behavior acceptable* (Simon and Gagnon 1987). This difference requires a charting of the ways in which an enhanced marketplace for sexual desire encourages shopping among the emotional products of current experience for their direct links to sexual excitement, as well as their indirect links to still older sources of sexual excitement (Stoller 1979). Such developments encourage a self more mutable in the scripting of its social commitments and one for whom the satisfactions derived from the inevitable insincerities of our own performance encourage the appropriation of the questionable sincerity of our sexual partners.

> For a mutable self may be subjected to "identity exchange", the reciprocal cognitive transfer of some of each partner's defining characteristics to the other during sexual intercourse. Identity exchange is central to both erotic experience and smut structure, providing the link between the sexy and the dirty. It is the "double helix" of sexuality, involved in both sexual attraction and repulsion. *Sex partners are attracted to each other because identity exchange allows for each to reproduce himself in the other and the other in himself.*
>
> (Davis 1983: 239, italics added)

THE MEANINGS OF PERVERSION

It is possible that at any one moment a society may contain a wide variety of forms of sexual perversion as I've defined it. Many such perversions are so obscure that they remain unknown and unknowable, if only because of the innocuousness of their practices. Still others occur with sufficient regularity that they become part of a society's canon of perversions. Of these, a small number become a special focus of attention and these frequently provoke an intense response; their appearances are not merely sanctioned severely, but their dangers advertised and their potential suspected, and actual practitioners are aggressively pursued.

The perversions that generally command the greatest attention are those whose incomprehensibility is being lessened by a diminishing of the differences that certify their very status as perversion. In other words, attention is paid to those "perversions" that begin to appear on the shadowy borders of plausibility and, as a result, where the increased scrutiny for signs of such taint in others occasions a similar scrutiny of the self. Such scrutiny is associated with a sense of impending epidemic as it brings to perception an enlarged number of decipherable signifiers. Collective and individual expressions of hostility to one or another form of perversion are obviously fed by the utility of such expressions. They offer demonstration of the remoteness of the individual from the taint of such perversions. They also become moments for unambiguous and

125

increasingly rare opportunities for heightening a sense of social integration. Much of the expression of homophobia that commonly permeates our culture, and in particular what might be termed the cultures of masculinity, tends to reflect these kinds of usage: a way of unambiguously affirming that the individual is not one of *them* and wholly a member of the group.

THE FUTURE OF PERVERSION

Masturbation and homosexuality over the past century have been repositioned with specific images that range from "normality" to tolerable or normal deviance. The continued oppressions associated with masturbation are largely confined to those that individuals are encouraged to impose upon themselves. Currently, masturbation is accepted in current schemata of individual development. Even for psychoanalysts, masturbation becomes a stage-appropriate behavior, though one not without its inherent dangers (Kaplan 1988; Laufer and Laufer 1989). Some consideration of the positive and enabling role it plays in psychosexual development has appeared (Freud 1914; Hillman 1975; Gagnon and Simon 1972). Outside of a concern for adolescence, however, it remains largely unexamined despite the research of Kinsey *et al.* (1948, 1953) and more recently the findings reported by Lauman and his associates (1994), which pointed to its persistent appearance in the lives of significant numbers over the longer span of the life cycle and as part of the sexual repertoire of many who are sexually active in other ways as well.

Most of the dominant institutions of society continue to define homosexuality as undesirable, but they do so with a dramatic erosion of credibility and confidence. For many at all levels of social life, lesbians and gay men no longer appear mysteriously hypersexual, but instead as disenchantingly pedestrian figures of everyday reality. Except for the most homophobic, the fear of homosexuality rests not upon its own claims, but upon what else must be reconsidered when homosexuality is reconsidered, not least of which is the already embattled privileging of marital sex. This is not to say that homophobia and its attendant irrationalities will not continue to occasion cruelties and pain, but that manifestations of homophobia must increasingly be seen as being irrational. The widened perception of homophobic practices as cruel, unjust, and irrational occurs because those practices must increasingly contradict and, at times, disrupt current conventional practices in areas of social life both immediately and remotely connected to the sexual.

The dominant claimants to the center stage of current perversions are pedophilia (the violation of norms of age) and sadomasochism (the extreme elaboration of the often hidden or denied norms of hierarchy, the language of power). These seem to provoke the qualities of widely publicized indignation that indicates that their presence may be known in the sexual imageries of a large number of persons.

PEDOPHILIA

Pedophilia is generally defined as sexual desire for the prepubescent, a sexual desire for those who, aside from being seen as unable to give meaningful consent or to be fully sexually responsive, are seen as objects who lack many of the qualities of the semiotic of the body that suggest erotic significance. This lack, or deficiency, appears to challenge our capacity to comprehend this desire empathically. However, the idea of children as sexual objects is not so remote that it cannot be viewed as potentially attracting a growing number of devotees. While the incidence of this kind of behavior is almost impossible to establish with any accuracy, it is becoming a more *visible* part of current social discourse than in any other period in history. Pedophiles are no longer exclusively an obscure type emerging out of unusual circumstances, known only in terms of their hypersexuality; in many instances they are our parents. The belated recall of histories of victimization, which now frequently occurs and with a widespread endorsement by parts of the psychotherapeutic community, gives substance to the image of the dysfunctional family as highly prevalent, if not nearly normal. Concerns for potential "victims" and commitments to various forms of prevention, such as legislation against child pornography and its stringent enforcement, suggest a widespread and growing anxiety approaching a moral panic.

The issue of child sexual abuse, both within and outside the family setting, has become one of the dominant themes in current public sexual talk. Independent of the actual frequency of such events, the sheer amount of such talk brings the behavior closer to the horizon of plausibility. Even those accepting the view that the sexual is a powerful, innate drive tainted with dangerous appetites and propensities to aggression must address the question of how and for whom is the body of the child or pre-adolescent eroticized.

The capacity for sexual interest in the very young is not unknown across either the cross-cultural or historical literatures (DeMause 1974, 1991). What is relatively unique to the current situation is the combined effect of the intensity of moral disapproval attached to the behavior and the implausibility of the desire. It is this that raises the question of motivation. Here the clinical literature, which typically seeks out the conspicuous differences between pedophiles and non-pedophiles, tends to point in two directions, only one of which speaks directly to a specifically sexual outcome. The first addresses the character "disorders" that distinguish the pedophile, such as ego defects or separation trauma. The second "explains" pedophilic behavior as the product of having been the object of sexual uses by others during childhood (Finkelhor 1984). This latter "explanation" tends, of course, to reinforce the image of a potentially sexual responsive child or one whose childhood experiences may have direct sexual consequences (DeMause 1991). The critical question is: what establishes this potentiating capacity? And the answer, at least in part, must be that it depends not upon the nature of the event itself but upon the kinds of desire that become prevalent, the representations of desire to which we are trained, and the kinds of individuals who must manage them.

The *plausibility* of pedophilic behavior has markedly increased in recent years. Increased plausibility, by itself, need not imply an increasing incidence of pedophilic behavior or that such behavior would be increasingly seen as being acceptable. As with all forms of behavior whose very implausibility becomes suddenly more plausible, it is necessary to scrutinize those behaviors, not only for changes in the characteristics and motives of its participants but for insights into the practices, sexual and nonsexual, such behavior appears to ignore, if not violate.

Norbert Elias (1978) provided a potent insight when commenting on the relatively recent emergence of a protected status for children, when it became important that children be sheltered from exposure to the appearances of adult sexual activity. He noted that previously there was little concern for what children were present to observe because the adults did not have to worry about maintaining psychological distance from their children as there was a sufficiency of social distance already in place. The civilizing (modernizing) process, which required that we learn to see the adult in the child as well as the legacies of childhood in the adult, has significantly eroded that social distance.

Much of the indignant astonishment that accompanied the introduction of Freud's image of the psychosexual life of the infant and child was clearly defensive. Yet, more surprising than the initial hostility was how quickly much of it evaporated. All things considered, how quickly the Western mind accepted the idea that the child could be both the object and subject of love and perhaps of lust as well. In the increasingly psychologically dense environment of the modern Western family, children were treated with an almost constant, but rarely fully conscious, anticipation of the adult person they were expected to be. The child could be seen in both experience and memory as accessing almost the entire range of human emotions. Erotic interest by the child, as well as the projection of erotic interest from the child, could be as ordinary as fear, anger, resentment, or envy, as well as loyalty, dedication, or love of the purest kind. The potential for pedophilic incest within familial settings that viewed children as property may have been far less than in those settings where the bonds of the family rest upon emotional attachment.

It is likely that pedophilia will remain a significant aspect of sexual deviance, maintaining its character as a major form of perversion for the immediate future. However, its plausibility is strengthened by the plausibility of other evolving practices. Just as the seeming universalism of gender, with its ability to naturalize a wide range of social practices and yet encompass and bracket great social differences, has been subjected to radical deconstructions, aspects of age appear vulnerable to similar deconstructive criticisms. The resulting uncertainty is reflected in the increasing ambiguity surrounding what is considered age-appropriate sexual costuming, postures, and behaviors.

As age loses a substantial portion of its seeming objectivity, its ability to organize independently the narrative of the self is correspondingly diminished. The uses of childhood in the narration of the self are exemplified in the ability of the psychoanalytic tradition to conceptualize most human experience as being framed by the repetitions of the experiences and meanings of childhood. As the traditional "family romance" turns into the horror story of the dysfunctional family, the sexual potential of childhood present and childhood past becomes something of an atmospheric presence: Saturn pursues Oedipus.

Of great general significance, the enlarged and empowered domain of psychic reality makes behavior the servant of sexuality, as it makes sexuality the servant of the narrative of the self. The narration of the self becomes less a continuous chronicle than a series of vivid episodes, episodes that often occur within settings that were rarely predicted. Moreover, the experience of sexuality in service to self-solidarity increasingly rivals the experience of sexuality in the service of social solidarity. Thus, the acting subject can become the object of its own desires by appropriating the experience of the other. For some, being in a quasi-parental role is the only acceptable route to the reconstruction of the fantasied desires of the child, an imagery we have been trained to enrich with meanings that derive from different ages beyond childhood. The degree to which pedophilic imageries begin to describe the construction of the sexual for significant numbers of persons suggests why the current intensity of responses to the issue of pedophilia is required as much as an act of self-protection as by a desire to protect the child.

SADOMASOCHISM

Sadomasochism directly touches and sometimes embarrassingly illuminates the degree to which hierarchy, with the immediate implication of power and control, permeates virtually all aspects of social life (Burke 1966; Foucault 1978; Chancer 1992). Aspects of social life that claim for themselves an egalitarian character tend to do so with a self-consciousness that announces its intention to avoid hierarchy. It is love, for example, that is supposed to have the power to level all, though the same folk psychology just as easily admits to an inevitable appearance of the dominant and dominated, even when gender does not predict all outcomes.

It should not be surprising, then, that past and current experiences with hierarchy should provide both motives and metaphors critical to the self-recognitions of the individual. The permeation of the sexual by such motives and metaphors should not be surprising. To the degree to which gender costumes power, the manifest significance of gender signs in the construction of sexual scripts speaks to the most general capacity of themes of hierarchy to elicit or give permission for sexual excitement as a general phenomenon (MacKinnon 1987).

The term "sadomasochism", as discussed below, does not refer to specific individuals, such as sadists and masochists, but to those who participate in the enactment of consensual "sadomasochistic" episodes in which at least one participant explicitly experiences sexual excitement as a result of overt sadomasochistic gestures. Great emphasis must be placed upon "explicit" because suggestions of the sadomasochistic, if only in obscure nuances, may play a role in sexual experiences for many, just as the comedic often disguises the very hostility upon which it depends. Because of the exclusion of hierarchy from most current cultural scenarios legitimating the erotic, themes of hierarchy are often hidden from the other, as well as from the self. Perhaps for that very reason, hierarchical themes tend to play a pivotal role in the processing of those gestures that inspire and reinforce sexual excitement (Stoller 1979, 1985a).

Among the most compelling and earliest of the experiences of hierarchy are those that involve critical dependencies of infancy and childhood. Emotionally infused issues of hierarchy also re-emerge with the ambiguities of adolescence, ambiguities that tend to be accompanied by an enlarged attention to the sexual. These ambiguous themes of hierarchy and power figure pre-eminently, but by no means exclusively, among the experiences that provide both an imagery of occasions and the raw materials of feeling-states from which sadomasochism in both its sexual and nonsexual guises subsequently arises.

There are very few forms of behavior more commonly dialogical than the modern experience of the sexual. It is dialogical in the sense that participation often requires an attribution, accurate or inaccurate, of the emotional responses of sexual partners, as well as a chorus of others who are not present but whose sense of judgment is invoked (Simon and Gagnon 1987; Bakhtin 1981). When uncertainty and dialogical requirements meet, actors are situated as an audience to the unfolding interaction; and, as such, they are split not only between activity and reflexivity but between identification with self and other as well. It may be that the lighting within the sexual chamber is dimmed, as often occurs, not to obscure what can be seen, but to see what is not present but must be seen.

As we read ourselves to meet our own socio-emotional requirements, so do we of necessity read the other. This is a problem that becomes more common with a decline in culturally prescribed specifics of sexual inter-action, a situation where each participant has the capacity to betray or embarrass the performance of the other.

The sadomasochistic script plays upon the potential absolutism of hierarchy not merely to experience hierarchy with the relief accompanying the elimination of its attending ambiguities, but to experience the emotions that invariably accompany its exercise: the rage and fear of rage in both the other and ourselves; rage that follows from our inability to be a perfect (guiltless) god or a perfect (will-less) servant of god; rage that follows from bondage to mutual dependencies where we endure an exercise of hier-archic power that occasions an intoxicating legitimacy precisely because of the illegitimacy of the behavior to which it is applied.

> Sadomasochism strives to avoid the dialectics of master and slave –
> Hegel's con game – which in the "real world" perverts all the energies
> in dubious confrontations. The purpose of the sadomasochistic
> contract is to make sure that power is never at stake. The bottom
> doesn't compete with his master; he manages with his help to
> challenge his own limits. The two configurations overlap, both
> struggle to achieve separately their own singularity.
>
> (Lotringer 1988: 22)

Such a "singularity", however, is fully infused with the dialogical, the social requirements that give permission to experience the desire, as well as the interplay of signifying gestures, without which the activities of each participant lose legibility. In a sense, then, sadomasochism represents an escape from both the practice and legacies of hierarchy by playing past its realistic imperatives, and it does so by creating an objectified locale within which the rules of the intrapsychic dominate, unimpeded by the consid-erations that tend to turn most acts into the product of both intrapsychic and interpersonal considerations.

The most general approaches to the appearance of sadomasochism have identified three elements: a strategy for managing guilt, continuing repair-ing of narcissistic wounds, and seeking relief from continuing threats of fragmentation. The latter is seen as increasing as a reflection of the increasing fragmentation and instability of social life (Socarides 1991). These three elements are far from being independent of each other. Each undoubtedly plays some role in the creation of the very possibility of sadomasochism. However, this kind of formulation, conceiving of the sexual as "serving" guilt, the temporary repairing of wounds, fails to see the possibility of the ways in which the guilt and a possible history of narcissistic wounds come to serve a version of the sexual that may arrive permeated and enlarged by our more general history from infancy on-wards with the intoxicating experiences of interpersonal power. Guilt may be more important as the metaphoric coinage of sadomasochism than it is as its inspiration.

The social segregation of the sexual ensures its limited claims upon larger, more visible identities; for example, it allows those who are professional aggressors in public contexts to become submissive children within the sexual script as it allows what in public are timid subordinates to become the most demanding despots. In a sense, then, sadomasochism can represent an escape from both the practice and legacies of hierarchy by playing past its realistic imperatives. Consensual sexual sadomasochism emerges as an exercise of hierarchy that occasions authenticity precisely because of the illegitimacy of the behavior to which it is applied; its eroticism and attending sexual excitement create a comforting sense of reality to what otherwise often appears as a childishly theatrical performance. The sexual, often too real to be taken too seriously, can become an occasion for a visceral confirmation of a *version* of self that is not obtainable in other configurations of the self (Lichtenstein 1977).

Though much of the sexual, and sadomasochism in particular, has been viewed as a desire to dissolve interpersonal boundaries, sadomasochism can actually serve to orchestrate a heightened sense of difference between self and other by affirming a felt absolute symbiosis of self and other in a parable of social order. It does so by playing upon divisions within the self, creating an objectified space within which the rules of the intrapsychic dominate, where authority uncovers all secrets, allowing truth, justice, and desire to coincide – albeit momentarily. Sadomasochistic sexual desires, as discussed here, can only be conceived of by segments of humanity capable of contemplating a fragmentation of self as well as a loss of social order.

To the degree that sadomasochism can be seen as "tainting" the sexual practices of many individuals, it may not qualify as an issue of perversion as we have used the word thus far. That is, the degree to which images, gestures or, to employ Stoller's (1979) useful descriptive term, "microdots" implicating sadomasochistic themes are generally prevalent in both the intrapsychic and interpersonal scripts of individuals should narrow the space between the thinkable and the unthinkable. For some time, film and art critics have instructed us in just how much the erotic is a game of power played within (or at) the rules of power. This is typified in discussion of the predominant representation of women as passive recipients of the male gaze, as the object of desire and only rarely the subject of desire (Berger 1972; Mulvey 1975). An enlarged capacity to empathically comprehend sadomasochistic attractions may account for the nervousness with which the popularization of its clearly related symbols (leather, chains, studs) has been greeted.

It is also important to understand that, as with most forms of sexual behavior, the attributes that appear to encourage a commitment to the specific enactment of erotic desires may be distinct from, rather than essential to, those attributes that give rise to the desire in the first place. While there are critical differences between those who only fantasize and those who risk performing a version of the fantasy, such differences may be independent of the shared capacity to dream in certain similar modes.

Sadomasochism looms large on the horizons of the current sexual landscape in ways that require that it be approached as a "disease of desire". One source of this marginalization is the dominant cultural scenarios that insist upon nonhierarchic motives, scenarios that are allowed to serve lust only in the guise of love, that place all emphasis upon the relationship to the object and very little, if any, upon other motives that might occasion sexual excitement (Benjamin 1972; Simon 1973; Stoller 1979, 1985a). It is possible that the experiences of recent years have created new pressures to modify this position. This has been particularly true for many among recent cohorts who experience the decline of Eros' imperatives as a crisis of identity, as a crisis of viability. Typical of this shift is the current abandonment of Freud's idea of genital maturity as occasioning an easy and gentle confluence of the sentimental and the erotic.

> There is a growing awareness of the importance of these polymor-phous perverse tendencies [e.g. exhibitionistic, voyeuristic, sadistic, and masochistic sexual games] as part of normal love relations, in contrast to their subordination to genital intercourse. I have proposed that normal polymorphous perverse sexuality is an essential compo-nent that maintains the intensity of a passionate love relation, and recruits – in its function as the receptacle of unconscious fantasy – the conflictual relations and meanings that evolve in a couple's relation-ship throughout time.
>
> (Kernberg 1988: 65)[2]

Kernberg's observation points us to an important potential bias char-acteristic of almost all scientific discourse on sex, including the present effort. Established as a central focus, sexuality is too easily seen as possessing a quality of importance that may not be descriptive of many individuals or most individuals most of the time. Related to this bias, perhaps reflecting also the degree to which Freud has influenced the thinking of all of us, there is a tendency to seek the deep sources of sexual desire within the history of the individual. Another biasing aspect is the continuing nervousness about sexual behaviors beyond the most conven-tional. Oral sex, for example, has only in recent times begun to shed the aura of being inherently deviant. Similarly, same gender sexual interac-tions seemingly continue to require some basic developmental, character-ological or genetic explanation. As a culture we take sex seriously, perhaps too seriously; in its appearance, something emblematic of "true" character is assumed to be revealed.

While inevitably drawing upon the resources of the intrapsychic, at specific times and possibly for growing numbers of persons, specific sexual acts may be engaged in for superficial or contextual reasons. Examples that come to mind are such phenomena as "political lesbianism", sexual engagements as an act of gender politics, or the use of articles and costumes associated with sadomasochism, including tattooing and piercing, as acts of identification with specific youth subcultures. Similarly, behaviors indicative of the sadomasochistic scripting of sexual interactions may be occurring more frequently not as the unleashing of previously repressed sadomasochistic desires but as a tactic for enhancing and elaborating sexual performances.

Periods of heightened sexual permissiveness frequently bring problems of their own, a kind of sexual anomie of affluence. The sexual, now less a scarce experience in its own right, one less shrouded in silence and less masked by the protections of pluralistic ignorance, faces an implicit challenge to live up to the promises made on its behalf. This challenge has been heightened by an increase in recent decades in the belief that sexual desire is a direct expression of the viability of a relationship. Moreover, this burden of demonstration is possibly being extended over a longer time span than ever before. This is particularly pressing in regard to long-term relationships where marked declines in the frequency of sexual interaction are commonly associated with the length of the relationship (Blumstein and Schwartz 1983). Long-term relations, as Stoller (1985a) noted, provide the comforts of familiarity and predictability (the orgasm of reassurance), but often at the expense of excitement (the orgasm of bliss). The elaboration of sexual play involving elements of the sadomasochistic is one of the few scripting materials available to heighten the production values of interpersonal sex-play, in a context where the orgasm of reassurance, in order to reassure, must be garbed as the orgasm of bliss – or its simulation.

The sadomasochistic charade, particularly for those adapted to the shifting of temporary roles, can sustain a sense of pressing an edge that eroticizes the extended performance beyond the immediately genital. This can be increasingly attractive in a context of communication systems where virtually all are given immediate access to intimacies of social power, but access projected through cool media and where bureaucratic rationalization depersonalizes the causes of frustration and outrage.

CONCLUSION

The legacies of the moral, social, and psychological significance previously assigned to the sexual continue to color our actual experience of the sexual. Few reared in the Western tradition can be indifferent to the sexual or be unaware of the ambivalences it generates, though the degree to which individuals are affected may differ widely within and between cohorts. The great significance accorded the sexual has tended to privilege it in the sense that its mere presence has often either created a near blinding glare or provoked such nervousness that a detailed examination of what in fact was occurring was nearly impossible.

The growth of an erotic consciousness in the modern West was occasioned, as Foucault (1976) argued, by the oppressive presence of efforts to banish it from visibility. This situation, in recent years, has changed profoundly. Erotic images, direct and indirect, conventional and unconventional, are abundantly visible. Patterns of behavior have changed in numerous ways, and the erotic status of individuals has become a more overt aspect of the reciprocal surveillance that accompanies many aspects of social life. At the risk of dissolving parts of what little we think we may know about sexual behavior, we must begin to address the questions of the *changing* nature of sexual desires, the *changing* nature of their uses. Very much in the spirit of Foucault, we must begin to see sexual behaviour as an evolving phenomenon whose meanings and truths are part of the continuing production of social reality, of the continuing production of our current versions of the human.

7

SEXUALITY
A discontinuous discourse on a
discontinuous subject

INTRODUCTION

To attempt to present the following ideas in some logical and, consequently, linear way would amount to a deception. To offer a coherent and
explanatory logic, as is perhaps too common to contemporary social
science, is to fashion a rhetoric that sustains the illusion of a corresponding
logic inherent in actual practice that is rarely to be found in actual practice.
This tendency is reinforced by the ability of labels, such as homosexual,
heterosexual, or bisexual, to homogenize what are significantly pluralized
phenomena.

How then can one write in a postmodern style? A partial answer is that
there will be no one postmodern style. Different adaptations will obviously
depend upon such diverse factors as the qualities of specific subject
matters and the constraints of representation, responses to the strains
existing between what we know and what must be lost and added in
communication, and, always, the conflict between what we know and
what we believe. The problem is one of finding a space for the articulation
of what I believe, without the distortions that inevitably follow the
conventional ways of making the believable believable.

What I have done in the present instance is merely to have started
thinking about the meanings of sexuality as I tried to understand it; they
tended to derive as "side-bar" elaborations that occurred while what has
gone before was initially being composed. Lines of thought were allowed
to develop without a self-conscious awareness of what would be included,
excluded, or what it would look like when finished. I started writing,
allowing what had come before to move me forward in a journey combining discovery with invention. If by the end of this journey I have not fully
contradicted myself more than once, I shall have failed.

Lastly, I have entered brief quotations from works that prompted some
line of thinking or that were called to mind by some line of thinking. Often
they were prompts that followed one of those "of course" responses that
denote an addition to perception; often it was the occasion for a dialectical

136

response. Not all those who have shaped my thinking are represented, and even these are rarely acknowledged to the full extent of my reliance on them or the full extent of my appropriations of their thoughts.

*   *   *

The sexual appears rooted in our very nature, as an ultimate, if obscure truth of the human being, and we continue to believe this bedrock conception of the sexual even though we rarely expect to find it in its quintessential form. Though we expect it to appear variously costumed and occasioned, we do not doubt that, at its origins, the sexual is an unchanging creature of nature, a touch of the original, a universal starting point, the illusion of the starting point of a desire that is what it is and not the creation of some historically burdened negotiation.

This belief is necessary if sexuality is to serve as an ultimate anchor for a multiplicity of semiotic chains. However, like Barthes's view of the photographic image, the appearance of the sexual is most typically a moment of deception: sex is rarely what it appears to be and it is never more deceptive than when it appears to be what it is.

*   *   *

> It is in sexual encounters that solitude is sharpest, that the imagined wealth of remembered, alternative, or illusory possibilities devastates the pretended truth of the moment. Men and women sleep not with each other but with the regrets, the hopes of unions yet to come. Our adulteries are internal; they deepen our aloneness.
>
> (George Steiner, 1995)

*   *   *

Among the most significant contributions of Freud is the insight that not all of sexuality (desire, physical excitement, and heightened emotional productivity/sensitivity) is experienced within the context of recognizable sexual acts. And, by the same token, not all recognizable sexual acts are ever totally in the control of sexuality.

*   *   *

Even when many of us dream the same dream, such similarities are not as important as the sense of their being our possession, our very own secret.

*   *   *

Even at moments of purest composition, when it is least burdened by service for other ends, sexuality remains a (com)promise. And moments that occasion a sense of completion may satisfy only through complicated psychological book-keeping.

137

*   *   *

We often experience our sexual selves as coming from within largely because the moment is illuminated with a sense of knowing yourself as you have always been for the first time, knowing yourself in an especially confirming way. The feeling is something like being well fitted for a pair of fine shoes. However, you have just become the kind of person capable of that experience and that capacity is the property of that moment and not that person.

How rare are the instances where this coalescence of past and present occurs without strain, inconsistency, fracturing, and reckless misrepresentation?

*   *   *

The fabric often tears along ragged, often hastily sutured seams.

*   *   *

Sexuality, under certain conditions, is transformed into eroticism. Eroticism can be defined as the images of desire that, independent of their immediate possibility of realization (enactment), are capable of initiating and sustaining sexual arousal. These "certain conditions", despite many very general aspects, find the appearance of the erotic following discouragingly unpredictable paths. But once constituted as eroticism or as an aspect of a subjective erotic culture, such images of desire approach hyperreality, resembling Lacan's notion of the recycling of desire. The erotic comes to function like the mock rabbit at dog-racetracks: while tempting with the scent of flesh, it is constituted never to be consumed.

*   *   *

The salience of the sexual circles from an absolute refusal to be sexual (possibly the most erotic response of all) back upon itself, where almost all experience is colored with sexual possibility or where that which is not colored with the sexual is lost to an under-attended backdrop.

*   *   *

Satisfaction can be defined as the "experience of judgment", something close to Kohut's concept of "ego-autonomy", or the self observing the self, and often the self observing the self observed or observable. Pleasure reverses this, it occurs as the "judgment of experience", close to Kohut's concept of "ego-dominance", the self thoroughly into its experience. The difference between these two – satisfaction and pleasure – is like the difference between doing something that you know to be fun and having fun.

*   *   *

138

All sex is a form of longing, even as it happens.

(DeLillo 1991: 90)

*   *   *

Desire, as experienced by the self, is not merely the experiencing of a lack or absence. It is the labeling of a lack that is the initiation of desire, the initiation of a process of layered interrogations hidden in the deceptively singular question: What is it I desire? Individual biography is the layered history of such interrogations, and personal character (as against "social character") may be little more than the practices by which the interrogations are most typically carried out.

*   *   *

Desire is the scripting of potential futures ("when I act"), drawing upon the scripting of the past of desire as experienced in the contingent present. Desire, in the fullness of its implicit ambiguity, can be described as the continuing production of the self.

*   *   *

I am as you desire me. This is what sounds the differentiating human experience: other animals may hunger; only the human experiences and is shaped by an awareness of what others desire of us. We are rarely only what others desire of us, but we never fully escape the fact of their desiring.

*   *   *

The functions of the orgasm: at times it appears as an exclamation at the end of a sentence. A link between pleasure and satisfaction? A way of avoiding the panic of pleasure or a way of returning from the pleasure of panic? The homage or ransom that "ego-autonomy" offers "ego-dominance"?

*   *   *

The *dream of desire* produces pleasure; the *desire of the dream* produces satisfaction. What makes satisfaction possible is not always an enhancement of pleasure (though it can be), just as what makes pleasure possible is not always an enhancement of satisfaction. There is an overlap of the two that permits one to speak of the pleasures of satisfaction and the satisfactions of pleasure; however, each of these represents a muddied, derivative or echoed character.

*   *   *

PLEASURE – (1) DESIRE, INCLINATION; (2) a state of gratification; (3a) sensual gratification; (3b) frivolous amusement; (4) a source of delight or joy.

139

SATISFACTION – (1a) the payment through penance of the temporal punishment incurred by a sin; (1b) reparation for sin that meets the demands of divine justice; (2a) the fulfillment of a need or want; (2b) the quality or state of being satisfied: CONTENTMENT; (2c) a source or means of enjoyment: GRATIFICATION; (3a) compensation for a loss or injury: ATONEMENT, RESTITUTION; (3b) the discharge of a legal obligation or claim; (3c) VINDICATION; (4) convinced assurance or certainty.

(Webster's New Collegiate Dictionary 1975)

      *   *   *

The desire of the dream and the dream of desire are both constructions. The former is the product of interpersonal scripting, the latter the product of intrapsychic scripting.

      *   *   *

The essence of the nature of the desire is not merely the experiencing of a lack or absence. It is the labeling of a lack that is the initiation of desire. One of the distinctive features of the modern experience was the tendency either to leave ambiguous or to pluralize potential labels for specific desires. This was accomplished by creating private spaces, both within and without, that sheltered the quest for desire that preceded desire's quest. Postmodernity extends ambiguity, pluralization, and sheltering to the point where the coercive legacies of surviving tradition become uncertain of themselves.

      *   *   *

Recognition of the fundamental and extensive difference between behavior directed towards these two ends ["satisfaction" and "pleasure"], and hence the fact that individuals living above the level of subsistence are likely to be faced with a choice between them, made it possible to distinguish traditional from modern hedonism. The former was identified as a preoccupation with sensory experience, with "pleasure" regarded as discrete and standardized events, and in the pursuit of which there is a tendency for the hedonist to seek despotic powers. Modern hedonism is marked, in contrast, by a preoccupation with "pleasure", envisaged as a potential quality of all experience. In order to extract this from life, however, the individual has to substitute illusory for real stimuli, and by creating and manipulating illusions and hence the emotive dimension of consciousness, construct his own pleasurable environment. This modern, autonomous, and illusory form of hedonism commonly manifests itself as daydreaming and fantasizing.

(Campell 1989: 202–3)

*   *   *

The erotic, that which endows something – a person, feature, posture, object, shape, texture, odor – with the capacity to elicit sexual excitement, can claim very little as its own. The construction of an erotic preference, aside from its coincidental biological inputs, can draw from many, often conflicting desires. For the moment, what is important is that we understand that these same desires can invariably be attached to many behaviors.

*   *   *

The experience of sexual desire might be described as a handful of M&M candies; a handful that for some persons is dominated by a few colors and for others is expressed as mosaics of conflicting tints, complementary tints, and – more than we realize – changing configurations of desire. Each M&M candy, in cross-section, can be seen as an oval of chocolate covered by a thin layer of candy, which is itself followed by a third, still thinner layer of dye. The chocolate oval at the center may represent the most primitive and inarticulate responses of the human: a very basic, undifferentiated core of longing that subsequently can be attached to a plurality of qualities of experience (the candy coating) that are associated with some specific gestural tone (the specific color).

*   *   *

Sexual behavior in its direct reproductive forms is not discovered; it is there all the time. Motivation (eroticism) may have never rested in biological uses, but in socially reinforced, expressive statements. For example, Freud's notion of the primal horde, where presumably a dominant male controlled all or most of the females to the exclusion of other males, suggests this relationship. The behavior makes more sense as an expression of a desire for power or social recognition than as the expression of a sex drive. The sexual becomes the vivid signifier and empowers the signified. Being the dominant male could be described and experienced as one of the more oppressive burdens of power. Having sex or, somewhat more dramatically, denying sex to others became a display, if you will, a confirmation and respectful acknowledgment of hierarchic position. This, or something like it, is necessary, given the absence of periodicity in women and similarly programmed responses by men: sex must be given a value.

*   *   *

Sexual deviants, like other marginalized categories of individuals and groups who resist the conventional or normal, become the occasion for the diffusion of disobedient desires as they become the uninvited presence at almost all demonstrations of conformity.

*   *   *

141

The "solution" of the pervert is unique to her or him, but the "problem" whose solution is being attempted is anything but unique. The pervert is frequently "solving" a problem that others are solving in different ways, ways that at times serve the conventional and at other times occasion change in the construction of the conventional.

*   *   *

Gender is an erotic signifier whose most common attributes are power and power relations. It is the difference between what I want to do and what I must be in order to do it well or merely to be allowed (to allow myself) to do it. As gender issues diminish dramatically, does sadomasochism replace them as the eroticizing of power after gender has been too compromised to serve?

*   *   *

We must consider the role of masturbation in training people to the illusion of empathy. Empathy must both follow and lead "the desire to be both sexes", the desire that, like many desires, is burdened with gender codes and prohibitions.

*   *   *

A poorly kept yet under-advertised secret: our sublimations are often richer in their capacity to sustain cycles of emotional production than the ghostly forbidden desires that may have infused them with significance in the first place. The sexual, both the object and subject of sublimation, often must be refurbished and elevated to approximate the qualities of expression found through other well-founded sublimations. At the core of our lusts is a falsified history of prosaic successes and failures.

*   *   *

It is the lust for orgasm and not orgasm itself that is the sexual in its purest form, lust that is nurtured in the continuing commerce of the self.

*   *   *

The most important permanent truth about sexuality is that there may be no important truths about sexuality that are permanent. Those of its aspects that appear to be permanent are rarely important and those that appear important may rarely be permanent. This is especially relevant to the seeming permanence of the link between the sexual and reproduction. This is another way of saying that there is little truth to be found in the body as such, and even less truth to be found in the body abstracted from life. Anatomy or body chemistry, as such, is rarely, if ever, the unmediated source of our destinies.

*   *   *

What we try to possess, then, is not just a body, but a body brought to life by consciousness .... The importance we attach to the body and the contradictions of love are, therefore, related to a more general drama which arises from the metaphysical structure of my body, which is both an object for others and a subject for myself. The intensity of sexual pleasure would not be sufficient to explain the place occupied by sexuality in human life or, for example, the phenomenon of eroticism, if sexual experience were not, as it were, an opportunity, vouchsafed to all and always available, of acquainting oneself with the human lot in its most general aspects of autonomy and dependence.

(Merleau-Ponty 1962: 166–7)

*   *   *

The deception that we have practiced – often too knowingly – was that when we talked about the sexual, whether across spans of time, cultural boundaries, or what others "down the block" were doing, it was as if we were always talking about the same thing.

*   *   *

Sexual psychopaths, like almost all psychopaths, differ from many apparently non-pathological persons in only a few, often relatively unimportant ways. The ability to act upon some fantasy, some congealed desires, generally has little to do with the capacity to have the fantasy.

*   *   *

"Cultural skin" describes the occasions where cultural scenarios evoked by the contingent moment are comfortably appropriate for the scripting of both interpersonal and intrapsychic responses: the moments when I am what (I sometimes pretend) you desire me to be and when you are what (I sometimes pretend) I desire you to be. This might be described as a situation where identity controls desire by containing desire within the prison of the dream.

*   *   *

PLEASURE IS FOUND IN METAPHOR, SATISFACTION IN NARRATION.

*   *   *

The desire of the dream is not the same as the dream of desire. The pleasures of the dream are the satisfactions of narration; the satisfactions of desire are the pleasures of metaphor.

*   *   *

143

The sexual act as performed in anticipations, in enactments, or as part of the changing narration of the self, while giving the impression of constituting a unitary act (an impression heightened by the singular focus often given by the experience of or aspiration for orgasm), might better be described as an ecology of desires, one that generates and sustains a highly variable economy of pleasures. The relationship between the intensity of desire and the intensity of pleasure is not necessarily very direct. Not everything that is strongly desired in the sense of being associated with heightened levels of sexual excitement is equally pleasuring.

*   *   *

Sexual intercourse is often more poetry than prose as it represents a sequence of metaphoric gestures whose interdependencies or claims for coherence are rarely articulated. And when they are articulated it is invariably through the arts of fictionalizing the truth to protect the innocence of the guilty.

*   *   *

The deconstruction of the desire of the dream, if possible, would reveal the desires hidden behind, or more accurately within, the dream. This is another way of saying that the dream, i.e. what the actor wants, wishes or desires to happen (which, even or especially in the dream, is most often quite different from what actually happens) is itself not the direct expression of her or his sexual desires, but a transformation of them into a narrative, i.e. a script for a sexual drama, a sexual drama with its own claims for plausibility, for – in most instances – a minimal assumption of mutual recognition, and appropriateness.

The desire of the dream, then, occasions the consideration of a wide range of sexual desires, i.e. those associated with an increase in sexual excitement, as it references a still larger universe of desires, many of which come tainted by other past and present uses. And with the invoking of any specific sexual desire there is an invoking of strings of associated desires, sexual and nonsexual, that have both negative and positive consequences for sexual excitement. The desire of the dream is a negotiated product that both produces sexual excitement for the actor and is offered, under varying terms and conditions, for negotiation with the other.

*   *   *

To consider a desire is to begin the experiencing of that desire. Many sexual desires have the capacity to generate excitement merely by being invoked, though the negativity of the response to its being invoked rarely permits its explicit inclusion or enactment. To understand that X or Y is not acceptable is different than X or Y being unthinkable. The negotiated *dream of desire* is often what makes the unacceptable at least thinkable.

*　　　　　　　*　　　　　　　*

> I felt obliged to study the games of truth in the relationship of the self
> with self and the forming of oneself as a subject, taking as my domain
> of reference and field of investigation what might be called "the
> history of desiring man".... Not a history that would be concerned
> with what might be true in the fields of learning, but an analysis of the
> "games of truth", the games of truth and error through which being is
> historically constituted as experience; that is, as something that can
> and must be thought.... What were the games of truth by which
> human beings came to see themselves as desiring individuals?
>
> (Foucault 1985: 6–7)

What Foucault is raising as an essential issue is central to the sociology of
emotions as it directly addresses the fundamental question of the evolving
nature of the self that "experiences" such emotions. To ignore this connection, proceeding with a directory of emotions as a given, i.e. fixed starting
points like something akin to a concept of primary colors, is to miss the
point, like seeing all sexuality as if it rested upon some unchanging truth.

*　　　　　　　*　　　　　　　*

Human sexuality is really nothing, at least nothing specific. It is nothing
specific in an almost infinite number of ways. It is almost never the same
even when it looks the same. At the same time, it often finds compelling
kinships of motive or feeling among even the most bizarre comparisons. By
the latter I mean that people doing strikingly different things may be
experiencing very similar feelings, very similar experiences of the self. And
of course the reverse: people engaging in what look like identical activities
may have very little in common with regard to what they are feeling or how
they are experiencing themselves. Sexuality is really nothing that is
constant. At least it is not a constant if you want to think about sex as
referring to something more than gender. Of course, it is difficult for us,
living late twentieth-century Western lives, to think about sex independent
of concerns for gender or recognition of its implication for species reproduction. However, it is equally difficult for us to think about human
sexuality as if it were only an issue of gender or reproduction. That might
constitute a sexuality, but surely not a human sexuality.

Even where aspects of gender and species reproduction seem to provide
some near universal commonalities, such commonalities are rarely very
informing. While all but the most ephemeral of groups facilitate some kind
of heterosexual genital intercourse, not all individual members of the
group necessarily engage or are allowed to engage in heterosexual genital
intercourse and, among those who do, not all will engage in it in the same
way or for the same reasons.

*   *   *

Hate between men comes from our cutting ourselves off from each other. Because we don't want anyone else to look inside us, since it's not a pretty sight in there.

(Ludwig Wittgenstein)

*   *   *

The picture does not create desire, desire creates the picture. The picture evokes desire, but only the desire that was lying in wait.

*   *   *

Self-cohesion might better be described as the degree of self-solidarity characterizing the subject. The use of "solidarity" should be explicitly linked to its Durkheimian richness: the ways in which the various aspects of self establish continuity-enhancing reciprocities. Indeed, Durkheimian imagery is very appropriate, particularly if a slight spin might be put on his terms. Mechanical self-solidarity is the degree to which the subject has achieved, experienced, or blundered into an integration of roles in ways that make them mutually reinforcing, creating a seamless identity, one whose comfort with self is accompanied by great interpersonal and intrapsychic silences. A realm where almost all language is public language and almost all utterances are in the service of *social* solidarities.

As the achievement or experience of self-solidarity becomes more problematic, those aspects of the self that are most directly implicated in the management of self-solidarity become more significant and so the human is transformed. The problematics of self-solidarity become greatest when the specific roles the individual plays increase in number, in fluidity (changing rapidly in the number of alternatives and significances), and in commanding respect (the degree of influence in the negotiation of behavior) both internally and externally. Which, in turn, suggests the fullest implications of the term "organic solidarity", the solidarity that derives from the potential reciprocities and pluralizing complexities that inevitably accompany increasing depths of differentiation and specialization. As the division of labor increases, all politics, including the politics of the self, become the politics of coalitions.

*   *   *

Disorders of mechanical self-solidarity produce rage and apathy; disorders of organic self-solidarity produce anger and anxiety. The former tends to freeze perceived options prematurely, while the latter inspires an exhausting constancy of scanning.

*   *   *

146

The feminine, it has been argued, is the accepting of the responsibility of being *other*, of willingly becoming the desire of the subject of the gaze, of being receptive in accepting the identity components desired by the subject's gaze. Allowing the subject to be what the object mirrors, implies, or mandates, completes one – and only one – of the circles of power surrounding the sexual.

*   *   *

Do pleasure and satisfaction necessarily war with each other? Is satisfaction the imposition of the past upon the present? Is pleasure a constant threat to the present moment? Martin Jay's characterization of the millennial postmodernist as wanting to stand forever at the very edge of an end that never comes is something the contemporary sexual experience increasingly prepares us for.

*   *   *

To say that all sexuality is a deception is not to affirm some special or unique character of the sexuality; rather, it is to recognize that sexuality, a kind of desire, shares this with human desire at the most general level. Sexual behavior is more often the representation of desire than its direct expression. And this too is a reflection of a more general attribute of the human. If deception, or the complexities of representation, describes all sexualities, the conventional or perverse appearance of desire does little to certify the conventional or perverse meanings intended. Nearly identical desires (Are there any identical desires?) may derive from different experiences. Identical archaeologies (sources of the desire of the dream) may find varied expression depending upon the contingencies that make available representations (the dreams of desire).

*   *   *

Unlike Magritte, I cannot inscribe under the preceding words these additional words: "This is not sex." Both public and private talk about sex constitute a form of sexual activity, a form of sexual behavior. Sexuality, more than any other aspect of behavior, first and foremost, is talk; it is rooted in discursive formations; it cannot speak until it is spoken. Its most clever disguises are ways not of hiding itself but of finding itself.

For many, if not most, readers trained in the Western tradition, these words have sexual meaning. A range of associations with meanings is immediately established; collaged images of experience are evoked; a history and possibility of fantasy is reconnected; in some cases, even the very preliminary biophysical manifestations of arousal commence. Similarly, in what follows, different degrees of sexual provocation will be experienced; some thoughts and images pull us away from the text, others return us to the text somehow made different by the digression. Much that is sexual, much that is intensely sexual, can be experienced without what is commonly regarded as sexual behavior occurring.

With increasing recognition of this, we learn to ask, "How is the sexual represented?" Often the answer is that it can be found in appearances seemingly remote from an explicit sexual act or gesture. What is more rarely asked is the still more important question, "What does the sexual represent?" In other words, the sexual may be far less the origin of our desires than a way station, a marketplace at the intersections of the trade routes of desire.

*   *   *

But what is eroticism? It is never more than a word, since practices cannot be so coded unless they are known, i.e., spoken; now, our society never utters any erotic practice, only desires, preliminaries, contexts, suggestions, ambiguous sublimations, so that, for us, eroticism cannot be defined save by a perpetually elusive word.

(Barthes 1976: 26)

*   *   *

Sexuality involves deception. This includes not only the deceptions we commit and those committed by others, but also the self-deception involved in not perceiving certain deceptions of certain others. Deception is not the sole property of sexuality. Rather, it is the signature of social life; it is what, to varying degrees, sexuality shares with most of social life. Among its singular attributes is its ability to convince us of the very possibility of truth regarding human behavior.

*   *   *

Sexuality is far more rooted in the poetic than the physical or biological. Sexual behavior, like many other forms of human behavior, is dependent upon myth ("a story that is not history" – where the truth of telling is more important than the telling of truth) and metaphor ("a relationship between symbols [representations] that is not logical"). (Definitions of myth and metaphor are those of Northrop Frye.) And it is this poetic aspect that explains why we tend to act out our sexuality less often than we can and more often than we need to.

*   *   *

To understand my sexuality, you must understand my life. However, it may be possible to understand a great deal about my life without understanding much about my sexuality. Does it involve osmosis between sexuality and existence, as Merleau-Ponty suggests? It seems so. But what is hiding behind those two words? Sexuality as both outside and inside meeting (trying to meet or colliding) in experience.

148

*　　　　　　*　　　　　　*

Sexual excitement, Stoller suggests, inevitably involves the objectification of the other because she or he is the carrier and bearer of what elicits sexual response. This attribution to the other has the capacity to be associated with sexual response prior to having met the particular other who occasions the response. This inevitable fetishizing is a way of making the other both more and less than she or he is. That may be one of the inevitabilities of social life. However, this seeming objectification of the other is a way of accomplishing the experiencing of a version of the other as a subject. Objectification of the self by the self, which may also be occurring as the necessary accompaniment to sexual excitement, is also a way of accomplishing the experiencing of a *version* of the self as a subject.

*　　　　　　*　　　　　　*

The urgencies and improbabilities, if not the absurdities, of our sources of sexual excitement often conflict with the idealizations that socially costume most of our sexual performances. Our desires for sexual activity, as a result, are not always synonymous with our sexual desires. It is in this sense that we might say that the scripting of sexual performances (the desire of the dream) is not necessarily the same as that which may have inspired the desire for the performance in the first place (the dream of desire). The tyrannies of sexuality are multiple; its threats of pleasure and promises of danger are many and only rarely, if ever, can they be separated.

*　　　　　　*　　　　　　*

The erotic, that which is associated with sexual excitement, does not adhere to behavior as such, but is only found in conduct (or the idea of behavior) after it is costumed with meaning. "Raw sex" can only be found as a sequel, as a last sentence.

*　　　　　　*　　　　　　*

Central to the transpiration of sexual practice into erotic feelings is its potential for combining an intensity of feeling with some complex idealization. Eros – "love directed towards self-realization". (One must ask, which version of the self?) Where the sexual, like other aspects of life, is eroticized there we will also find, virtually by definition, an instance of the "precession of the simulacra": the empowering and, in some instances, the "libidinizing" of an ideal that will henceforth lead our desire, becoming the judgment of behavior awaiting the coming of the real.

*　　　　　　*　　　　　　*

Hyperreality is the natural character of eroticized desire in the sense that it

149

always points to what is sought, never to the merely discovered. Nothing may be so rare as truly "unexpected" sexual pleasure.

* * *

Erotic cultures, like certain kinds of religious cultures, specialize in transforming the real or nearly real into the possibility of the hyperreal. Where the object (or occasion) of desire for sex is found, it is entirely consumed in the finding, allowing us to find more in less and, sometimes, less in more. Like religious cultures, erotic cultures struggle to routinize the exceptional and, like religious cultures, they succeed more often than we realize. (Which is possibly why they war with each other so often?)

* * *

Desire is not a thing but a variable presence in the production of behavior. Even as a sexual event occurs, levels and uses of desire may fluctuate. At its best, sexual activity is the coordination of fragments of narrative within the confines of an episode.

* * *

To embrace desire fully is to run grave risks, not least of which is the risk of disappointment. For most of us, most of the time, merely to invoke its presence is sufficient.

* * *

Kundera observes that eroticism tends to feed upon ambiguity – the greater the ambiguity, the greater the excitement that is generated. This requires a suggestive, and always incomplete, typology of ambiguities. And ambiguity, of course, is a relatively gentle expression for the increasingly common pluralized (heteroglossic/polyvocal) psychic life of the individual in late modern or postmodern social contexts. It is possibly for this reason that the democratization of preoccupation with the sexual, the transformation of the sexual into the erotic, occurred.

* * *

Well-integrated individuals, whether this integration is achieved through the coercion of external expectations or the happy, if rare, confluence of roles and role commitments, tend to have relatively uninteresting sex lives. The sexual flourishes at the margins, as well as in dark corners that generate a sense of risk at the approach of consuming warmth.

* * *

An additional dimension is sensuality – at last we get to acknowledge the body – the pleasures of bodily sensations that are scripted to generate pleasure. Not all touching or being touched feeds on or is fed by erotic

150

possibility, by sexual excitement. The pleasures of these do not always feed on pleasure, but on the pleasures of feeding and, at times, of being fed.

*   *   *

The deceits and impersonations of the erotic vampire, who produces pleasure or the appearance of pleasure in the other only to appropriate it for her or his own nourishment, speak to the merger of ambiguity and sensuality. The erotic vampire must generate the simulation of her or his own pleasure in order to encourage the production of the pleasuring pleasure in the other. The erotic vampire may be among our most successful erotic possibilities.

*   *   *

A man can bare himself before others only out of a kind of love. A love which acknowledges, as it were, that we are all wicked children.
(Ludwig Wittgenstein)

*   *   *

My premise is that recognition of the other is the decisive aspect of differentiation. In recognition, someone who is different and outside shares a similar feeling; different minds and bodies attune. In erotic union this attunement can be so intense that self and other feel as if momentarily "inside" each other, as part of a whole. Receptivity and self-expression, the sense of losing the self in the other and the sense of being truly known for oneself all coalesce. In my view, the simultaneous desire for loss of self and for wholeness (or oneness) with the other, often described as the ultimate point of erotic union, is really a form of desire for recognition. In getting pleasure *with* the other and taking pleasure *in* the other, we engage in mutual recognition.

Understanding desire as the desire for recognition changes our view of erotic experience. It enables us to describe a mode of representing desire unique to intersubjectivity which, in turn, offers a new perspective on women's desire.
(Benjamin 1972: 126)

An alternative view:

The love between women is a refuge and an escape into harmony. In the love between a man and woman there is resistance and conflict. Two women do not judge each other, brutalize each other, or find anything to ridicule. They surrender to sentimentality, mutual understanding, romanticism: Such love is death, I'll admit.
(Anaïs Nin)

151

*   *   *

What is particularly striking is that Benjamin who, like most who operate from an object relations perspective, credits the pre-oedipal stage with being the context for the most critical aspects of character formation and the initial structuring of the agenda of desire. What is for her one of the most essential desires of this the earliest of periods of existence, "the desire for recognition" by another, constitutes the essence of the erotic experience. But recognition is not a form, it is a content. What is one recognized for being, and by what authorization is the other as a mirror privileged to judge? Benjamin's erotic act is pure form, which is what makes it both utopian and anything but erotic.

*   *   *

The very idea of "healthy" sex rests on the assumption of the possibility of a quality of relationship, a quality of experience that is inherently pathogenic in its utopianism.

*   *   *

The questions that must be asked are these:

- Who (what) is the identity of both participants?
- How do they make their presence known?
- Which of the alternative identities must be transformed?
- What history of negotiation brings them to this moment?

In other words:

- Who are they?
- What have they come to do?
- What provides permission for them to do it?

*   *   *

In "erotic union" the experience of inter-subjectivity is the exclusive province of the intrapsychic. Togetherness is an individual experience that, at best, two individuals might have at the same time without ever knowing whether they were having it or having it in the same way.

*   *   *

In a social context seemingly with more signs than signifieds, there follows an understandable anxiety about the effectiveness of efforts at communication. Does the other receive what I am sending in ways that I anticipated or desired? Questions whose very plausibility reminds us of the capacity of pleasure to hinge on our ability to perceive others as perceiving us as we desired them to perceive us and responding appropriately. At a minimum, two sets of emotions must be scripted. Which of the two is the

152

most significant contributor to pleasure cannot be determined. However, we can know who is scripting the emotions. At the same time, the potential confusion makes communication more self-conscious, heightening reflexivity (What shall I un-wear today?). To varying degrees, this has the potential for shifting the locus of pleasures, as sending messages (anticipation/assembly/creation) becomes a locus of pleasure that becomes independent of how such messages are received. This, in turn, heightens the importance of "undercoding", the increasing eroticization of *underwear* which slowly begins to work its way to the surface (Davis 1992).

* * *

Sometimes one experiences oneness and the other does not. We only experience oneness one at a time.

* * *

There are times when the only way the subject can rest fully confident of the *authentic* presence of the other is to play the role of the other. This should be particularly relevant when the burdens (complexity) of the performance fall to the other. This should occur most often when the initial commitment to the performance (script) is experienced by the self as the object's object or what happens when the object of desire must provide not pleasure but the responses that engender pleasure.

* * *

Intensity of feeling derives not from revealing ourselves to the other, but in revealing ourselves to ourselves. The other is often merely the occasion.

* * *

But in losing the intersubjective space and turning to conquest of the external object, the boy will pay a price in his sense of sexual subjectivity. His adult encounter with woman as an acutely desirable object may rob him of his own desire – he is thrown back into feeling that desire is the property of the object. A common convention in comedy is the man helpless before the power of the desirable object (*The Blue Angel*); he is overpowered by her attractiveness, knocked off his feet. In this constellation, the male's sexual subjectivity becomes a defensive strategy, an attempt to counter the acute attractive power radiating from the object. His experience parallels woman's loss of sexual agency. The intense stimulation from outside robs him of the inner space to feel desire emerging from within – a kind of reverse violation. In this sense, intersubjective space and the sense of an inside is no less important for men's sexual subjectivity than for women's.

(Benjamin 1988: 164)

*   *   *

Masturbation as a way of holding onto, developing, extending, and becoming fixated within the inner space.

*   *   *

Psychoanalytic discourse continues to predicate an emotionally dense infancy and childhood and, more than dense, an emotionally consequential infancy and childhood. The discussion – particularly Benjamin's – contains too much by way of borrowed meanings: meanings and intensities derived from later experience represented by metaphors of earlier experience. "Castration anxiety" has the ring of plausibility to the post-pubertal man because it so neatly sums up, for all but the insensitive and unconflicted, his continuing fear of failing as a man.

*   *   *

Two defects in the psychoanalytic approach to sexuality:

1 Desire in earliest childhood is inherently sexual. (Sexual desire is always inherently something else.)
2 That sexuality is the expression of the permanent conflict between the individual and the collective. (It is humanity at its most social.)

*   *   *

Freud's "where id is, ego will be" makes sense only in terms of drive theory. Without drive theory we might have to rewrite this as "where ego was, id will be". Ego – the organism trying to avoid discomfort and panic – gives rise to a developing self system, with those fragments, self objects and versions of self objects that cannot be incorporated within the self system constituting the id-like intrapsychic functions. Some were excluded when they were inconsistent with the emerging self, others are abandoned because they are outgrown. Others just abandoned and forgotten – it does happen. Some are "repressed" because they engender conflict, others because they cause depression.

*   *   *

> Fundamentally, the agent is not he who has power or pleasure, but he who controls the direction of the scene and the sentence (as we know that every Sadean scene is the sentence of another language) or: the direction of meaning.
>
> (Barthes 1976: 31)

*   *   *

The basic dialectic of modernism: the constancy of change is contained within the normalizing of the very nature of change which anchored the

154

stability of the human or the normalizing of its evolution. My attempt to make sense of the sexual required calling into question not the biological substrate but its explanatory powers.

*   *   *

The pleasures or rewards of interpersonal scripting are something analogous to ego libido, the motivational source that encourages the individual to engage in self-enhancing behaviors, a center of motivation that often conflicts with desires to engage in psychic pleasures less rooted in immediate social interaction (intrapsychic scripting). An emphasis on the urgency of "a sex drive" obscures just how rich the pleasures of eliciting confirmations from others can be.

*   *   *

Behavior that is not particularly pleasuring or persistently mysterious often enhances the pleasures at the interpersonal level. This occurs when we fail to experience existentially the pleasures that prevailing cultural scenarios promise are associated with the behavior. At any rate, we may have excessively focused upon the desires of the intrapsychic.

*   *   *

Love, which minimizes the difference, which would abolish the difference, also permits the revelation and revelry of the difference. Romantic love retreats to the middle ground of merger, to the celebration of a loss of identity such that neither lover is experienced as complete without immediate reference to the other. Romantic love is risk aversive, the dancing on the edge of mutual permission is fatal; transgression becomes a terminal crisis. For those who celebrate the difference risk is vital, transgression the occasion for its inevitable confirmation: a sharing of wickednesses that cannot be experienced alone.

*   *   *

Myth is totally dependent upon the powers and mysteries of the other; to know her and be known by her in a costumed nakedness that confesses more than there is to confess and that forgives only enough to preserve the difference.

*   *   *

How terrified we are of not being anchored by the brutal reality of economic interest; we are required to adore its implacable objectivity, its capacity for ruthless logic.

*   *   *

How poorly sex serves sexuality.

155

NOTES

INTRODUCTION

1   One of the consolations, if not seductions, of working within conventional or "normal" social science paradigms is that they tend to shelter the coherence of the world and thereby protect the cohesiveness of the self. Revisionist or revolutionary "theory" is often a confession of a loss of the coherence of the world and of the cohesiveness of the self. At their very best, revisionist or revolutionary theories thus are often over-determined attempts at the restoration of what has been lost or the replacement of what no longer serves.

While most of the discourses of postmodernism have occurred in the context of the humanities, the most substantial inputs have their origins in traditional social science discourses. Unfortunately, the dominance of positivist styles in the social sciences – from academic psychology's fragmenting of the human, in its aping of the laboratories of the natural sciences and fetishizing of the quantitative to the medicalization of psychoanalysis – has produced an anti-intellectualism that in the main led to the abandonment or devaluation of this heritage. As a result, the renewal of "critical cultural studies", though continuing to draw on traditional social science literatures, has come to us predominantly from the humanities and within the humanities, significantly from the growing tradition of feminist studies.

2   "Natural paradigms", or what some term "basic schemata", are the representations produced by our experiences in social life as first we come to comprehend it. They represent the world as it first was and, as a result, they become the operative markers of change for ourselves and the world.

3   The emergence of what some have termed "the executive self" follows an absence of integration of the multiple social roles most are required to perform and a corresponding uncertainty as to their eventuality. Implicit is a shift of behaviors from those expressive of a sense of "natural identity" to those more accurately described as a "staged identity". The increased salience of the latter can be seen in the recently expanded interest in the works of G.H. Mead and Erving Goffman.

4   Additional dimensions along which the development of postmodernity might be charted are the ways in which nature is conceptualized and commitments to the concept of progress (Simon *et al.* 1993). There has been a decline in the view of nature as a lawful phenomenon, accessible to reason because it embodies reason. Similarly, the concept of progress, the idea of a future realization that organizes and makes sense of both personal and collective history, is being called into question. Perhaps for the first time since the

156

Renaissance, the Western world seemingly is without a future that is superior to the present in ways that imply a moral obligation to work and sacrifice for its achievement (Bury 1932).

5   The term "deconstructive" is used in a limited way. Overused and often misused, its present use shares some meanings with the critical approach associated with Derrida. Among these common uses is an acceptance of an inevitable relativism following from the increasing pluralization of contexts of social experience and changing contexts of texts that shape all discourse. We also share an acceptance of the possibility that there is no fixed truth or meaning to be discovered, that the very effort at both description and understanding, research and theory, indissolubly mixes discovery with invention, and that attempts at understanding social life, like social life itself, will remain an unfinished, continuing process (Cohen 1987). In the main, we share a view that the "gap" between experience and representation, its entry into existing discourse, is a condition to be understood and not a problem to be solved.

6   Marx, for example, despite rhetorical disguises, clearly had a vision of socialism that preceded and informed the critique of capitalist society. Another example is observable in current feminist writing where embarrassing essentialisms often seem to follow the effective "unmasking" or "debunking" of many earlier versions of what was essential to gender that are implicated in the maintenance of existing patriarchal constructions of gender. Having exposed much of the constructed nature of gender, the question invariably arises, "What then? Can the preoccupation with gender, which until now has been one of the dominant factors in shaping social life, merely be dissolved?" A common response is to turn this same critical apparatus to the discovery of either the "true" meaning of gender or to the advancement of some truer or more attractive uses of gender. The constructed nature of gender often becomes as politically and psychologically uncomfortable as the larger issue of the constructed nature of all social life.

7   Distinctions between these three types of self-constructs are never wholly isomorphic with the predominant character of the surrounding social context. Rather, like Riesman's well-known typology, tradition directed, inner directed, and other directed, they represent that which is both occasioned by and most easily accommodative of the predominant character of the surrounding context. Few individuals – particularly in modern and postmodern settings – are entirely describable in terms of any one of these distinctions. The same might be said of their social settings.

8   The major originating image that informed this line of argument was a display I observed in the Boston Museum of Science, a display that at the touch of a button would produce a normal distribution and do so over and over again with great regularity. Balls of a uniform size would drop from a hole at the topmost center of the display. Placed on the rear wall was a series of evenly spaced, fixed pegs. As each ball, one at a time, fell from the hole at the top, it would fall to the bottom in a seemingly irregular way. Within minutes, as all the balls fell to the bottom, the familiar bell-shaped curve was created with lawful regularity. I could not help being struck by how unlike this process was from the patterns of contemporary social life where entry occurs at a multitude of places, where entering "units" can be viewed as uniform in only the most abstract ways, and where intervening sources of deflection, now including other "units", are rarely uniform or stable.

9   The tyranny of the normal should not be overstated. Normalization obscures heterogeneity, but it does not eliminate it. At best, normalization sets the

conceptual context within which further redefinition can occur. This is what Foucault intended when he noted that "[i]n a sense the power of normalization imposes homogeneity; but it individualizes by making it possible to measure gaps, to determine levels, to fix specialties and to render the differences useful by fitting them one to another" (Foucault 1979: 184).

10   There are also immediate implications of postmodern perspectives for the practice of research. Among these is a critical view of current treatment of complex social phenomena with multivariate statistical techniques that condense representations and order them on the basis of some assumed uniformity of meaning or arbitrary dimension of magnitude. In contrast, postmodernist perspectives aim at preserving intrinsic heterogeneities, at preserving and exploiting different orders of otherness.

This, in effect, suggests a compensatory privileging of naturalist research technologies, an approach consistent with sociology's continuing responsibility for societal book-keeping. What is important is that problem-driven or theory-driven research be constrained to respect the fullness of its subject matter, that it be open to scavenging, leaving behind the descriptive resources with which to examine all "deviant cases" as if they were possible versions of alternative normalities. In another sense, no specific research methodology can be justified beyond a vagary of conceptual boundaries that can both inspire and satisfy curiosity. There can be no privileging methodologies, except those that recognize that there is little hope for a reduction in the confusions with which social life presents itself and that the effort to produce the enduring truth of either representation or understanding is not unlike attempting to produce the truth of a river.

1 THE POSTMODERNIZATION OF SEX

1   While it was perhaps Freud who did more than anyone else to place sex on the scientific agenda of the Western world, it is also clear that, past what he viewed as the experiences of infancy and childhood, he did little to encourage a direct examination of sexual behavior. Thus, we find only about a dozen references to orgasm in his remarkably prolific body of published works. Moreover, attention to the sexual within psychoanalytic discourse was more than disproportionately focused upon "infantile" and "childhood" sexual experience. Almost all that followed by way of post-pubertal experience was essentially seen as metaphoric references to the meaning of these early experiences and, in these, the erotic is more often than not largely confined to the latently sexual. The explicitly erotic gets very little attention in psychoanalytic discourse. Moreover, even where the erotic is explicitly referenced, it is discussed in the most abstract language.

In the following chapter there will be little attention payed to psychoanalytic theory, partly because this has been addressed elsewhere (see Chapter 3) and partly because there is relatively little direct material to reference. However, it is clear that Freud, and his students, directly and indirectly contributed to the naturalization of sex. This contribution is of such a profound magnitude that all who deal with the human sexual remain in his debt, though perhaps less for what he taught us about the nature of the sexual than for what he taught us about the nature of the human.

There are three related "errors" in Freud's thinking that had pervasive influence in virtually all subsequent thinking about human sexuality. "Errors" is placed in quotation marks to highlight the fact that these represented what might be termed normal errors. Normal is used in the sense that they represented derivatives of the conventional scientific wisdom of his day.

The first of these is the assumption of the idea of inherited characteristics (Lamarckianism). Much of what would otherwise have to be viewed as the precocious wisdom of the infant-child organism had to depend upon its ability to draw upon the experience and wisdom of its ancestors. The oedipal issue, dramatized by the occasion and recognition of the "primal scene", from Freud's perspective, was only partially dependent upon the experience of the individual; the phylogenetic stood ready to provide what otherwise eluded experience.

The second was a questionable extension of the generalization that "onto-geny recapitulates phylogeny" – a generalization that has itself been called into question in recent considerations. The very notion may be dependent more upon a metaphorically enriched reading of the developmental process than upon experience. Moreover, for Freud this generalization was translated into the proposition that the history of the individual recapitulates the history of the race or species, adding sociohistorical evolution to the even less articulate process of organic evolution.

Connected to this latter assertion was the assumption that the origins of the species were necessarily to be found in the most brutal kinds of savagery. This was a view of preliterate social life that combined the interrelated romanticism of the popular culture of the time with the rationalizations of Western imperialism. What followed was the image of the infant organism as a brutal savage whose primitive impulse must be reshaped before she or he would be fit for "civilized" living.

Thus a dubious anthropology, drawing upon an anthropomorphic zoology and linked to a now discredited approach to genetics, shaped and gave credence to Freud's view of both psychosexual development and the impact of the psychosexual upon the most general aspects of human development.

2 SEXUAL SCRIPTS: PERFORMANCE AND CHANGE

1   There is an obvious similarity between our conceptions of interpersonal scripting and intrapsychic scripting and the much earlier formulation of Mikhail Bakhtin.

In the Bakhtinian model, every individual engages in two perpendicular activities. He forms lateral ("horizontal") relationships with other in-dividuals in specific speech acts, and he simultaneously forms internal ("vertical") relationships between the outer world and his own psyche. These double activities are constant, and their interactions in fact constitute the psyche. The psyche is thus not an internal but a boundary phenomenon.

(Emerson 1983: 249)

However, our conception is not rooted in an ontological given, but in the interactions of individuals that constitute certain qualities of social life. Such distinctions would have limited significance in contexts where persons cannot conceive of being anything except what they are.

2   In most discussions of anomie it is the image of Durkheim the positivist that tends to dominate the discussion. However, of possibly greater significance is the image of Durkheim the evolutionary theorist, an image that is rarely invoked, if only because of the embarrassment this image creates for

contemporary structuralists. However, consistent with this evolutionary perspective, Durkheim applied the evolutionary principle to the major product of sociocultural evolution: the human.

> In so far as societies do not reach certain dimensions nor a certain degree of concentration, the only psychic life which may be truly developed is that which is common to all the members of the group, which is found identical in each. But, as societies become more vast and particularly, more condensed, a psychic life of a new sort appears. Individual diversities, at first lost and confused amidst the mass of social likenesses, become disengaged, become conspicuous and multiply. A multitude of things which used to remain outside consciences because they did not affect the collective being become objects of representation. Whereas individuals used to act only by involving one another, except in cases where their conduct was determined by physical needs, each of them becomes a source of spontaneous activity. Particular personalities become constituted and take conscience of themselves. Moreover, this growth of psychic life in the individual does not obliterate the psychic life of society, but only transforms it. It becomes freer, more extensive, and as it has, after all, no other bases than individual consciences, these extend, become more complex, and thus more flexible. Hence, the cause which calls forth the differences separating man from animals is also that which has forced him to elevate himself above himself. The ever growing distance between the savage and the civilized man has no other source.
>
> (Durkheim 1964: 347–8)

3 This is a commonplace contemporary event that may represent the most prototypical postmodern response. The evolved sexuality of the contemporary Western world may represent, in general, some of our most general conditioning for the existential events posed by the conditions of postmodernity. The special link between the sexual and postmodernity may rest in the fact that for perhaps most persons it is one of the earliest and most emotionally involving experiences with the *hyper-real*, that which prompts a quest for what can never wholly be found within social reality because it was never there in the first place (Baudrillard 1988).

4 Not all behavior that is defined, perceived, or experienced as sexual need necessarily be experienced as erotic. However, the reverse is probably not true; it is hard to conceive of an erotic experience that is not sexual in the sense of involving the physiological and psychological processes associated with sexual arousal. The term erotic is frequently applied to other behaviors, but more often than not with an "as if" implication. Only in a metaphoric sense, i.e., "viewing something from the perspective of something else" (Burke 1969), can one speak of eroticizing work or food. The reference, of course, is to an intense, potentially obsessional, and possibly addictive pleasure. An implicit question is whether it is appropriate to speak of sexual pleasure as if it was a very special pleasure, a pleasure – one might say – all its own. An alternative and somewhat more reasonable question is whether it is appropriate to speak of the varied and often simultaneous pleasures that are served by the experience of the sexual, just as they may be served by other kinds of experience.

5 The power of the gaze has its embarrassments as well as its seductions. The late Robert Stoller once observed that what ordinary people might think about while engaging in sexual intercourse is "enough to make a monkey's hair

stand up straight". Following Freud's belief that most of us would rather confess our worst sins than describe our fantasies, overt socio-sexual acts may be as close as many of us come to confessing our fantasies even to ourselves. However, even then, such enactments are more likely to provide an environment for the shadow-play of fantasy elements than to be even an approximate enactment.

3 ADOLESCENCE AND SEXUALITY: UNREMEMBERED YOUTH

1   The following comment of Freud on the precocious insights of young children typifies some of the conceptual problems associated with the concept of infantile sexuality.

These scenes of observing parental intercourse, of being seduced in childhood, of being threatened by castration are unquestionably an inherited endowment, a phylogenetic heritage, but they may just as easily be acquired by personal experience. All that we find in the prehistory of neuroses is that a child catches hold of this phylogenetic experience where his own experience fails him. He fills in the gaps in individual truth with prehistoric truth; he replaces occurrences in his own life by occurrences in the life of his ancestors.

(Freud 1918 [1914]: 97)

This position, resting as it does upon the discredited Lamarckian view of genetics, was understandable for Freud himself. Lamarckianism was, to a large extent, part of the conventional wisdom of his era (Sulloway 1979). It was also convenient; Lamarckianism accounted for how the child intuitively responds with insights that only later childhood or adolescence can struggle to acknowledge.

4 ADOLESCENCE AND SEXUALITY: ALMOST REMEMBERED YOUTH

1   The very possibilities of fantasizing may be as specific to the modern Western world as are the meanings associated with the concept of adolescence. The uncertainties about the future that confront the adolescent in situations where lineage guarantees little by way of specific outcomes, and the unevenness and often contradictory expectations surrounding the adolescent, make fantasy a component of a larger process that culminates in an enlargement of internal psychic space (Durkheim 1893; Aboulafia 1986).
2   Implicit in the traditional psychoanalytic view was the idea that genital satisfaction, psychological satisfaction, and erotic satisfaction were virtually identical. One almost senses behind this position the legacy of Freud's earlier, more primitive, and inherently sexist notion of sexuality involving the discharge of accumulated substances through phylogenetically determined channels and methods. This may be contrasted with a Lacanian perspective that accepts the near constancy of sexual desire and views sexual pleasure not as relieving the individual from desires for the erotic, but as confirming and even heightening such desires. Satisfaction and pleasure often have independent and warring interests.
3   The ease and naturalness with which the concept of the nuclear is joined to the concept of the family provide one of the dramatic illustrations of the complex

role that language plays in influencing both culture and personality. To describe the contemporary family as being not *a* but *the* nuclear family is clearly to suggest that it – this form – is the family at its most basic reality, the bedrock of both individual and societal wellbeing. This position appears to be reinforced in current debate regarding pressing social problems where, in the midst of profound global economic, technological, demographic, and geopolitical change, the family and family "values" appear as both cause and/or impediment to solutions of these problems.

4   The perception of this extension of empathic response as being inherently dangerous is held by those who view gender as phylogenetically fixed and requiring rigorous segregation of indexical behaviors. However, as "the two sex model" (Laqueur 1990) is effectively deconstructed, this position becomes difficult to maintain.

5   This implies a historically specific image of homosexual behavior in a homophobic culture that generates the image of a devalued other who permits the heterosexist to experience being the object of desire without experiencing a threat to claims of masculinity. In other words, creating a desired object (an erect penis) whose pleasure (orgasm) certifies power. The homosexual (the queer) in this cultural scenario produces orgasms for others – a bribe and a tribute; the homosexual rarely has culturally scripted orgasms of her or his own.

5 ADOLESCENCE IN RETROSPECTION: MOVIES, MEN AND MYTHS

1   This inevitable bias serves to reinforce an anti-libertarian tendency in the social sciences, where the unequal availability of data constrains us to know more about how the individual serves culture than we know about how culture serves the individual.

2   This theme might be contrasted with the recent ascendancy of a variant of this theme: the experience of the fixated frontier personality trapped in worlds that have exhausted their frontiers. In this case it offers rituals of dying that affirm an idealized self embattled by aging and social change and begin to replace earlier rituals that confirmed and legitimated an idealized version of the self. Heroes no longer ride off into the pages of history but find their end in anonymous graves. *Liberty Valance* might be seen as a transitional phenomenon in this dramatic shift (Wright 1977).

3   The implicit analogy between this "trinitarian" construction of the self – narcissistic grandiosity, narcissistic honor, and social honor – and that constituting the trinity describing the Freudian vision of the self system is as obvious and suggestive as it may be misleading. Among the most significant differences is that the narcissistic grandiosity of *Liberty Valance*, despite its resemblance to common descriptions of the id and the drives associated with it, does not precede social experience, but is as much the product of social experience as the others.

4   Where the family remains a strong and permanent source of social identity, narcissistic honor, as used here, is unlikely to appear as a significant aspect of the lives of most individuals. The centrality of the family in such circumstances promotes the dominance of collective identities over individual identities. Thus social honor flourishes where "identity is essentially . . . linked to institutional roles" (Berger 1970). Oren (1984) has pointed to the striking parallels between the John Wayne persona as the embodiment of "narcissistic

honor" and Warshow's earlier conception of the "westerner" (Warshow 1962). Honor, for the westerner, Warshow observes, "is a style, concerned with harmonious appearances as much as with desirable consequences, and tending therefore toward the denial of life in favor of art" (1962: 141).

5   For example, though I would like to think of myself as a committed feminist, I also know that having been raised in this culture my unmonitored feelings are full of preferences that are embarrassingly sexist. More often than I like to admit, I feel my gender insecurities eased by the deference accorded me by women. I vicariously enjoy physical dominance when ritualized in sports. Part of me feels a curious gratification when I win arguments with other men that is different than when I win arguments with women. Too often I pretend to mechanical competence I do not possess and I feel humiliated when it becomes obvious to others that I have little of such traditional male competencies. Some part of me rejoices when Dirty Harry "wastes" some loathsome miscreant in ways that violate both decency and the protection of constitutional rights. I think I have this sexism in check, but that doesn't mean that any ritual of psychic cleansing will make such feelings go away; they continue to frame who I am at the moment. They are the residues of the "normality" of another time, and that part of me continues to protest when I announce to myself and the world that I am happier having subdued them.

6   It is worth noting, in retrospect, that the confrontation of the three dominant men prefigures the ultimate outcome. Valance and Doniphin play out their joint charade; but Stoddard walks off with the prize, though there is some doubt about its ultimate consummation.

6 DEVIANCE AS HISTORY: THE FUTURE OF PERVERSION

1   Changes in the family and other changes in social life are often reflected in what might be termed the changing ecology of the self. This, in turn, poses the possibility of a disordering or altering of prior commitments to expressions of the sexual. Commitments at each earlier stage of personal history reflected accommodations to specific and now different ecologies of the self. Even when a disordering of the ecology of the self culminates with a re-consolidation of the previously existing ecology, the sexual will often become an initial focus of change as previous commitments and renunciations must be reprocessed (Kohut 1977).

2   It is worth noting that even this concession to the possible acceptance of perversities, such as sadomasochism, is admitted only on the condition that they serve to enhance a domesticated relationship. The origins of the lusts that somewhat belatedly are allowed to serve love are seen as limited to the universal residues of inarticulate infancy and early childhood. There is no concern for the recent history or current condition of individual existence; "the conflictual relations and meanings" that occur within extrafamilial roles, as well as within other regions of the self.

REFERENCES

Aboulafia, M. (1986) *The Mediating Self: Mead, Sartre, and Self-determination*, New Haven, Conn.: Yale University Press.

Auden, W.H. (1970) *A Certain World: A Commonplace Book*, New York: Viking.

Bakhtin, M. (1981) *The Dialogic Imagination: Four essays*, ed. M. Holquist, trans. C. Emerson and M. Holquist, Austin, Tex.: University of Texas Press.

Barthes, R. (1968) *Elements of Semiology*, trans. A. Lavers and C. Smith, New York: Hill & Wang.

—— (1973) *Mythologies*, trans. A. Lavers, London: Paladin.

—— (1976) *Sade/Fourier/Loyola*, trans. R. Miller, New York: Hill & Wang.

—— (1977) *Rolland Barthes*, trans. R. Howard, New York: Hill & Wang.

Baudrillard, J. (1983) *Simulations*, trans. P. Foss and P. Patton, New York: Semiotext(e).

—— (1988) *Selected Writings*, ed. M. Poster, Stanford, Calif.: Stanford University Press.

Bell A. and Weinberg, M. (1978) *Homosexualities: A Study of Diversity among Men and Women*, New York: Simon & Schuster.

Bell A., Weinberg, M. and Hammersmith, S.K. (1981) *Sexual Preference: Its Development in Men and Women*, Bloomington, Ind.: Indiana University Press.

Bell, D. (1989) *New York Times*, 7 February.

Bellah, R., Madsen, R., Sullivan, W.M., Swindler, A. and Tipton, S.M. (1986) *Habits of the Heart: Individualism and Commitment in American Life*, New York: Harper & Row.

Benjamin, J. (1972) *The Bonds of Love: Psychoanalysis, Feminism, and the Problem of Domination*, New York: Pantheon.

Berger, J. (1972) *Ways of Seeing*, Harmondsworth: Penguin.

Berger, P. (1970) "On the obsolescence of the concept of honor", *Archives of European Sociology* XI.

Bernstein, B. (1972) *Class, Codes, and Control*, vol. 1, London: Routledge & Kegan Paul.

Blackmur, R.P. (1989) *Selected Essays*, New York: Ecco Press.

Blos, P. (1962) *On Adolescence: A Psychoanalytic Interpretation*, New York: Free Press.

—— (1985) *Son and Father: Before and Beyond the Oedipus Complex*, New York: Free Press.

Blumstein, P. and Schwartz, P.W. (1983) *American Couples*, New York: William Morrow.

Bourdieu, P. (1977) *Outline of a Theory of Practice*, Cambridge: Cambridge University Press.

—— (1993) "Censorship", in *Sociology in Question*, trans. R. Nice, Thousand Oaks, Calif.: Sage Publications.

Brome, V. (1983) *Ernest Jones: Freud's Alter Ego*, New York: Norton.

Browning, F. (1994) *The Culture of Desire: Paradox and Perversity in Gay Lives Today*, New York: Vintage.

Burke, K. (1935) *Permanence and Change: An Anatomy of Purpose*, reprinted 1965, Berkeley: University of California Press.

—— (1941) *A Grammar of Motives*, reprinted 1967, Berkeley: University of California Press.

—— (1966) *Language as Symbolic Action*, Berkeley: University of California Press.

Bury, J.B. (1932) *The Idea of Progress*, 1955 edn, New York: Dover.

Campell, C. (1989) *The Romantic Ethic and the Spirit of Modern Consumerism*, New York: Basil Blackwell.

Canguilhem, G. (1989) *The Normal and the Pathological*, trans. C.R. Fawcett, New York: Zone Books.

Castoriades, C. (1987) *The Imaginary Institutions of Society*, Cambridge, Mass.: MIT Press.

Chancer, L.S. (1992) *Sadomasochism in Everyday Life: The Dynamics of Power and Powerlessness*, New Brunswick, NJ: Rutgers University Press.

Cohen, S. (1987) *Visions of Social Control*, Cambridge: Polity Press.

Cooley, C.H. (1902) *Human Nature and the Social Order*, New York: Charles Scribner's Sons.

Darnton, R. (1994) "Sex for thought", *The New York Review of Books* XLI(21): 65.

Davidson, A.I. (1987) "How to do the history of psychoanalysis: a reading of Freud's 'Three essays on the theory of sexuality'", *Critical Inquiry*, Winter: 252–77.

Davis, F. (1992) *Fashion, Culture, and Identity*, Chicago: University of Chicago Press.

Davis, M.S. (1983) *Smut: Erotic Reality/Obscene Ideology*, Chicago: University of Chicago Press.

DeLillo, D. (1991) *Mao II*, New York: Viking Press.

DeMause, L. (1974) *The History of Childhood*, New York: Psychoistory Press.

—— (1991) "The universality of incest", *Journal of Psychohistory* 19(2): 123–64.

Denzin, N.K. (1991) *Images of Postmodern Society: Social Theory and Contemporary Cinema*, London: Sage.

Durkheim, E. (1893) *The Division of Labor in Society*, 1964 edn , trans. G. Simpson, New York: Free Press.

Elias, N. (1978) *The Civilizing Process: The Development of Manners*, New York: Urizen.

Epstein, S. (1987) "Gay politics, ethnic identity: the limits of social construction", *Socialist Review* 93/94: 9–54.

Erikson, E.H. (1950) *Childhood and Society*, New York: Norton.

—— (1975) "Once more the inner space", in *Life History and the Historical Moment: Diverse Presentations*, New York: Norton.

Escoffier, J. (1985) "Sexual revolution and the politics of gay identity", *Socialist Review* 82/83: 19–53.

Fenichel, O. (1953) "On masturbation", in *Collected Papers: Series Two*, New York: David Lewis.

Ferenczi, S. (1931) *Final Contributions to the Problems and Methods of Psychoanalysis*, 1980 edn, New York: Brunner-Mazel.

Finkelhor, D. (1984) *Child Sexual Abuse: New Theory and Research*, New York: Free Press.

Ford, R. (1981) *The Ultimate Good Luck*, Boston: Houghton Mifflin.

Foucault, M. (1978) *The History of Sexuality: An Introduction*, trans. R. Hurley, New York: Pantheon.

—— (1985) *The Uses of Pleasure: The History of Sexuality, vol. 2*, trans. R. Hurley, New York: Pantheon.

Freud, S. (1898) "Sexuality in the aetiology of the neuroses", trans. J. Strachey, *Standard Edition*, vol. III, London: Hogarth Press/Institute for Psychoanalysis.

—— (1905) *Three Essays on the Theory of Sexuality*, trans. J. Strachey, *Standard Edition*, vol. VII, London: Hogarth Press/Institute for Psychoanalysis.

—— (1906) "Psychopathic characters on stage", trans. J. Strachey, *Standard Edition*, vol. VII, 1942, London: Hogarth Press/Institute for Psychoanalysis.

—— (1907) "Creative writers and day dreaming", trans. J. Strachey, *Standard Edition*, vol. IX, 1908, London: Hogarth Press/Institute for Psychoanalysis.

—— (1908) "Civilized morality and modern mental illness", trans. J. Strachey, *Standard Edition*, vol. X, London: Hogarth Press/Institute for Psychoanalysis.

—— (1912) "Contributions to a discussion on masturbation", trans. J. Strachey, *Standard Edition*, vol. XII, London: Hogarth Press/Institute for Psychoanalysis.

—— (1914) "From the history of an infantile neurosis", trans. J. Strachey, *Standard Edition*, vol. XVII, 1918, London: Hogarth Press/Institute for Psychoanalysis.

—— (1915) "Instincts and their vicissitudes", trans. J. Strachey, *Standard Edition*, vol. XIV, 1954, London: Hogarth Press/Institute for Psychoanalysis.

Gagnon, J.H. (1973) "Scripts and the coordination of sexual conduct", in J.K. Cole and R. Diensbrier (eds) *The Nebraska Symposium on Motivation*, vol. 23, Lincoln: University of Nebraska Press.

Gagnon, J.H. and Simon, W. (1973) *Sexual Conduct: The Social Sources of Human Sexuality*, Chicago: Aldine.

—— (1987) "The sexual scripting of oral genital contacts", *Archives of Sexual Behavior* 16: 1–25.

Gay, P. (1989) *Freud: A Life for Our Times*, New York: Doubleday/Anchor Books.

Gellner, E. (1992) *Reason and Culture*, Oxford: Blackwell.

Gergen, K. (1991) *The Saturated Self: Dilemma of Identity in Contemporary Life*, New York: Basic Books.

Gilligan, C. (1982) *In a Different Voice: Psychological Theory and Women's Development*, Cambridge, Mass.: Harvard University Press.

Goffman, E. (1959) *The Presentation of Self in Everyday Life*, Garden City, NY: Doubleday/Anchor.

Guy, D. (1992) *The Autobiography of My Body*, New York: NAL/Dutton.

Haeberle, E. (1983) "Sexology: conception, birth, and growth of a science", paper presented at the Sixth World Congress of Sexology.

Halperin, David M. (1990) *One Hundred Years of Homosexuality: And Other Essays on Greek Love*, New York: Routledge, Chapman & Hall.

Harry, J. (1982) *Gay Children Grow Up: Gender Culture and Gender Deviance*, New York: Praeger.

Herdt, G. and Boxer, A. (1995) "Bisexuality: towards a comparative theory of identities and culture", in R.G. Parker and J.H. Gagnon (eds), *Conceiving Sexuality: Approaches to Sex Research in a Postmodern World*, New York: Routledge.

Hillman, J. (1975) "Towards the archetypal model for the masturbatory inhibition", in *Loose Ends*, Dallas: Spring Publications.

—— (1979) "An essay on Pan", in *Pan and the Nightmare: Two Essays*, Dallas: Spring Publications.

Honneth, A. and Joas, H. (1988) *Social Action and Human Nature*, trans. R. Meyer, Cambridge: Cambridge University Press.

Horney, K. (1937) *The Neurotic Personality of Our Times*, 1964 edn, New York: Norton.

Ionesco, E. (1987) *Fragments of a Journal*, trans. J. Stewart, London: Quartet Books.

Irvine, J.M. (1990) *Disorders of Desire: Sex and Gender in Modern American Sexology,* Philadelphia: Temple University Press.

Isbister, J.N. (1985) *Freud: An Introduction to His Life and Work,* Cambridge: Polity Press.

Jones, E. (1953) *Sigmund Freud: Life and Works,* New York: Basic Books.

Kagan, J. (1985) *The Nature of the Child,* New York: Basic Books.

Kallen, D.J. and Stephenson, J.J. (1982) "Talking about sex revisited", *Journal of Youth and Adolescence* 11(1): 11–23.

Kaplan, L.J. (1988) *Adolescence: The Farewell to Childhood,* New York: Jason Aronson.

Katz, J.H. (1990) "The invention of heterosexuality", *Socialist Review* 90/91: 7–34.

Kinsey, A.C., Pomeroy, W.P., and Martin, C. (1948) *Sexual Behavior in the Human Male,* Philadelphia: Saunders.

Kinsey, A.C., Pomeroy, W.P., Martin, C., and Gebhard, P.H. (1953) *Sexual Behavior in the Human Female,* Philadelphia: Saunders.

Klumpner, G.H. (1978) "A hypothesis regarding the origins of Freud's conception of the psychology of adolescence", *The Annual of Psychoanalysis,* vol. VI: 3–29.

Kohlberg, L. (1969) "Stage and sequence: the cognitive-developmental approach to socialization", in D.A. Goslin (ed.) *The Handbook of Socialization Theory and Research,* Chicago: Rand McNally.

Kohut, H. (1977) *The Restoration of the Self,* New York: International University Press.

—— (1978a) "Forms and transformations of narcissism", in P.H. Ornstein (ed.), *The Search for the Self,* New York: International University Press.

—— (1978b) "Thoughts on narcissism and narcissistic rage", in P.H. Ornstein (ed.), *The Search for the Self,* New York: International University Press.

Krafft-Ebing, R. von (1876) *Psychopathia Sexualis,* 1965 edn, trans. H.E. Wedeck, New York: G.P. Putnam.

Kubie, L.S. (1972) "The drive to become both sexes", *Psychoanalytic Quarterly* 43: 349–426.

Lacan, J. (1977) *Ecrits, A Selection,* trans. A. Sheridan, New York: Norton.

Lampl-de Groot, J. (1961) "On adolescence", *The Psychoanalytic Study of the Child,* vol. XVI, pp. 95–104, New York: New York International University Press.

Laplanche, J. and Pontalis, J-B. (1973) *The Language of Psychoanalysis,* trans. D. Nicholson-Smith, New York: Norton.

Laqueur, T. (1990) *Making Sex: Body and Gender from the Greeks to Freud,* Cambridge, Mass.: Harvard University Press.

Laufer, M. (1976) "The central masturbation fantasy, the final sexual organization, and adolescence", in *The Psychoanalytic Study of the Child,* vol. XXXI, pp. 297–316, New York: New York National University Press.

Laufer, M. and Laufer, M. (1989) *Developmental Breakdown and Psychoanalytic Treatment in Adolescence: Clinical Studies,* New Haven, Conn.: Yale University Press.

Lauman, E.O., Gagnon, J.H., Michael, R.T., and Michaels, S. (1994) *The Social Organization of Sexuality: Sexual Practices in the United States,* Chicago: University of Chicago Press.

Levin, C.D. (1992) "Thinking through the hungry baby: toward a new pleasure principle", in A.J. Solnit, P.B. Neubauer, S. Abrams, and A.S. Dowling (eds), *The Psychoanalytic Study of the Child,* vol. XLVII: pp. 119–37, New Haven, Conn.: Yale University Press.

Levine, M.P. (1986) "The gay clone", unpublished dissertation: New York University Press.

—— (1992) "The life and death of the gay clone", in G. Herdt (ed.) *Gay in America: Essays from the Field,* Boston: Beacon Press.

Levine, M.P. and Troiden, R.R. (1988) "The myth of sexual compulsivity", *Journal of Sex Research* 25: 33–45.

Lichtenstein, H. (1977) *The Dilemma of Human Identity*, New York: Jason Aronson.

Lotringer, S. (1988) *Overexposed: Treating Sexual Perversion in America*, New York: Pantheon.

Luria, S.E. (1975) *36 Lectures in Biology*, Cambridge, Mass.: MIT Press.

Lyotard, J-F. (1984) *The Postmodern Condition* (Theory and History of Literature, vol. 10), Minneapolis: University of Minnesota Press.

MacKinnon, K. (1987) "A feminist/political approach: pleasure under patriarchy", in J. Geer and W. O'Donoghue (eds), *Theories of Human Sexuality*, New York: Plenum.

Mannheim, K. (1936) *Ideology and Utopia*, New York: Harcourt, Brace.

Masters, W.H. and Johnson, V.E. (1966) *Human Sexual Response*, Boston: Little, Brown.

Merleau-Ponty, M. (1962) *The Phenomenology of Perception*, trans. C. Smith, New York: Routledge.

—— (1970) *Themes from the Lectures*, Evanston, Ill.: Northwestern University Press.

Merton, R.K. (1957) *Social Theory and Social Structure*, New York: Free Press.

Miller, P.Y. and Simon, W. (1980) "Adolescent psychosexual development", in J. Adelson (ed.) *The Handbook of Adolescent Psychology*, New York: Wiley.

Money, J. (1980) *Love and Love-sickness*, Baltimore, Md.: Johns Hopkins University Press.

—— (1985) "The conceptual neutering of gender and the criminalization of sex", *Archive of Sexual Behavior* 14: 3.

—— (1988) *Gay, Straight, and In-between: The Sexology of Erotic Orientations*, New York: Oxford University Press.

Mulvey, L. (1975) "Visual pleasure and narrative cinema", *Screen* 16(3): 6–18.

Nozick, R. (1989) *The Examined Life: Philosophical Meditations*, New York: Simon & Schuster.

Nunberg, H. and Federn, E. (1965–72) *Minutes of the Vienna Psychoanalytic Society*, New York: International University Press.

Offer, D. (1969) *The Psychological World of the Teen-ager*, New York: Basic Books.

—— (1982) "Adolescent turmoil", *New York University Education Quarterly* 16: 29–32.

Oren, M. (1984) Personal Communication.

Ortega y Gasset, J. (1963) *Concord and Liberty*, New York: Norton.

Ovesey, L. (1969) *Homosexuality and Pseudo-Homosexuality*, New York: Science House.

Plummer, K. (1975) *Sexual Stigma: An Interactionist Approach*, London: Routledge & Kegan Paul.

Reich, W. (1961) *The Function of the Orgasm*, New York: Farrar, Straus & Giroux.

Riesman, D. (1952) *Faces in the Crowd*, New Haven, Conn.: Yale University Press.

—— (1969) *The Lonely Crowd: A Study of the Changing American Character* (rev. edn), New Haven, Conn.: Yale University Press.

Robinson, P. (1976) *The Modernization of Sex*, New York: Harper & Row.

Rockeach, N. (1968) *Beliefs, Attitudes and Values: A Theory of Organization and Change*, San Francisco: Jossey-Bass.

Rogers, R.S. and Rogers, W.S. (1992) *Stories of Childhood*, Toronto: University of Toronto Press.

Samois (1982) *Coming to Power*, second edn, Boston: Alyson.

Sarnoff, C. (1976) *Latency*, New York: Jason Aronson.

Schmidt, G., Klusmann, D., Zeitzschel, U., and Lange, C. (1994) "Changes in adolescents' sexuality between 1979 and 1990 in West Germany", *Archives of Sexual Behavior* 23(5): 489–513.

Siegal, A.W. and White, S.H. (1982) "The child-study movement: early growth and development", in H.W. Reese (ed.), *Advances in Child Development and Behavior*, New York: Academic Press.

Simon, J. (1988) "The emergence of the risk society: insurance, law and the state", *Socialist Review* 17(5): 61–89.

Simon, W. (1972) "Reflections on the relationship between the individual and society", in *Human Futures*: A Special Issue of *Futures*, pp. 141–58.

—— (1973) "The social, the erotic, and sensual: the complexities of sexual scripts", in J.K. Cole and R. Diensbrier (eds), *The Nebraska Symposium on Motivation*, Vol. 23, Lincoln: University of Nebraska Press.

—— (1994) "AIDS: the archipelago of discourses", presented at the meetings of the American Sociological Association, Los Angeles, August.

Simon, W. and Gagnon, J.H. (1969) "On psychosexual development", in D.A. Goslin (ed.) *Handboook of Socialization Theory and Research*, New York: Rand McNally.

——(1975) "The anomie of affluence: a post-Mertonian conception", *American Journal of Sociology* 82(2): 356–78.

—— (1986) "Sexual scripts: permanence and change", *Archives of Sexual Behavior* 15(2): 97–120.

—— (1987) "The scripting approach", in J. Geer and W. O'Donoghue (eds), *Theories of Human Sexuality*, Plenum: New York.

Simon, W. and Simon M.B. (1958) "Beyond the visceral sleuth: reflections on the symbolic representation of deviance", *Studies in Public Communication* 3: 71–84.

Simon, W., Kraft, D., and Kaplan, H. (1990) "Oral sex: a critical overview", in J. Reinisch, B. Vollmer, and M. Goldstein (eds), *AIDS and Sex: A Biomedical and Behavioral Approach*, New York: Oxford University Press.

Simon, W., Haney, C.A., and Buenteo, R. (1993) "The postmodernization of death and dying", *Symbolic Interaction* 16(4): 411–26.

Sloterdijk, P. (1987) *Critique of Cynical Reason*, trans. M. Eldred, Minneapolis: University of Minnesota Press.

Steiner, G. (1995) book review, *New Yorker*, April 17, p. 102.

Stoller, R.J. (1975) *Perversion: The Erotic Form of Hatred*, New York: Pantheon.

—— (1979) *Sexual Excitement: Dynamics of Erotic Life*, New York: Pantheon.

—— (1985a) *Observing the Erotic Imagination*, New Haven, Conn.: Yale University Press.

—— (1985b) *Presentations of Gender*, New Haven, Conn.: Yale University Press.

Sulloway, F. (1979) *Freud: Biologist of the Mind*, New York: Basic Books.

Symons, J. (1979) *The Evolution of Human Sexuality*, New York: Oxford University Press.

Thorne, B. and Luria, Z. (1986) "Sexuality and gender in children's daily world", *Social Problems* 33: 176–90.

Trilling, L. (1972) *Sincerity and Authenticity*, Cambridge, Mass.: Harvard University Press.

Van de Berg, J.H. (1974) *Divided Existence and Complex Society: An Historical Approach*, Pittsburg, Pa.: Duquesne University Press.

Warshow, R. (1962) "Movie chronicle: the Westerner", in *The Immediate Experience*, Garden City, NY: Doubleday.

Weber, M. (1958) *The Protestant Ethic and the Spirit of Capitalism*, trans. T. Parsons, New York: Scribners.

Weeks, J. (1985) *Sexuality and Its Discontents: Meanings, Myths, and Modern Sexualities*, London: Routledge & Kegan Paul.

REFERENCES

Weinberg, M.S., Williams, C.J., and Pryor, D.W. (1994) *Dual Attraction: Understanding Bisexuality*, New York: Oxford University Press.

Weinberg, T. (1983) *Gay Men, Gay Selves*, New York: Irvington.

White, E. (1983) "Paradise found", *Mother Jones*, June 1993, reprinted 1994 in *The Burning Library*, New York: Knopf.

Wright, W. (1977) *Six Guns and Society: A Structural Study of the Western*, Berkeley: University of California Press.

Wrong, D. (1961) "The oversocialized conception of man in modern sociology", *American Sociological Review*, 26: 2.

Zurcher, L. (1977) *The Mutable Self: A Self-Concept for Social Change*, Beverly Hills, Calif.: Sage Publications.

INDEX

psychobiologism, and deviance 113
psychotherapy 2, 9
puberty, psychological and social 72–4
puritanism 28

race, and object choice 35
rape 117
reflexive me (Mead) 44
reflexivity 29, 41–2, 49; *see also* self-
reflexivity
regression 67, 83–4, 100, 110
Reich, W. 22, 66
relativism 3, 10, 27, 157n5
religion 9; fundamentalist 28
Renaissance 3, 42
representation 74, 116–17, 118
repression 61, 68–9, 85, 94, 105
reproduction *see* species reproduction
research *see* scientific study of sex;
social research
Riesman, D. 2, 4, 9, 79, 157n7
rites of passage 54, 75
rituals of dying 162n2
Robinson, P. 24
Rockeach, N. 89
Rogers, R. S. 83
Rogers, W. S. 83
role reversal 102–3, 153
roles 51; and cultural scenarios 40, 69;
and life cycle 52; multiplication and
segregation of, in postmodernity 6, 7;
see also gender role
romantic passion 109
Romantic tradition 96, 114

sadomasochism 77, 78, 86, 95–7, 101,
126, 129–34, 142
Samois 96
Sarnoff, C. 74
satisfaction 29–30, 43, 138, 139, 140, 143,
147, 161n2
Schmidt, G. 55
Schwartz, P. W. 57, 122, 134
science 1, 10–11, 14, 16, 27
scientific method, application to
sexuality 22–3
scientific study of sex 19–26, 27, 29, 32,
34, 37, 72
scripting 34, 40–4, 139, 152–3;
adolescent as auteur 74–7;
masturbation 86–8; *see also* cultural
scenarios; interpersonal scripting;

intrapsychic scripting; sexual
scripting
scripting approach of recent
research 25
scripting self, production of 43–4
self: in adolescence 72, 75, 77; in
alternative realities 115–16; authentic
42; changing ecology of 163n1;
childhood and 129; decentered 6;
divisions and conflicts 97–8, 103,
119–20; eroticized 117; evolution of
abstract 89; fragmentation of 131,
132; and games of truth 145; in
Liberty Valance 105, 162n3; of limited
liabilities 5; and masturbation 87,
119–20; modern 8–9, 13, 66, 115–16;
and other 72, 77 (in sadomasochism
132); in paradigmatic/
postparadigmatic societies 13, 29;
and pluralization of experience 15;
postmodernity 13, 124; as
production of social life 7, 70; and
sexology 25; sexual selves 138; and
the sexual 25, 33–4, 120; staging of
50–1; *see also* scripting self
self-cohesion 89, 146, 156n1
self-control 50, 105
self-observation 50
self process 41–2, 52, 70
self-reflexivity 7–8, 95
self-revelation 153
self-solidarity 49, 57, 75, 129, 146
sensuality 150
sex 155
sexism 48, 110–11, 161n2
sexology *see* scientific study of sex
sexual 43–4, 134–5; denaturalization of
30–1; distinguished from erotic 29,
138, 160n4; language of 63; as master
and servant of desire 32;
modernization of 20, 21–2, 36–7, 39;
ontogenic significance of 45–6;
origins of 137; privileging of 97–8; as
problematic 31–4; sociogenic
significance of 45–6; visibility of 81
sexual abnormality 24
sexual abuse of children 82–3, 127–9
sexual activity 137, 144; as expression
of nonsexual motives 98; as merger
of identities 96
sexual addiction 124
sexual aim 35, 61